Praise for *The Cashless Revolution*

"China is profoundly important, fintech is profoundly important, so how they come together will have much to do with how the global financial system plays out. *The Cashless Revolution* is a very valuable and important summary of the relevant issues."

—LAWRENCE H. SUMMERS, Charles W. Eliot University Professor, Harvard University, and former secretary of the treasury

"A comprehensive, highly readable look at China's cashless revolution: what went right, what went wrong, and how we can learn from China's experience as we strive to modernize our own payments system."

—SHEILA BAIR, former chair of the US Federal Deposit Insurance Corporation

"In this superb account, Chorzempa chronicles the breakneck speed in the development of the fintechs in China, starting from their humble origins as payment add-ons in e-commerce to all-seeing big techs that later incur the ire of the authorities, all within the space of ten years. Chorzempa's sure grasp of the political economy provides much-needed context to understand current developments. *The Cashless Revolution* is a must-read for any serious observer of digital innovation and of China."

—HYUN-SONG SHIN, Bank for International Settlements

"Chorzempa brings us an extraordinary look into the future of money and with it, the future of both global power and daily life. Having taught himself Mandarin and immersing in Chinese life, he tells the incredible story of the rise of China's powerhouse fintechs—their reining in by the Chinese government, and the dilemmas now facing all the world in seeking to harness the leveling power of technology while protecting privacy and averting state power on a scale never seen before—enabled by financial technology. Equal parts business chronicle, social and political analysis, and storytelling, *The Cashless Revolution* is one of those rare books that opens readers' eyes. The world will never look the same."

—Jo Ann Barefoot, CEO and founder, Alliance for Innovative Regulation, and former deputy controller of the currency

"*The Cashless Revolution* is a fascinating analysis of how Chinese entrepreneurs, despite setbacks along the way, transformed Chinese finance from a low-tech backwater to the world's largest and most-advanced market for digital finance."

—Nicholas Lardy, author of *The State Strikes Back*

"China is at the forefront of digital financial innovation, from mobile payment to online investment, and from digital lending to central bank digital currency. While rapidly transforming the financial structure, Chinese fintech also created immense new challenges for the policymakers. *The Cashless Revolution* offers an authoritative analysis of this very dynamic new financial sector—what happened, which factors contributed to the dramas, and where it will likely head."

—Yping Huang, Peking University

"This outstanding book on digital money provides a captivating account of the transition of China's financial system from financial repression to big tech-led financial liberalization. Chorzempa masterfully describes the back and forth between China's big-tech platforms and its regulators with their shifting attitudes. The possible erosion of people's privacy carries important lessons for the West."

—MARKUS BRUNNERMEIER, Princeton University

THE CASHLESS
REVOLUTION

THE CASHLESS REVOLUTION

CHINA'S REINVENTION OF MONEY
AND THE END OF AMERICA'S DOMINATION
OF FINANCE AND TECHNOLOGY

MARTIN CHORZEMPA

PUBLICAFFAIRS

New York

PublicAffairs
Hachette Book Group
1290 Avenue of the Americas, New York, NY 10104
www.publicaffairsbooks.com
@Public_Affairs

Printed in the United States of America

First Edition: October 2022

Published by PublicAffairs, an imprint of Perseus Books, LLC, a subsidiary of Hachette Book Group, Inc. The PublicAffairs name and logo is a trademark of the Hachette Book Group.

The Hachette Speakers Bureau provides a wide range of authors for speaking events. To find out more, go to www.hachettespeakersbureau.com or call (866) 376-6591.

The publisher is not responsible for websites (or their content) that are not owned by the publisher.

Print book interior design by Jeff Williams

Library of Congress Cataloging-in-Publication Data

Names: Chorzempa, Martin, author.
Title: The cashless revolution : China's reinvention of money and the end
   of America's domination in finance and technology / Martin Chorzempa.
Description: First edition | New York, NY : PublicAffairs, [2022] |
   Includes bibliographical references and index.
Identifiers: LCCN 2022006946 | ISBN 9781541700703 (hardcover) | ISBN
   9781541700727 (epub)
Subjects: LCSH: Finance—China. | Finance—Technological
   innovations—China. | Digital currency—China. | Money—China. |
   China—Economic conditions.
Classification: LCC HG187.C6 C463 2022 | DDC 332.0951—dc23/eng/20220608

LC record available at https://lccn.loc.gov/2022006946

ISBNs: 9781541700703 (hardcover), 9781541700727 (ebook)

LSC-C

Printing 1, 2022

For Natalia, Rafi, and Henry

Contents

III. PARTY CONTROL
AND INTERNATIONAL EXPANSION

Uncharted Territory

"If someone must go to prison for it, I'll go"

T he future of finance—the way Wall Street operates and how you manage your personal finances—is on the verge of upheaval. And the force underlying the change comes not from usual suspects such as Goldman Sachs, JP Morgan Chase, or Bank of America but China, where finance and technology are being merged into a system that could either be Orwellian or liberating. The changes of this global revolution in finance and technology ("fintech") will be just as powerful as those wrought in social media, retailing, and advertising by giants such as Amazon, Facebook, Google, and Twitter, which have overturned how we shop and communicate.

It all started close to two decades ago, when Jack Ma, a former English teacher and founder of Alibaba, took on China's backward financial system.

In January 2004, Ma made one of the most consequential decisions in recent financial history, one that would revolutionize China's backward financial system and spark the new financial model making waves around the world. Ma was at the World

Economic Forum in Davos while his team in Hangzhou was nearly ready to launch Alipay, a payment system for Alibaba's online marketplace for selling goods. Few Chinese had credit cards, so Alibaba had to create its own payment system to allow people to pay for what they ordered online. Ma and his team knew Alibaba would need that system to achieve its e-commerce ambition, but neither he nor Chinese officials were sure whether it was legal. A powerful state-owned company had a monopoly on most payments, and there was no procedure to ask the government for permission. While hearing the world's top CEOs speak about social responsibility, Ma made up his mind to take the risk. In the middle of the night, he called his team and said, "Set Alipay in motion immediately, at once, right now. If someone must go to prison for it, I'll go."

Ma is the quintessential Chinese entrepreneur of the twenty-first century, among a group that took huge risks to build what has become the foundation of China's prowess in technology. Instead of going to jail, Ma built an empire of companies that was at one point worth more than a trillion dollars, and he accumulated strong influence in the most powerful circles of the Chinese Communist Party. Alipay would be accepted everywhere in China, along with dozens of other countries. Yet in late 2020, after he dared to take on the government with a blistering speech criticizing regulators, the government cut its most famous and popular entrepreneur to size, canceling what would have been the world's largest initial public offering (IPO), that of Ma's fintech giant Ant Group. Ma suddenly disappeared from public view, sparking rumors that he had finally been locked up, while the government hit Chinese technology companies with a wave of regulation that wiped a trillion dollars from their wealth. What happened that could bring such a reversal of fortunes?

In 2013 I moved from Berlin to Beijing to learn Chinese and to study the Chinese economy. It was China, not Europe, that was the rising global power, a more foreign place with a perplexing economy impossible to understand without being immersed in it and learning its famously difficult language. To my surprise when I arrived, I discovered not an economic leviathan but a backward, antiquated, and low-tech financial system. The system's primary virtue, it seemed, was that it enforced government control over people's financial lives. I could see the limitations through my personal experience navigating the system. When I wanted to invest my meager savings, I walked into a dusty bank branch and was offered interest rates that were capped by the government below inflation, a policy that allowed the bank to siphon off savers' money to fill Communist Party coffers. Everyone went about their daily transactions paying in cash.

Economists call this situation "financial repression" because it robs consumers of choices and funnels money to the government's priorities. Banks offered credit cards to only an elite few. All debit cards bore the mark of the only player in the market: a state monopoly called UnionPay, and most merchants didn't accept them. Cash was hardly a convenience. Fraud was rampant, and even the tiniest local restaurant would obsessively run any bills worth more than a few dollars through a scanner to detect counterfeits. My friends in the United States were using the Venmo app to make payments—for example, splitting restaurant bills by using their phones. But my Chinese friends still settled up in cash.

No one expected then that China would within a few years be on the cutting edge of finance, bringing unprecedented financial liberty to a billion Chinese and making China the global leader in the fusion of finance and technology. Chinese fintech developed so quickly that my return to the US in 2015 felt like going back in time—leaving a world of ubiquitous mobile finance for paper checks and plastic cards. Major financial firms in the United States are now wondering how to catch up and avoid being left behind in a new wave of innovation. Then almost unknown outside of China, Jack Ma used his e-commerce empire and political influence as a springboard to disrupt the monopoly of the Chinese banks. He founded a new financial technology giant, Ant Group, which was recently assessed as one of the most valuable financial companies in the world—on par with JP Morgan Chase or Mastercard.

The United States was the source of much of the early funding, ideas, and technology for mobile-payment systems like Ant's Alipay and its main competitor, Tencent. However, Ant and Tencent have now developed a powerful new alternative to how finance is done on Wall Street. Both companies run "super-apps" more powerful than anything available outside of China, allowing their billion users to pay, borrow, invest, buy goods and services, travel, chat, and far more—all fused together in one mobile-phone application.

China's fintech revolution is not just a curiosity for scholars of the middle kingdom but a preview of a potential digital financial future that is already spilling over to the rest of the world. Facebook founder and CEO Mark Zuckerberg's strategy for his global empire, including launching a private digital currency that many feared could replace the national currency of many countries, appears to have been modeled on Tencent's WeChat super-app. The US government is worried about the rise of Chinese internet firms that are now strong enough and advanced enough to compete with Silicon Valley. It blocked Ma's attempt to buy a US payment company regularly used by members of the American military and attempted to ban WeChat Pay in the United States. Even so, Alipay is accepted everywhere from Walgreens stores in Washington, DC, to shops in Thailand that waved away my plastic American credit cards as useless relics. Chinese tech companies now compete all over the world with US tech firms. Even if governments ban these Chinese companies, their ideas cannot be contained within China's borders.

China's fintech revolution is an invaluable source of lessons about harnessing the new possibilities of technology in finance while avoiding the pitfalls inherent in entering uncharted territory. China has taken risks the West could not stomach. At times, its experiments have exploded spectacularly, with the fallout contained by a heavy-handed regime of censorship and suppression of protests that is anathema to democratic values. The rest of the world is unlikely to take a similar path, but we need to learn from the power of what China has unleashed and where it is leading, especially in how it reveals the importance of payments for what is possible in online business.

The issues posed by these transformations in commerce, banking, and transactions in China, which its policy makers have been grappling with for years, are not unique. They are the same kind of concerns about privacy, monopolies, and national security that the giant US tech firms are raising worldwide. The story of Chinese fintech suggests that adding finance to the existing big-tech empires can unlock impressive innovations that bring convenience, inclusion, and lower costs, shaking up incumbents accustomed to outsized monopoly profits. Yet that potential is not without risk. In the absence of effective antimonopoly controls, data-powered fintech behemoths that no financial or technology upstart could hope to compete against could become entrenched monopolists, harming rather than encouraging innovation. The near-total view of the data on the activities of users and the influence over what they see could also turn fintech apps into the perfect locus of control for governments, with the potential to undermine autonomy and liberty.

We need to understand the Chinese government's response to these challenges as we aim to create a digital future that does not give too much power to either big tech or the government. We need to embrace financial innovation without it leading to financial crises and maintain our competitive edge in finance and technology in the face of a Chinese system that has proven innovation can thrive even under an authoritarian regime.

China's fintech revolution started in June 2013, when hundreds of millions of regular Chinese took nearly $100 billion out of the state-backed banks to entrust to Yu'E Bao, an investment fund that one could buy in the Alipay mobile-phone app introduced by Ma. He offered savers 6 percent interest on money they could use anytime, far better than the state banks' offer of zero. Banks raised their rates and tried to compete, but Yu'E Bao still became the world's largest money-market fund, outpacing global giants like JP Morgan and Vanguard. Ma blew up financial repression across China, forcing innovation and competition on a sclerotic banking system. Today, a billion Chinese have abundant choice for payments, loans, and investments thanks to big-tech apps such as Alipay and its rival WeChat.

These super-apps have reinvented money. The financial lives of people in China no longer revolve around governments and banks but around tech ecosystems, bundling finance with functions that would take dozens of apps to even approximate in the United States, Europe, Japan, or Korea. Super-apps power a lightning-fast payment system that is far cheaper than US credit-card payment systems. It is this system that created the foundation for the rise of China's powerful internet companies. Citibank is now sending its bankers to China to get an early glimpse of the future. One said after visiting Shanghai, "If you're a banker in the United States, trying to envision what consumer banking could be like, this is pretty close to the end state."[1] Nearly a decade after I walked into that decrepit bank in Beijing, mobile payments are now so ubiquitous that beggars hang QR codes for Good Samaritans to scan with phones for donations because no one carries cash anymore.

Yet the reinvention of money and finance in China poses enormous risks. The fintech revolution may be poised to deepen China's authoritarian control over its people's lives, inspiring the government to take control with its own initiatives like social credit, a digital tool for social control that brings Mao-era dossiers of political loyalty into the twenty-first century. After accusing an official of corruption, investigative journalist Liu Hu found himself on an automated blacklist that prevented him from getting a loan, buying many goods, or even taking a fast train. Millions more get added to those blacklists every year. When COVID-19 hit China, it was through the fintech super-apps that the Chinese government controlled people's mobility. Tech firms' algorithms determined whether millions of Chinese were free to leave their homes, demonstrating that super-apps would be the perfect means to control the population.

Control over the operation of the digital wallets of Alipay and Tencent could lock unfavored groups such as dissidents out of the modern economy. As China's politics becomes even more authoritarian and statist, the innovative new financial system built by China's entrepreneurs may well be replaced by one focused on control and surveillance. Fintech would then cease to be the force for financial freedom in China that Ma made a reality for so many years. The move from a laissez-faire system that incubated China's booming tech sector and the response to Ma's speech criticizing regulators are stark illustrations that China's government wants innovation only if it does not threaten its control and that it will not tolerate concentrations of power outside the party—even if Ma is a party member.

A central-bank-backed digital currency, the most advanced of any major economy, will enable real-time government tracking and control for every transaction anyone makes, and central banks around the world are considering building similar systems. As the new digital currency replaces paper cash, the Chinese people will no longer have a way to transact anonymously.

Successful entrepreneurs and government control are only part of the story, much of which involves serious failings in China's grasp of what is going on regarding rampant illegal behavior successfully masquerading as innovation. There is a dark, seedy side of fintech innovation in China—the paths to be avoided for anyone following China's model. Ding Ning, a technical college dropout, used outlandish claims about advanced financial technology to earn plaudits from high-ranking Communist Party officials, hoodwinking nearly a million investors out of billions of dollars to fund a Ponzi scheme that bought him a Singaporean villa and pink diamond rings for his mistress.

Overworked local officials I spoke with admitted to sticking their heads in the sand about such frauds. They covered them up in order to look good to a willfully ignorant central government until massive protests shocked them into action. Millions lost their savings in such get-rich-quick schemes, and some of the entrepreneurs hoping to ride tech and finance to riches are now languishing in jail. What emerges is a portrait of regular humans in a flawed system grappling with unprecedented challenges, not a decisive government of enlightened central planners with full control of their economy.

This book is based on hundreds of interviews and meetings, from multiple visits to the Communist Party's leadership compound in Zhongnanhai to meet Politburo-level officials all the way down to the underresourced district government officials responsible for implementing the party line, from top executives at Ant Group and Tencent down to bosses and staff of failed peer-to-peer lending companies that ran off with millions of people's savings.

Researching China has taught me not only to read, listen, and speak Mandarin but also to gain a grasp of China's complicated political and economic system. That involves parsing the turgid prose of hundreds of party documents and censored news reports for what is not said or finding the one-word change to a boilerplate speech that signals a coming crackdown on an industry worth trillions.

Years of research have made me determined to paint a portrait of China's rise that blasts through stereotypes. It is often more a story of unbridled entrepreneurship and even lawbreaking than it is one of state subsidies, five-year plans, and party-imposed order. It unveils the divisions and factions inside what many wrongly consider to be a unified authoritarian government, such as when reformist bureaucrats like Zhou Xiaochuan invited big tech into finance to compete with state-owned banks and force them to shape up, realizing that simply ordering banks to become more innovative was bound to fail.

My analysis shows that Chinese people care about privacy just like we do but that they see themselves having much less ability to protect it. It reveals the limits of the party's control, from powerful companies refusing to hand over credit data to the central bank to entrepreneurs going above the heads of regulators to neuter rules that would hold back their companies. Whereas press reports often exaggerate the technological power of the social credit system, the story of fintech shows that the party's surveillance and control methods are often less than meets the eye, suffering from technical and political difficulties that rarely make it into the public discourse.

The story of fintech is fascinating in its own right and full of implications for the future of finance and technology around the world. It is also the perfect lens through which to understand what China, the world's rising power, is today. The narrative arc of fintech, from the 2013 paradise for entrepreneurship and innovation to today's tight controls after a messy period reining in excess, mirrors a China under expanding control and surveillance as Communist Party general secretary Xi Jinping has consolidated power. After years as a liberalizing force for freedom, digital money now looks darker, becoming instead a tool for surveillance and control in the hands of a government that demands absolute loyalty from even its most powerful and independent-minded business leaders. In turn, the darkening climate in the Chinese homeland makes the expanding reach abroad of major Chinese technology firms look like more of a threat, for it is hard today to argue that these firms can stand up to party demands to hand over data on either Chinese or foreign users. It is up to the rest of the world to present an alternative vision, avoid the same fate, and instead employ the new possibilities of digital money to enhance freedom and autonomy.

· · ·

Part 1 of this book covers the origin of China's fintech revolution, a triumph of entrepreneurial energy. Chapter 1 starts with entrepreneurial solutions from Jack Ma of Alibaba and Pony Ma of Tencent to the problem of China's antiquated financial system. Competing against each other, they launched China's fintech revolution, all supported by Zhou Xiaochuan, the technology-embracing central-bank governor who helped these upstarts with loose regulation and political protection. The underdeveloped, repressed financial system that then existed did not provide what tech companies needed to get off the ground. There was no venture-capital-type funding for innovative business. Contrary to what many would expect about China, these companies had to go to foreigners for capital to fund their young companies, not get by on state subsidies.

In fact, China's technology success depended on foreign capital and financial expertise. Back then, Chinese firms engaged in copying ideas and importing technology from the more mature internet sector abroad. They would take whatever was working well in the United States and try it in droves in China soon after, so a look at US technology gave a preview of what would soon be coming to China. To earn revenue, Chinese tech firms needed to create their own payment systems because they lacked what we take for granted in the United States, Europe, and Asian countries such as Korea and Singapore: a modern, well-functioning payment system. In doing so, the tech firms liberated themselves from a constrained, Communist Party–dominated financial system by building their own alternative. Fintech also helped them beat out foreign giants like eBay in the China market.

Chapter 2 describes the shortcomings of China's repressive, backward financial system that left it ripe for disruption by big tech—if the innovators could overcome the political barriers to entry that protected the state-owned players dominating the market. It outlines how and why the Chinese government was encouraging and open to innovation in payments, even more so than the US government, leaving the unruly online-payment sector entirely unregulated for about seven years.

The chapter shows why, by 2012, the Communist Party was willing to disrupt its own state monopolies to encourage innovation and competition. Premier Wen Jiabao, the party official in charge of the economy, denounced the banks and said their monopoly had to be broken up—despite their being owned and controlled by the state, with executives chosen by the party. I then introduce China's political economy, especially the fascinating shift and newfound challenge to China's growth model that in 2012 gave the reformist faction within the Communist Party the upper hand over those who wanted to keep the state in charge of the economy. This chapter is key to explaining why China was willing to take such huge risks to promote fintech, much more than the West was.

Part 2 describes the Cambrian explosion created when that political opening let tech companies leverage their technology, data, and user base to create financial products that went beyond payments. Chapter 3 shows how Tencent and Alibaba's competition with each other led them beyond copying foreigners to pushing the cutting edge of global payments and financial innovation. The flow of ideas began to reverse, with some in Silicon Valley learning from Chinese internet firms instead of the other way around. Alipay and WeChat Pay entered an arms race of bundling, adding more and more financial tools with services such as social media and e-commerce to their apps. They became more akin to operating systems that host many apps in them, gathering an unprecedented breadth of data to unlock a business model more powerful than anything that global giants like Facebook or Google have managed. The power of big tech to quickly scale up and compete ferociously to build out new markets made major improvements in bigger nationwide financial issues such as the paucity of consumer and small-business finance, payment digitization, inclusion, and competition in investments.

All countries, including the United States, struggle with ensuring access for all to financial products, especially for the poor and for small businesses. China leaped ahead with tech-enabled solutions. This chapter explains how and why Chinese tech firms were able to revolutionize finance while Silicon Valley failed: digital wallets from the US tech giants have made minimal changes to our financial system. Chinese tech companies, on the other hand, disrupted the state monopolies. Thankfully, they had the political power and support from patrons like Governor Zhou to fight back against incumbents that tried to nip their innovations in the bud.

Chapter 4 describes the issues that emerged with the boom in fintech, from Ponzi schemes running off with millions of people's savings to black-market margin financing that helped crash China's equity markets. Once they opened the door with loose regulation, authorities had to figure out how to keep the good side of innovation and winnow out what was bad or too risky—all without causing a financial crisis. This delicate balancing act is what governments in the West avoided by holding back fintech, largely refusing to adjust regulation to accommodate new ways of doing finance.

Many old-fashioned fraudsters masqueraded as innovators to benefit from fintech's political favor, which illustrates the difficulty of knowing ex ante whether a given business model that appears innovative will be beneficial or create serious headaches. None exemplifies these issues more than peer-to-peer lending, which once seemed like the future of finance but would underperform in the United States and cause a disastrous wave of frauds in China, suggesting lessons for how to make sure that regulators properly monitor the more shadowy corners of financial innovation before they can cause carnage.

Part 3 describes attempts by the government and the Chinese public to reassert control over the behemoths that emerged in the previous boom and rein in their excesses to protect financial stability, privacy, competition, and state power. Chapter 5 covers the campaign against financial risk, including how the government reasserted control of financial infrastructure and data, as well as the social credit system that has terrified Western observers as the quintessential Orwellian, tech-enabled system for surveillance and social control but has yet to become nearly as advanced or ambitious as its detractors fear. It also shows how Xi Jinping's consolidation of power began to take out major Chinese tycoons, eliminating bases of power outside the party and serving as a warning to Jack Ma and Pony Ma that they would need to stay on the right side of the political line to retain their commercial empires.

Chapter 6 delves into the ambition and challenge of expanding abroad in a world that increasingly looks on Chinese firms with suspicion—especially when those firms have become so close to their government in order to succeed at home. It explores the fascinating new pattern of global competition in finance, with fintech wallets backed by Chinese super-apps competing with Visa, Mastercard, and other US giants around the world. The new global reality is that Chinese innovation is spreading everywhere. The chapter explores how Chinese fintech is coming to the United States, despite attempted bans, by inspiring people such as Mark Zuckerberg to follow the Chinese model because of its alluring power. He was surely guided by China's fintech revolution in his attempt to bring about a global fintech revolution centered on Facebook's plan for a global digital currency that could upend global finance and give Facebook the kind of reach worldwide that

WeChat had amassed in China. Governments around the world viewed this possibility with alarm.

Chapter 7 then moves to the backlash against big tech, a global phenomenon of even greater urgency in China, considering big tech's newfound financial power gained by leading the fintech revolution. It starts with a privacy awakening, as even government officials find themselves victims of identity theft and the booming market in hacked or sold data. It outlines the challenges of finding a privacy framework that does not hold back innovation, a hot topic in the US, Europe, and around the world. It provides counterintuitive examples, such as Ant Group being admonished by the public and regulators for bad privacy practices that are accepted as the norm in the United States. Counterintuitively, in some areas the Chinese have more control than we do—at least when it comes to how private companies use data.

Especially after the peer-to-peer lending bubble imploded, and with it millions of Chinese people's savings, the government began to realize that inviting big tech into finance created a host of new issues and got to work pushing back, preparing tougher rules across the board. Meanwhile, the once-popular tech firms began to lose the support of the populace to which they brought so much freedom and convenience, as patience thinned with worker exploitation and monopolistic practices.

Chapter 7 also discusses how the Chinese central bank wants to gain the commanding heights of global financial power with its own digital currency to take on cryptocurrencies such as Bitcoin, the US dollar, and perhaps even its own tech companies as a way to cut down on risk and impose control over the powerful firms and their users. It situates the reassertion of control in the context of a China that has reversed important liberalizations across society to put the Communist Party and Xi Jinping in command.

During COVID, fintech apps became a new locus of control for the Chinese population. The apps helped the government determine who was a health risk and who was confined to a red code on their Alipay app, meaning forced home isolation. The program helped China successfully handle the pandemic for years while infections raged abroad, and it showed the ability of Chinese tech to help its country, but at the same time it gave a glimpse of a scary potential future of app-based government control. In the background, but permeating the narrative, is Xi Jinping's increasing assertion of power and the way that fintech companies and their users were dragged into the net of control.

Chapter 8 discusses the spectacular fall from grace of fintech and Jack Ma, who on the cusp of the world's largest IPO put it all on the line for a second time to push against further regulation of fintech and to criticize the party. His miscalculation broke the dam of political support that long kept big tech relatively unfettered, leading the government to cancel the deal, costing him tens of billions of dollars, and embark on a campaign of rectification that would see a flood of regulations imposed on big tech, from new privacy and competition rules to tighter financial regulation.

In Chapter 9 I explore scenarios for the future, both in China and implications for the rest of the world, including which elements should be replicated and the measures needed to avoid the bad parts of the model, from monopoly power to privacy violations and financial risk.

· · ·

I take seriously the scary scenario that the new digital money becomes a tool not of freedom, which it initially promised, but of control. Super-apps would then become the locus of control for government, with digital currency monitoring all transactions. China then would export this model abroad to countries hoping to develop their financial sector, undermining US national security. But this is not fated in China or anywhere else that adopts the model. There are forces in China, including the populace, officials, and companies wanting to become global, that are pushing back. Let's hope they succeed.

PART I

Financial Repression and the Rise of Chinese Tech (2002–2012)

1

The Rise of the Super-apps

"Time is money, efficiency is life"

Following a trip abroad in the early 1990s, Zhou Xiaochuan, a lifelong bureaucrat who was then vice president of the state-owned Bank of China, arrived back in Beijing convinced that the internet was the future of finance. He had just returned from a banking conference where every person attending received a floppy disk with software to go online and send emails. He saw a chance to make a big difference back home, where no one was using the internet even though the necessary ingredients like computers and telecom connections existed. When he dropped by the state telecom bureau to request an email account for the Bank of China, surprised workers informed him that he was the first person in the city to ask for one.[1] Luckily for financial technology—fintech—in China, Zhou focused on developing Chinese finance through new technology. He would soon become one of the country's most powerful officials and fintech's most important protector.

China's fintech revolution transformed its financial system from the backward, low-tech, and repressive one that I encountered as recently as 2013 to today's financial technology powerhouse. A billion Chinese people who were starved for financial and other services a few years ago now have an abundant choice of investments, loans, payments, and a host of conveniences, some of which surpass what is available in the United States and elsewhere in the West. In turn, the symbiotic relationship between technology and finance helped fuel the growth of big Chinese technology companies, which have gone from imitators of Silicon Valley to innovators that compete with and inspire US tech giants.

If we want to understand how this happened—how technology firms disrupted the state-dominated banking system to build a new financial model around super-apps that started with e-commerce, social media, and games and expanded into financial empires spanning payments, investments, and loans—we have to probe the three larger-than-life characters who brought this revolution about. First is Zhou, the brilliant pro-market and pro-technology official who over decades designed key financial reforms in China and made sure that incumbents could not use political power to end fintech's disruptions to monopolies. Second is "Pony" Ma Huateng, the quiet engineer/founder of Tencent, China's largest social-media and gaming company, who launched China's first successful digital currency. And third is the outspoken, controversial "Jack" Ma Yun, the swashbuckling founder of Alibaba and Ant Group, which more than any other company drove fintech forward.* We also have to understand China's fascinatingly complex political economy, a paradoxical mash-up of Marxist-Leninist political system and state ownership coexisting with a vibrant scene of entrepreneurship and innovation.

The story of financial technology in China had its origin in 2002 with Zhou's first year as governor of China's central bank and the beginning of the forays of China's technology companies

---

*Although Jack and Pony share the same surname, they are not related. Ma is one of the most common surnames in China.

into finance. Tencent and Alibaba, the tech companies that would become threats to powerful Chinese banks, were still fragile and focused on copying the established ideas and technologies from more-advanced countries. They were far from posing any threat to Chinese banks or competing with Silicon Valley outside of the Chinese market. Importantly, the money that fueled their growth came not from master plans hatched by Communist Party officials but from foreign investors who saw potential in China's nascent but rapidly growing technology sector.

The Western technology companies that China was emulating grew to become innovative and powerful without entering finance, but Chinese firms took a different path because of a necessity that became the mother of innovation. For decades, finance in China was focused on state repression, siphoning off resources from savers to provide cheap loans to the government and largely state-owned companies. It provided neither the financing that innovative companies like Tencent and Alibaba needed to get off the ground nor the kind of payment tools that online businesses needed to charge customers for digital goods or physical ones ordered online. One of the secrets behind the rise of Chinese tech, alongside foreign investment, was the way that Jack Ma and Pony Ma overcame the payment issue.

Both stumbled on payments as a serious roadblock to their businesses. Tencent, an online gaming and social-media company, had to figure out how to collect payments for cheap digital goods. Alibaba, trying to construct an e-commerce marketplace, had to find a way to get merchants and buyers to trust each other when they were accustomed to paying in cash only after personally verifying that the goods checked out. Unlike companies in the West, which could simply accept the credit cards that virtually no one had in China, Tencent and Alibaba could not rely on banks or the only payment company in business, a government monopoly, to build a workable system for online payments. Therefore, they had to create far more extensive and robust systems to collect payments than did tech companies in the West, which could just plug into the infrastructure of the credit-card system.

That initial backwardness would become a blessing in disguise. It laid the groundwork for Tencent and Alibaba in particular and Chinese tech in general to build full-fledged payment systems. Once they had a successful payment system integrated into their tech platforms, Tencent and Alibaba could add all sorts of other services, financial and nonfinancial, to become one-stop hubs for everything from loans to taxis and social media to food delivery. How they did so could become a blueprint for aspiring super-apps throughout the world.

None of this triumph of entrepreneurship and perseverance would have been possible, however, if it had not been for political support that permitted their risk taking and experimentation. After all, China's financial system was backward because government control had forbidden market forces from playing more of a role in finance. Jack Ma, for one, was acutely aware that his firm's entry into payments, an area usually reserved for state companies, could end up with him and his colleagues being thrown in jail. In no small part thanks to Governor Zhou and his allies, the Chinese government instead took a hands-off approach to the sector, providing the political cover that entrepreneurs needed. They also locked out foreign payment and tech companies that might have been tougher competition than the lumbering state-owned companies that then dominated, although the threat of foreign competition from eBay and PayPal were important motivations for Jack Ma to launch Alipay.

The wait-and-see approach that China applied to fintech regulation might seem surprising coming from an authoritarian government, but it is consistent with how China transformed from a poor centrally planned economy with a GDP per capita three times lower than sub-Saharan Africa in 1978 to a thriving economic superpower.[2] Communist Party leadership set the overall direction and parameters for reform, and local governments or industries were given space for experiments that the central government could learn from, evaluate, and scale up. Political scientist Yuen Yuen Ang calls this "directed improvisation," a flexible combination of top-down and bottom-up policy.[3] Online payment was the latest in a long line of experiments in which China allowed "implementation first, and drafting universal laws and regulations later."[4] In fact, the Chinese approach to fintech was more flexible and encouraging than the more cautious approach of authorities in the United States and Europe.

As Chinese technology companies grew more powerful and capable, around 2012 benign neglect turned into explicit support. China's most-powerful officials, like Governor Zhou Xiaochuan, saw that inviting technology companies into finance could help the party stay in power by maintaining the economic growth that helped legitimize its rule. Loose regulations and a blanket of political protection made it possible for fintech companies to break through the moat surrounding state-owned banks and disrupt them. In addition to this political breakthrough, the rise of mobile internet made it possible to take online finance anywhere, neutering much of China's financial regulation and threatening the state monopoly that held a vise grip on online payments.

Tencent Creates an Online Economy and Virtual Currency

Tencent, then a little-known social-media company, helped kick off the fintech era when it issued a virtual currency called the Q coin in 2002. Now one of the world's most important companies and the largest gaming firm worldwide, with a market valuation that at one point neared a trillion dollars, Tencent is little known outside of China. Its WeChat super-app has more than a billion active users who depend on it for everything from news, chats, and social media to payments, loans, and investments. It would take Facebook, Instagram, your banking app, and many more apps used by people in the West to do all that WeChat can. It has its own offerings in gaming, social media, cloud computing, and more, as well as large stakes in non-Chinese companies such as Epic, whose *Fortnite* game has made billions around the world. Tencent's success and creativity have made it a model for emulation abroad, including by Facebook, but it began like many Chinese companies: as a thinly veiled copycat. Far from being embarrassed by this record, Pony Ma Huateng, who cofounded Tencent in 1998 with four friends in Shenzhen, once said that "imitation is the most dependable innovation."[5]

Pony Ma spent his childhood in a small town on Hainan island, where his parents worked for the port. His family moved to Shenzhen in 1984 when he was thirteen, where he soaked in an entrepreneurial atmosphere unique in China at the time. The reform era was young, and capitalists would not be officially let into the Communist Party for eighteen years, but that year Shenzhen dared to contribute a float with the slogan "time is money, efficiency is life" to a parade in Beijing celebrating the People's Republic of China's thirty-fifth anniversary. Originally a small city across the river from Hong Kong, Shenzhen became a boomtown after China's early market reforms designated it a "special economic zone" encouraged to experiment with business-friendly policies. Massive investment, migration from the rest of China, and breakneck economic growth followed.

Ma has had a lifelong interest in science and building things, both physical and digital. His first product was a makeshift telescope, and he earned his first RMB after he entered a contest in Beijing by submitting a report with his detailed observations of Halley's comet.[6] He passed the college entrance exam in 1989 and entered Shenzhen University with a major in engineering, where he showed an early knack for computer programming. He was competitive, studious, and mischievous, writing viruses that would freeze fellow students' progress on their work.[7] His skills and reputation were such that he was the first person the university administration would call to deactivate the viruses that locked up shared computers.

Pony's first job out of college in 1993 was as a software engineer at a start-up pager company, where he worked quietly for five years and was nicknamed "Little Ma." His programmer job paid only about $2,300 per year, but it was an astronomical sum for China then. The GDP per person at the time was only $377 in today's dollars, less than Sierra Leone or Afghanistan today.[8] Ma may not have been perceived to be star material by his company, but outside of it he showed the trappings of a budding, risk-loving entrepreneur. He made thousands of RMB selling stock-quotation machines he built in his spare time, and he plowed the profits into equipment and four phone lines to host a sort of pre-internet website at his home, putting him in contact with many others who would also become star tech entrepreneurs.[9] When one of them, Ding Lei, founded his own company and became rich selling email systems, Ma saw his own chance to get in on the ground floor of the new possibilities that the internet brought. He left his job and launched Tencent with a group of cofounders on November 11, 1998.

Tencent was part of a wave of Chinese start-up companies following the promise of dotcom riches by copying successful Western tech products just as the tech bubble was nearing its peak in the United States. Tencent's first product, OICQ, was a copy of ICQ ("I seek you"), an online messenger owned by AOL. OICQ users could chat on a PC online or pay to receive news and messages on pagers. Tencent's naming of this product made the brazenness of its copying all too obvious. It was forced to change to the more original "QQ" after AOL sued it for intellectual property theft. Tencent had a million users at the end of 1999, yet it had little revenue. Like other dotcom companies at the time, Tencent had focused on user growth by making its product free, hoping to someday figure out how to make money. Without any revenue, Pony Ma and his cofounders ran so low on cash that they tried and failed to sell the company. Prospects were so bleak that a friend bailing them out with loans told them, "You really have no money, it's ok if you do not pay me back, but I do not want your equity."[10] This would turn out to be one of the greatest financial mistakes of all time.

It's difficult for the powers that be in Beijing to own up to the fact that the tech titans of China depended on foreign investment, especially by US-based venture capital and stock markets, to survive their early years. Tech companies popped up in China quickly, but local venture capital was scarce to nonexistent, and Chinese stock markets set the bar for listings too high for new companies like Tencent.[11] The Chinese government was not willing to open sensitive technology sectors fully to foreigners, but it also pragmatically knew that it needed foreign capital to develop a homegrown tech sector. It tacitly allowed work-arounds that enabled Chinese tech firms like Tencent to accept foreign money through holding companies located offshore.*

Without this foreign help for companies in this sensitive sector, Tencent (and other companies) would not have survived the dotcom crash. A well-timed venture-capital infusion in 2000 from the US-based International Data Group (IDG) and the Hong Kong–based PCCW Global saved it from running out of funds. One of the best investments in history would come from Naspers, a South African conglomerate that took a 32 percent stake in Tencent in 2001 for around $20 million (years later, the stake would be worth over $100 billion).[12] Soon after Tencent raised all this

---

* These holding companies are called "variable interest entities" (VIEs), and they are not allowed to have legal equity in some of the key Chinese domestic entities, such as internet content providers. Instead, Chinese nationals have a contract to manage the local firm on behalf of the holding company and its shareholders, and to ensure that the holding company gains the economic benefits that a shareholder normally would. I recommend this piece by Paul Gillis—www.chinaaccountingblog.com/vie-2012septaccountingmatte.pdf— for a detailed look at VIEs in China.

money, however, the tech bubble burst, and foreign venture capital dried up. Tencent was burning through cash, and bankruptcy loomed unless it could find a way to make money fast.

• • •

China's financial backwardness, especially its lack of a payment system, was an existential threat for online companies like Tencent. Start-ups in the United States and other countries brought in revenue by selling advertisements. But even with a large user base, ads were less than 5 percent of QQ's revenue. The average disposable income for urban workers in China in 2000 was around $758 *per year*, about the same as in Haiti.[13] QQ's young users would have made even less on average—not enough purchasing power to entice advertisers.[14]

That left charging users directly for services. Even if customers wanted to buy online products from Chinese tech companies, there was no easy way to pay online. "At that time," noted Pony Ma, "almost none of China's young consumers had a credit card. They had to run to the post office to make a transfer, which few netizens were willing to do for a 10 RMB payment every month."[15]

China lacked the payment infrastructure that allowed people in the US to simply input their card information on a website and hit "pay." Credit cards were extremely rare, and the debit cards that millions of Chinese held could not really be used to make online purchases. Early debit cards could be used only in the city they were issued in, and only at the ATMs of the card-issuing bank. Thus, a Shanghai card would be useless on a business trip in Beijing, forcing the traveler to bring piles of cash. Since the 1990s, the Chinese government had been working to establish a payment network like Visa and Mastercard, connecting banks in the same retail payment network. Payment cards from different banks and different cities could then be used to pay at the point of sale (POS) or take cash out of ATMs anywhere in the country.

That effort culminated in the creation of China UnionPay in 2002, a government monopoly owned jointly by the central bank and Chinese commercial banks. UnionPay's creation was motivated in part to enhance the banking system's competitiveness with coming foreign competition after China entered the World Trade Organization, which opened its domestic markets to foreigners.[16] Government orders, not competition, created China UnionPay's role in the market: all processors of card payments in China were forced to accept it. All card payments inside China denominated in RMB had to run through its network. It would become powerful, but it was just starting when Tencent needed to quickly raise revenue. UnionPay's initial focus was on the huge potential in offline businesses such as physical retail, restaurants, and hotels, not fledgling online businesses that had no good way to handle online billing with cards.

Tencent's first solution involved billing users through one of China's state-owned telecom companies. Tencent fees for news updates and other content could be added on to a user's phone bill. China Mobile would then collect the payment and hand it over to Tencent, minus a 15 percent fee. Telecom companies are well placed to build payment systems in countries with weak banking sectors because they have many users and a large network of locations and agents that can accept cash. In China's case the partnership opened 65 million China Mobile subscribers to Tencent billing in early 2001.[17] A 15 percent fee may seem steep, but it is only half of the 30 percent fee that Apple and Google long charged App Store and Google Play Store developers for payments made in apps for digital goods.[18] This billing work-around probably saved Tencent from bankruptcy and the dustbin of history, for the ability to bill millions of people was key to Tencent making its first profit, in 2001.[19]

But Tencent still could not collect payments from its users logging into QQ from internet cafés or home PCs. The strategic calculus was even more important. Tencent aimed to create its own ecosystem, under its control, rather than leave itself at the mercy of the state-owned telecom company. When Tencent first tried to go outside the telecom's system to make money, charging users 10 RMB per month (about 1.20 USD) for premium accounts, inconvenient payment tools, as Pony Ma said, doomed the effort. Even if premium accounts were worth 10 RMB per month to users, it would not have been worth a trip in person to the post office to send a money order every month to pay such small amounts.

A Payment Solution: Virtual Currency

Tencent's solution was to create its own virtual currency, the Q coin, in May 2002. Once again, Tencent borrowed the idea from elsewhere. Virtual currencies had existed at least since the late 1990s in online games like Sony's *EverQuest*.[20] Tencent was probably most inspired by the Chinese gaming company Nine Cities, which made millions in revenue by selling a virtual currency for use in its games in early 2001. However, Q coins were much more useful than simple in-game currency. They could be bought for 1 RMB each and then used for any of Tencent's digital services. Instead of making multiple trips to the bank or post office, users could simply make one larger purchase of Q coins from a network of sellers that Tencent developed that included banks, internet providers, telecoms, and even internet cafés.[21]

Tencent would not redeem Q coins for anything other than its own products. So it seemed like an uninteresting sort of gift card, except for one key addition: users could transfer Q coins freely among one another online, meaning that Tencent was running a payment system—with no permission or regulation from the government. The Q coin thus became the foundation for a seamless online economic system under Tencent's control, one with a more convenient payment system than the government had built in the physical world.

The Q coin largely solved Tencent's payment woes. At the end of 2004, there were about 63 million Q coins outstanding, which nearly quadrupled in 2005 to 234 million (worth about 28 million USD at the time), more than two Q coins for each of the 111 million people then using the internet in China.[22] No longer needing to rely on the backward financial infrastructure built by the state for every transaction, it was suddenly easy for Tencent to sell virtual outfits, game items, and chat avatars for a few Q coins each. At the same time, in the US the easy ability of merchants to accept credit cards was a double-edged sword. It was easy for customers to make payments that way, but high fixed fees for credit-card transactions, with a common range from 10 to 30 cents, meant that charging small amounts would end up costing more in payment fees than the company would make selling a digital item for a few cents.[23] The US system was not inconvenient enough to justify US tech giants creating an equivalent to the Q coin, but it still restricted online business models to either larger transactions or making money from advertisements, as most did.

However, Tencent was unprepared for the implications of running a real payment system that in the end it could not control. A thriving black market embraced Q coins as its currency of choice. Professional gamers sold the coins they won, gambling rings used them to launder money, and hackers broke into people's QQ accounts to steal their coins. So-called QQ girls engaged in racy online chats in exchange for coins, and an online gamer even murdered another in real life over a weapon used in an online game that sold for 7,200 RMB (more than 1,000 USD).[24] Alibaba, the emerging rival of Tencent, became an informal exchange, posting buy and sell offers for Q coins on its e-commerce marketplace.[25]

Facing a loss of control, Tencent restricted transfers in late 2006 to make Q coins more like gift cards. But even gift cards can be bought and sold outside the control of their issuer. Users could create as many QQ accounts as they wished, put coins in, and then transfer those coins by handing over the log-in information to a buyer. In April 2007 the black market sold Q coins for about .82 RMB, making it a sort of parallel currency unmoored from the government's bottom line of a single stable currency under its control.[26] The government warned that it would take action to "prevent virtual currencies from assaulting the real economic and financial order."[27] Yet it took two more years to figure out what to do with this unregulated payment system. In June 2009, regulations finally came that banned use of gaming companies' virtual currencies for anything other than the issuer's digital services, largely shutting down the Q coin's black-market economy.

The mania around Q coin foreshadows the enthusiastic Chinese embrace of Bitcoin, an innovative digital currency that appeared in an obscure online white paper just as regulators shut off the Q coin's use outside Tencent's ecosystem. Though important in enabling Tencent's growth in its early years, the Q coin ended up as a dead end, a flash in the pan that briefly powered online commerce but did not change the broader payment system because it threatened government interests and was essentially shut down. A new contender was about to take the fintech torch from Tencent.

• • •

"Jack" Ma Yun founded Alibaba in his hometown of Hangzhou in April 1999, four months after Pony Ma started Tencent. Two hours from Shanghai, Hangzhou is the capital of Zhejiang province, known for entrepreneurship and small business—not politics and state planning. Ma would later say about his company's home in Hangzhou that "it's better to be as far away from the central government as possible."[28] Ma's father worked in a factory, and his mother was a photographer, but Jack wanted something much greater for his life. Fascinated by American culture and seeing English as a way to connect with the outside world, in the late 1970s and early 1980s he biked early every morning to greet foreign visitors to Hangzhou, trading a free tour for English practice. Despite such tenacity and curiosity, he failed to pass the Chinese college entrance exam in his first two tries. Surprisingly, the man who would become one of the world's most successful technology entrepreneurs could not pass a math test, and he would never develop technical skills such as coding. In many ways he is the polar opposite of Pony Ma.

After Jack's failures with the examination, the best job his father could find him was manual labor hauling bundles of magazines, an inauspicious start for someone who would become one of the world's richest people. Yet in a theme for Ma's career, he would not let failure hold him back. The third time sitting for the entrance exam, he scored a place in the local teacher's college, where he thrived and built political connections, eventually becoming president of the city's student association. He got a teaching job after college, but when Deng Xiaoping relaunched economic reforms in 1992 with the mantra of "let some people get rich first," Ma jumped on the bandwagon.

His first company was a translation agency that he started on the side of his government teaching job. It never generated enough business to survive, but failure did not deter him. His English skills scored him a trip to the United States in 1994. As with Zhou Xiaochuan, a fortuitous trip abroad led to his early discovery of the internet. Ma vowed to use it to connect China to the world. His next business, Chinapages.com, was an online directory for people abroad to find Chinese companies, but it was ahead of its time—many thought he was a scammer because few of the clients he hoped to sign up had even heard of the internet.

He already showed a knack for public relations, garnering national attention for his colorful and engaging speaking style, including fabricating Bill Gates quotes to lend his words more authority.[29] However, China Pages failed to take off, and the ailing company then entered a joint venture with a state-owned company that promptly used its capital and political muscle to take over full control. From this failure, Ma learned a valuable lesson about the government, which he later summarized as "Be in love with them, but don't marry them."

After a brief, unhappy stint as a bureaucrat in Beijing, Ma was ready for his third try at entrepreneurship. This time it worked like a charm. Internet companies in China and the US were reaching stratospheric valuations, and he was not about to miss the boat that he recognized years earlier. From the start, Jack Ma aimed to start a global company. He named it Alibaba because of its positive associations and global recognizability. Based on the *One Thousand and One Nights* story about Ali Baba incanting "open sesame" to enter a treasure-laden cave, Ma's company would connect Chinese businesses with foreign buyers directly through the internet, eliminating expensive middlemen.

Like Tencent, Alibaba.com started off free, using the classic Silicon Valley strategy to gain users first and make money later. The strategy worked but required large fund-raising from investors abroad. Early investors included Goldman Sachs, SoftBank, and others from Hong Kong, Singapore, Sweden, and the United States. Alibaba also borrowed and adapted ideas. Shirley Lin, who made the investment for Goldman, later said that "Jack's ideas were not entirely original. They had been tried in other countries. But he was completely dedicated to making them work in China."[30]

Alibaba started with e-commerce that linked businesses from China and overseas for wholesale orders such as ten thousand corporate T-shirts, but it expanded in 2003 to helping regular consumers buy online with a site called Taobao, which translates to "search for treasure." Ma feared that eBay, which had just entered China with a massive investment, would take control of the Chinese market and leave no room for tiny companies like his. It is hard to imagine today, but China's homegrown tech companies back then were miniscule compared to global giants from America and were therefore vulnerable. The outcome for Alibaba and other homegrown companies competing with the likes of eBay,

Google, and Yahoo! was uncertain. Most foreign websites were not yet blocked in China, and the foreigners had considerable advantages in capital and experience, which were matched against Chinese upstarts' more nimble nature and knowledge of the local market.

Jack Ma's response to competition made Alibaba into what it is today—China's Amazon and a great deal more—as he launched Taobao, Alibaba's first consumer-facing e-commerce site. Building Taobao forced Alibaba to face even-thornier issues with the payment system than those that had led Tencent to the Q coin because it was a platform for independent sellers with online shops, more like eBay but without auctions. It not only needed to collect payments from users all over the country; it also had to route them to a host of third-party merchants. Alibaba would run into two key problems: trust and clunky infrastructure.

· · ·

Taobao had serious trouble in its early days from sellers who never received payment for the goods they shipped and buyers who paid but never received their shipment, so it was flooded with disputes that undermined consumer confidence in online shopping.[31] Most of us who buy online with a credit card do not think about the fact that an online purchase is like making a loan, an extension of credit. When shopping in person, money and goods are exchanged simultaneously, so parties who do not trust each other can still transact. (Of course, the product could still prove defective or the cash could be counterfeit, but generally each party can see what they are getting.) Online, one party has to take a leap of faith by providing something of value before knowing what she is getting in return. If a buyer pays right away when submitting an order, the seller could default by failing to ship the goods or sending a shoddy product. Conversely, if the buyer can pay later, she might refuse to pay even if the seller delivers. In the early days of e-commerce in China, buyers and sellers who found each other online would agree to deal only with people in the same city, whom they would meet in person and pay with cash, which severely limited the potential scope of e-commerce.[32] Without solving the trust issue, China would not be where it is today, by far the world's largest e-commerce market.

US consumers and businesses did not have to think nearly as much about the trust issue, thanks to consumer protections built into law and into credit cards. If goods ordered online with a credit card do not arrive or are not what was agreed, aggrieved customers can demand a "chargeback," which reverses the payment. The banks generally end up eating the cost if they cannot recover the funds from the merchant, so the credit-card system has an incentive to screen merchants to make sure they are not frauds before allowing them to accept credit cards, a sort of credit check. But credit cards were few and far between in China, and consumer protections were rudimentary at best, so consumers were hesitant to buy online. This difference between the US and China situations illustrates how the institutional environment and incentives need to be aligned for new markets to function properly, but Alibaba's eventual solution shows that missing parts of this environment can be added by a determined company.

Alibaba workers studied PayPal's business model and Tencent's Q coin, but neither seemed to solve the problem.[33] Instead, Alibaba would copy from eBay and its Chinese partner, which tried an escrow system that requires buyers to pay up-front but releases the money to merchants only when buyers confirm that the goods have arrived in satisfactory condition. Sellers knew that the buyers had paid up before they sent the goods. Buyers knew that the sellers could not run off with their money without sending the promised product. They did not have to trust each other. But both must trust Alibaba for it to work.

Alipay managed to start collaborating with a local branch of the Industrial and Commercial Bank of China (ICBC), China's largest bank, which is owned by the government, to directly handle holding the money and processing the payments between bank accounts. Alibaba would then deal only with areas of less legal risk: data and mediating disputes about the quality of goods or receipt of payment. ICBC put its reputation on the line by providing custodian services for Alipay, giving users credible assurance that their money was securely parked in and overseen by a state bank, not some unknown tech company with little track record.[34] Taobao's escrow system, which became Alipay, handled its first payment to a Chinese student who sold a used Fuji camera on Taobao in October 2003, and the transaction almost failed when the buyer got cold feet.

Still, issues remained. Buyers had to use China's clunky payment system to use Alipay. It was a major barrier that put pressure on Alipay to build more than just an escrow system. Few Chinese used online banking, even in China's most-developed cities, so people would often need to go in person and wait in line at the bank to make a transfer.[35] For those without bank accounts, Alipay partnered with China Post to allow people to fund Alipay accounts in person at post office branches, which was helpful but still very time consuming when compared to Americans typing in a credit-card number.[36] As Lucy Peng, a top Alibaba executive, remembered, "During Alipay's initial operations one department had a fax machine. After clients wired monies via banks or post offices, they had to fax bank slips to Taobao. We would then double-check and confirm."[37] In many cases it would have taken less time for a buyer to just visit a local store in person and pay in cash. Merchants were also frustrated that it could take weeks to receive payments for goods they had delivered, largely as a result of the slow payment system then in use between China's banks.

Much of Alipay's work had to be done by hand, far from today's automated marvel that can process hundreds of thousands of transactions per second. The low-tech model was passable in 2003, when the entire market for customer-to-customer (c2c) online e-commerce in China was only around 1 billion RMB, about 120 million USD. Then, Alipay handled only around thirty transactions per month, which it recorded in Excel spreadsheets.[38] As adoption snowballed, growing pains emerged. Merchants were furious because frequent errors led many payments to be reversed or delayed, sometimes for months. ICBC, which had to manually print Alipay's payment orders and have its employees type them into the central bank's payment system, was so overloaded that it wanted to sever the relationship, which would have killed off Alipay and dealt a blow to e-commerce's rise in China.

This existential threat sparked innovation. Alibaba started batching transactions, a first step toward becoming a real payment system.* The change cut by half the number of daily bank payments needed to support Taobao, but it was not enough: Alibaba was still hemorrhaging money on bank fees.[39] Jack Ma first tried working with the existing system. He approached UnionPay, the powerful government monopoly network for debit- and credit-card payments, hoping that a partnership would give Alipay one-stop access to the banks. However, UnionPay showed its disdain for the small tech sector by sending a low-level executive to meet Jack Ma. It was a miscalculation on UnionPay's part. Alipay had to build its own solution as a result, a fateful event that would change China's financial system and threaten UnionPay's monopoly.

The need to keep its banking relationship alive turned Alipay into a real payment system more by necessity than by design when it introduced so-called virtual accounts. As with the Q coin, a user could use the backward banking system once to put a sum of

---

* For example, Alibaba's payment team previously might have needed to order the bank to make dozens or more payments per day to a single Taobao seller with large sales volume. Under the new policy, they could wait until the end of the day and submit one payment that added together all the day's sales.

money in an Alipay account. Alipay could then process transactions within that ecosystem without any need for the banks until someone took the money out. Virtual accounts reduced the load on its bank partner, cut down on bank fees, and let Alibaba earn interest on funds it deposited in banks on behalf of customers. Although Alipay initially could be used only for purchases from Alibaba, it became the foundation for a system that could provide payments for any online merchants.

Alipay solved many problems by becoming a payment system, but it risked legal trouble. Though not officially illegal, neither was it strictly legal. Collecting money for investment without government authorization was then subject to the death penalty. The central bank had responsibility for payments, but no laws or regulations were on the books for what Alipay was doing. Jack Ma plowed ahead anyway.[40]

No businessperson can become as successful as Jack Ma in China without the political savvy to evaluate which risks are worth taking. The People's Republic of China is a Leninist party-state that has never bought in to concepts like the rule of law enforced by independent courts.[41] Breaking or bending the law was nothing compared to understanding the political implications of a business decision. Such calculations and conversations with political backers are too politically sensitive to talk about openly in China.

Ma would have known that China's financial system was generally reserved for powerful state companies, which might make privately owned Alipay hesitate to enter this space. The risk probably seemed worth taking because it stepped on no toes of those powerful companies. After all, UnionPay was not interested in this market, and the banks were profiting from their relationship to Alipay. He might have also taken note that the Q coin had many of Alipay's features but had not yet brought any trouble to Tencent or Pony Ma. Jack Ma's connections in government may have also told him that the government looked favorably on e-commerce but was not paying too close attention to it. However, the hardening in the party's attitude since late 2020 shows that such permissiveness is always of limited duration. Yesterday's successful risk taker can quickly become tomorrow's pariah if she is not able to adjust quickly enough when the political winds shift.

This is where Zhou Xiaochuan reenters the picture, ensuring that innovators like Jack Ma had the support from regulators they needed to experiment and grow. A report coauthored by the World Bank and the People's Bank of China (PBOC) later found that "Chinese regulatory authorities initially took a 'wait and see' approach, allowing the emerging industry to innovate and grow with relatively few restrictions."[42] Governor Zhou also had support from even higher up, when the top Chinese government organ issued opinions in 2005 that pushed for "advancement of the online payments system" to boost e-commerce, which could "change the way our economy grows and raise the quality and efficiency of citizens' economic activity."[43] Online payments fit in with the government's goals, which gave Zhou and the central bank leeway to treat it with a light touch. Instead of imposing rules, the PBOC issued "guidance" in 2005, as an official explained, to "create a relatively loose environment for the innovation and development of e-payment business." Official rules would not be imposed for five years.[44]

Not all parts of the government were fully hands-off. The local government in Hangzhou supported Alibaba, hoping that its homegrown business would stay there and invest instead of decamping to more-prestigious places such as Shanghai or Beijing. In an email published on the city's website, Mao Linsheng, then mayor of Hangzhou, told Jack Ma in 2003 that "if there are any difficulties and problems in the operation of [Alibaba], please tell us quickly, and we will try our best to help and solve them." The city provided land to Alibaba and policies encouraging other firms to go online too.[45] China's political economy is unique, but packages of subsidies, tax breaks, and other support to entice firms to invest are common at different levels of government around the world, including in the US. In a comprehensive review of Chinese industrial policy, University of California, San Diego professor Barry Naughton found that in the late 1990s and early 2000s the central government was focused on making "enterprises more fully market-oriented" and "stopped trying to enact specific industrial and technology outcomes."[46] Any planning was focused on heavy hard technology like semiconductors and telecommunications networks. Tencent and Alibaba succeeded early on mostly because they solved problems and adapted to the market, not because Beijing picked them as winners.

Underdog Alibaba
Beats eBay and PayPal in China

Alipay and Taobao helped Alibaba get the jump on powerful foreign competition. eBay purchased EachNet, the dominant local Chinese player in consumer-to-consumer e-commerce, in the early 2000s. eBay then brought PayPal to China in 2005. Started in the United States in 1998, PayPal grew fast as an online-payment tool for sellers on eBay's auction platform. Like Alipay, PayPal grew symbiotically with e-commerce. eBay bought it in 2002 for $1.5 billion. By the time that eBay brought it to China, PayPal was a global payment giant with more than 80 million accounts in dozens of countries and $25 billion in annual transfers.[47] One-year-old Alipay seemed to have little chance against eBay's resources and PayPal's experience and technical prowess.

Jack Ma memorably quipped about eBay that "they have deep pockets, but we will cut a hole in their pocket."[48] Unlike eBay, which charged sellers for listings, both Taobao and Alipay were free. SoftBank, which had funded Yahoo!'s successful effort to fend off eBay in Japan, invested millions in Alibaba. Yahoo! poured even more money into Alibaba, investing $1 billion in August 2005. Thanks to this large influx of money from abroad, Alibaba could afford to promote Taobao and also make it free. Jack Ma's quip at the time, "Thank you eBay . . . you made this all possible,"[49] is an indication of the positive effect that foreign competition can have on spurring improvement and investment.

Taobao was better adapted to the Chinese market. A remarkable reversal in fortune in China e-commerce markets in the mid-2000s resulted in Taobao obliterating eBay/EachNet's lead within two years. Taobao had half of China's customer-to-customer e-commerce market by 2005 and 80 percent by 2007, whereas eBay/EachNet market share in China fell from a dominant 70+ percent in 2003 to less than 10 percent in 2007. Serious mistakes doomed eBay, despite immense investments in its Chinese operations. For example, it moved the back end of its China website to the United States. Its traffic then needed to cross China's Great Firewall—the internet censorship system— to reach the computers of Chinese users.[50] The result was a poor user experience, with a slow website and pieces of its site blocked. Some of the blame lies with Chinese government censorship, but eBay's unfortunate decision exacerbated the problem. It also could not settle on one payment/escrow service that users could get to know and trust. eBay China promoted both PayPal and EachNet's homegrown escrow service An Fu Tong, which led to a confusing customer experience that frustrated users and undermined their trust in the service.[51]

A payment system is useless if the merchants that people want to buy from do not accept it. eBay/EachNet's plummeting market share deprived PayPal of the use cases that drive consumer adoption. Alan Tien, then head of PayPal China, wrote to colleagues that "Taobao's product development cycle is much faster. Jack Ma's right. We cannot fight on his terms," and later that "I think it's absolutely frightening that eBay doesn't take these threats more seriously . . . Taobao/Alipay has grabbed the mantle as the auctions/payments leader in China." Tight government rules around foreign exchange and cross-border payments neutralized many of PayPal's advantages over Alipay, like its global network that might have helped Chinese businesses sell abroad.[52] Nevertheless, my interviews with multiple individuals involved in PayPal's push into China were unanimous in naming the most decisive factor in Alipay's victory over PayPal as Taobao's success with customers, not protectionism.

Meanwhile, Taobao's rapid rise drove demand for Alipay. By mid-2006, Alipay had 20 million users transacting 30 million RMB (about 4 million USD) per day, and banks were eager to earn a cut of the fees from processing its payments. The major state banks and even Visa signed strategic partnerships with Alipay. Alipay even worked with banks to expand into plastic credit and debit cards.* Despite all the interest from banks, the Alipay user experience was still poor compared to, for example, purchases on Amazon with a credit card in the United States. Most users did not leave money in their Alipay accounts because these neither earned interest nor had state guarantees like bank accounts.[53] That meant users needed to log into their online banking system to "push" a payment into Alipay each time they wanted to buy something, a buggy and slow process that led nearly half of Alipay payments to fail, losing Alibaba a huge amount in sales. By contrast, Amazon's one-click ordering meant its users could enter their credit-card information on its website only once. The system would save these details and seamlessly pull money from their account for future payments.

Alipay's big breakthrough was called QuickPay. The easy online-payment experience taken for granted for years in the

---

* Construction Bank, one of the "big four" state banks, issued a special debit card that made it easier to pay on Taobao. China Post did so as well, and in 2010 Bank of China even issued a credit card tied to Taobao accounts.

United States then became an option in China. Users could use their debit card to link their bank account and Alipay account, which could then pull money from the bank to complete Alipay transactions seamlessly. QuickPay made the customer experience so much better that payment success rocketed to 90 percent. One underappreciated factor in China's fintech success was that most people in China already had bank accounts they could bind to Alipay, both as a way to verify their identity and as a way to get money into and out of the system. In 2011, 64 percent of Chinese had a financial account, twenty percentage points higher than the average of other middle-income countries.[54] It was much easier for Alipay to rely on banks to help it verify user identities and move money into and out of Alipay accounts than to have to build this capability itself.

Alipay had to make big promises to get banks to agree to allow it to pull money from their customers' accounts. Jack Ma personally visited bank presidents and chairmen at least ten times during 2010 to build these relationships.[55] Most of China's top banks agreed to participate after early trials indicated that the fraud risk was controllable and, even more importantly, that cards linked to Alipay accounts on QuickPay tended to be more active, generating more revenue.[56]

Online payment made it easier to shop online, and in turn Taobao's runaway success in e-commerce made Alipay a rising star with leverage over banks, which saw it as a cash cow for fees, not as a future competitive threat. By 2007, Alipay had a 50 percent share of the Chinese electronic payment market, with more than 47 million users making more than 750,000 transactions per day. Three years later, in 2010, Alipay had grown by a factor of ten to become the largest online-payment company in the world. Although it was active only in China, the domestic market was so big that Alipay passed PayPal's global user total with 500 million people transacting 2 billion RMB (300 million USD) daily.[57]

The End of Laissez-Faire

The government's laissez-faire approach did not require formal government approval to launch a payment company. That ended after a wave of scandals created pressure to regulate and clean up the sector. In late 2009, authorities discovered that Shenzhen NPS, a payment company, made 70 percent of its revenue by facilitating payments for overseas pornographic and gambling websites. Another, called Mingsheng, was busted in early 2010 for handling 130 million RMB in payments to 50,000 online gamblers.[58] In the wake of these scandals the PBOC issued payment regulations in 2010 and then in 2011 required online-payment companies to get a license and submit to government oversight to stay in business. The PBOC remained supportive, reserving for a later time much of the complex details that would make compliance so challenging.

The long period of loose regulation followed by rules installed after a scandal continued a pattern. For example, seven years elapsed between the introduction of financial innovations such as the Q coin and the first real regulation. The government did not want to cut off innovation. So it limited itself to reining in the worst abuses, such as reducing the risk for customers that payment companies could run off with their money or facilitate illegal activity. Alipay had not been not involved in the scandals, but Jack Ma must have felt political pressure building. He went out of his way to demonstrate fealty to the government in 2010, saying, "As long as the government needs it, Alipay can be prepared to give to the government anytime."[59] The statement implied that Ma would not object to nationalization if the government asked. Surely, he did not anticipate that it would. Alipay remained in the government's good graces, demonstrated by the fact that it obtained the first new payment license issued under the new rules.

The licenses, however, contained a protectionist provision that created a scandal, denting Jack Ma's reputation and making China look like an unreliable place to do business. The 2010 rules were tough in one respect: no foreign companies allowed.* When Yahoo! and SoftBank were giving Alibaba the capital needed to defeat eBay, China's government apparently did not object to their buying around 73 percent of Alibaba, with the usual work-around through a shell company. But Jack Ma claimed that this time the Chinese government's licensing regime was serious about keeping foreigners out. He argued that if Alibaba owned Alipay, it could be considered a foreigner and thus unable to obtain the license needed to keep Alipay running.

Just months after he said he would transfer Alipay to the government if asked, it emerged that Ma had instead transferred Alipay, an asset worth billions of dollars, out of Alibaba to an entity that he controlled. Jerry Yang, the Yahoo! cofounder who then had a board seat at both Yahoo! and Alibaba, was furious and claimed to have been blindsided. During the dispute, he met with a senior PBOC official in Beijing who reportedly told him to "accept the situation," which was "out of their [the PBOC's] hands."[60] Whether it was actually a government requirement or Ma expropriating foreign shareholders is unclear because Chinese laws are not uniformly enforced, and regulatory processes are not transparent. Tencent, for example, which had 20 percent of the online-payment market, received a license without carving its payment division off from its foreign shareholders like Naspers. Alibaba and its shareholders later gained some rights to Alipay, but far less than if it would have remained one company.

The Yahoo!-Alibaba case is a stark reminder of the challenges for foreigners of doing business in a place as opaque as China. They have to rely on local partners to manage relations with a government operating without the rule of law. That leaves them

---

* Officially, the regulations stated that requirements for electronic payment companies with foreign ownership would be determined later, a tactic often used to keep foreigners out of a market without an explicit ban that would run afoul of World Trade Organization rules.

vulnerable to expropriation if the government and the local partner act in cahoots or if their local partner makes demands that it
claims come from the government. There is no way for the foreign investor to know the truth in these situations, and to this day
the real story of Alipay's transfer is not known outside of perhaps
Jack Ma himself and a few high-ranking officials. The irony is that
these foreign investors helped a Chinese firm push out foreign
competition in payments, only to be pushed out themselves.

However, the separation of Alipay, which would later be renamed Ant Group, would have important positive implications
for the company. It would soon raise billions for expansion, including from politically powerful relatives of former high-ranking
officials and foreign investors undeterred by what had happened
to SoftBank and Yahoo! The separation also had important implications for its culture. It was now its own entity and no longer
a subsidiary of an e-commerce company, with more freedom to
build its own financial business, driving toward expansion beyond
payments. It would be far more aggressive than Tencent in expanding into finance.

Small businesses everywhere struggle with access to loans. Jack
Ma recognized the challenge and thought early on that Alibaba's
data could help evaluate creditworthiness and enable access to
credit. Alibaba's first steps in finance after payments took place in
2007, when it began an ill-fated partnership with two state-owned
banks to lend to businesses selling on its platforms. Alibaba would
provide a credit report for the companies to help banks control
the lending risk. The match was not meant to be. Yan Qingmin,
a senior financial regulator, wrote that the cooperation ended
"abruptly" in 2010 because of "great difference in the understanding of credit-related concepts among the parties."[61] Alibaba would
have to prove its data's usefulness another way, for the banks were
too inflexible with their lending criteria.

A more ambitious move followed in 2010, when Alibaba
founded its own microloan companies. As it gathered more data

and learned through experience, it improved. Alibaba knew much more about its borrowers than banks ever could. It saw, in real time, payments using Alipay, revenues, customer satisfaction, growth, and even the supplies that merchants bought on Alibaba's platforms. Alibaba could also have a higher risk tolerance with its own capital than banks could, and its existing relationship with its sellers also led to low customer-acquisition costs. Although its capital costs were much higher than a bank's, it had a different kind of leverage: the reliance of borrowers on Alibaba's platforms. Alibaba named and shamed defaulters, using public pressure to demand repayment, and the fear of being banned from Taobao or Alipay could be a powerful incentive.[62] Simply putting a defaulting enterprise lower on the list of product search results could be catastrophic for an online business.

By the end of June 2012, it had lent 26 billion RMB (4 billion USD) to 129,000 small businesses, and later that year it began funding its loans through partnerships with trust companies. China's leading e-commerce company now had success in payments and lending, and its ambition would only grow from there.

A Foundation for Fintech

The early years of Tencent and Alibaba are classic stories of leapfrogging. They found success by importing and adapting ideas and capital from more-advanced countries and companies. The government put in place the basic ingredients of a competitive economy needed for these companies to get off the ground and assimilate foreign ideas: from internet and mobile-phone connections to education and a stable economic environment conducive to growth. If anything, even though it had an alliance with the local government, Alipay succeeded in spite of Beijing picking other winners, big state companies, to subsidize.

It is striking that so much of the raw intellectual material that fed Alipay and Tencent's most-successful products and the capital for subsidizing years of free services to gain market share came from foreigners, not the government. The credible threat of foreign competition from eBay was the most important driver in the decision to launch Taobao, so protectionism cannot explain it either. Without Taobao, there would have been no need for Alipay. If China had engaged in protectionism that would have kept out eBay, it might have delayed fintech development.

Whatever their long-term ambition, Alibaba and Tencent's entry into finance was born of necessity. China's backward payment system and problems with trust were holding back their non-financial businesses. They had to build their own payment systems because credit-card acceptance was not an option, and the government let them do it without any regulation for years. The traditional reform playbook of improvisation worked extremely well by giving space for innovation that removed payments as a barrier to Chinese technology adoption. At least for the payment side of their businesses, the government's main contribution to their success was simply not getting in the way or paying them much attention. Financial authorities left these private firms alone until their financial products were mature and important enough to merit developing rules tailored to their benefits and risks.

Up to 2012, fintech's impact on Chinese finance and people's lives was limited to their purchase of online goods, not yet affecting most customers' financial lives even as it enabled e-commerce and online services to grow. It was a symbiotic relationship. As online services and shopping grew, so did demand and familiarity with online payments. Powerful incumbents had no reason to pressure the government to restrain the Q coin or Alipay. That made it politically tenable to give them so much latitude. Banks saw Alipay as a revenue generator that brought in transaction fees and deposits, and UnionPay's card-payment business was growing too rapidly to care much about online payments. But Jack Ma and Pony Ma would not stop at payments. As Jack said, "Once AliPay grows large enough, we can slip in direct payments. And as our

AliPay becomes more popular, someday it has the possibility to become China's largest bank."[63]

Mobile internet and smartphones were about to become the foundation for fintech to leapfrog the old financial infrastructure. At the end of 2012, 420 million Chinese accessed the internet with a mobile device, more than accessed it with a desktop computer.[64] Internet users totaled well over half a billion, or 42 percent of the population. Smartphone adoption accelerated as local technology companies such as Huawei, Lenovo, and Xiaomi competed for a thriving market in low- to medium-end smartphones that boasted features and performance similar to high-end devices like the iPhone but at a cost that regular Chinese could afford.

By mid-2012, the Chinese were buying more smartphones than Americans, over a quarter of the global total.[65] WeChat, Tencent's mobile-first chat app, which was launched in early 2011 and is covered in depth in Chapter 3, had 270 million users after only two years in operation, a hint at how quickly that established technology players could gain users for new services. China's mobile-first internet adoption laid the foundation for the boom in mobile payments because all the technology needed to make payments was in people's pockets even if they left their physical wallets at home.

Products and apps could be designed directly for mobile, and apps in turn generated data that could be used in the underwriting process for loans or marketing other financial products. Half a billion reachable internet users formed a lucrative addressable market, which in turn attracted waves of funding for financial technology start-ups.

China's place in the world was changing, and fast. During the decade of Chinese tech's rise (2002–2012), China boomed on just about every measure and gained confidence in its own model of managing its economy. GDP per capita rose 450 percent, from $1,100 to $6,300. The world bought up its exports. Domestic infrastructure such as high-speed rail sprang up to bring people to new cities with forests of skyscrapers. Hundreds of millions of Chinese flocked to cities to work in the world's factory instead of scraping by with subsistence agriculture in their hometowns. As the wealth of China's population rose, so did their demand for investment options other than buying up extra apartments or leaving the money in the bank. As entrepreneurship, rather than joining state companies for cushy lifetime jobs, increased in attractiveness, so did the demand for loans that Chinese banks could not provide. Thus, an enormous void of financial services developed that tech companies were well placed to fill—if the state would let them.

2

Repression Ripe for a Revolution

"We have to break up their monopoly"

Alibaba and Tencent's ability to create and operate innovative, game-changing payment systems for years without regulation might make Chinese finance seem like a libertarian's dream. However, online payment was unique, an outlier in a financial system repressed and dominated by the government. In virtually every other area of finance, government barriers to entry and restraints on competition protected inefficient incumbents focused on serving their real customer—the Communist Party. By contrast, the good investment and loan options that Americans take for granted, such as stocks, bonds, and credit cards, were difficult to come by for the average person in China.

Only a relatively short time ago, in 1978, China's financial system was essentially just one state bank, the People's Bank of China, which existed mostly to funnel money where government planners ordered it. There was no need to develop skills such as pricing risk or to perform functions such as allocating capital, crucial parts of financial systems in market economies like the United States. In reforms over the following decades, the government established new banks, trust companies, credit cooperatives, bond markets, and stock markets. Some competed with each other, but nearly all were state owned. Many sectors of China's economy opened to private capital and competition, but the state retained a tight grip on finance because of its strategic importance in controlling the movement of capital.[1]

China began its transition away from a centrally planned command economy in 1978, but China's financial system has been caught in a tug-of-war between two major factions of Communist Party officials. Though sometimes referred to as liberals and conservatives, in China's context these terms are somewhat different from how they are used in the United States. Conservatives hark back to the past, but in China this is a past of state planning and more control. Liberals are not like US progressives but are more likely advocates of traditional liberalism in economics.

The "liberal" camp, including Zhou Xiaochuan, supported market reforms that could raise the efficiency of China's economy and sustain its growth. They argued that government ownership and micromanaging tended to create bad loans and inhibit the formation of a modern financial sector that could support economic growth. Instead, state regulation, as in many advanced economies, could ensure that the financial sector stayed stable and supported policy objectives. However, these reformists contended with powerful "conservatives," from the top of the Politburo Standing Committee down to lower-level bureaucrats, who tried to quash any actions that would reduce direct government control over the banks. Some did so for ideological reasons, ensuring that the state controlled the "commanding heights" of the economy, but other vested interests that benefited from state influence over banks to access cheap capital for local projects and connected state companies also fought market reforms tooth and nail.

Zhou Xiaochuan:
Reformer and Future Fintech Protector

Zhou Xiaochuan's career illuminates the challenges of the financial system that fintech faced and then disrupted. Zhou is a "princeling," son of a high-ranking official who once was a mentor to Jiang Zemin—general secretary of the Chinese Communist Party from 1989 to 2002. China expert Barry Naughton described Zhou as "one of the very best and brightest" of his generation, whose "links to a broad array of political factions complement his technical expertise."[2] Those connections would prove important in his ability to get tough reforms done, even if they created powerful losers. He was well educated and curious about the world beyond China's borders. Even during Chairman Mao Zedong's violent Cultural Revolution in the 1960s and 1970s, when children of urban elites were banished to poor rural areas and showing interest in the "bourgeois" West could get one publicly beaten to death in mob-led "struggle sessions," Zhou collected a five-foot-tall stack of records that played Western classical music and musicals.[3]

Zhou started his career just when China began moving away from a command economy to one that was more market-based. He designed reforms by looking abroad for economic and financial expertise that did not exist in China. He even had an extended stay in the United States as a visiting scholar at the University of California, Santa Cruz. Foreigners from transition economies such as Hungary, experts from the World Bank, and even Milton Friedman came to China to teach how modern economies worked and to share the challenges faced by other countries transitioning to more market-based economies.[4] People like Zhou then had to figure out what would be feasible in China, considering its political and economic constraints.

In 1991 Zhou made the jump to finance when the Communist Party named him vice president of the government-owned

Bank of China and member of its Communist Party Committee. Senior bankers in China's state banks are politicians or techno-crats handpicked by the party. Top bankers are thus ultimately responsible for their position to the party or even to individual political patrons, rather than to the banks that they nominally run.[5] In his new role and subsequently in senior positions, Zhou would have gained insight on how local governments interfered with loan decisions, directing funds to wasteful pet projects. Local officials used credit to run up economic growth in their jurisdictions so they could get promoted, leaving their successor responsible for paying back the loans.[6] He would also have seen how government-directed lending led to the state bailing out bad loans. Executives at Chinese banks thus failed to acquire the skills these institutions needed to become modern commercial banks that could support a more market-oriented economy.

In the late 1990s, Zhou was promoted to head China Construc-tion Bank (CCB), one of the four largest state banks. He turned a crisis into a breakthrough for reform, just as later worries with state-led finance would open the door for the reforms that ush-ered in the fintech revolution. Decades of state-directed lending to failing state companies had brought China to the brink of finan-cial crisis. To put China's challenge in context, over 40 percent of the biggest state bank loans had gone bad, whereas the peak non-performing loan rates for US banks during the 2008 financial cri-sis was only 5 percent.[7] Zhou published his plan to fix the banks in the *People's Daily*, the party's official mouthpiece. He urged China to invite foreign investors in and to sell shares outside mainland China in order to "have more clearly defined operational goals, resist government intervention, and help turn around . . . the tra-dition of non-market operation." Foreign capital would also help ensure that Chinese taxpayers would not be entirely on the hook for staggering losses. Much of Zhou's plan was adopted, bad loans declined, banks became profitable, and they listed their shares on the Hong Kong stock exchange. When Goldman Sachs and others invested in the Industrial and Commercial Bank of China (ICBC), the bank's chairman emphasized opportunities for China to learn from foreigners, saying that the bank "is not simply looking for some capital. Rather, it is more important to bring in internationally state-of-art management concepts and technologies to strengthen corporate governance."[8]

The government also learned from abroad in overhauling its financial regulation. In 2003 it followed international practice by creating a stand-alone bank regulator, the China Banking Regulatory Commission (CBRC). Liu Minkang, its first head, had an MBA from the United Kingdom and "relentlessly drilled his subordinates on the importance of global regulatory norms . . . officials joked that Liu would terrify them by landing unannounced in their departments and putting them through an impromptu grilling on 'Basel II,' the international accord on bank capital."[9] Reformers still had to be careful to avoid touching nerves with their pro-market policies, coming up with contortions like saying maximizing returns for shareholders was realizing communist principles and "socialism with Chinese characteristics."[10]

The Unmet Demand for Finance Leaves Fintech with an Opening

Yet even with Zhou heading the central bank, financial reforms had stalled in the mid-2000s as political resistance kept banks from evolving fully into commercial institutions. Zhou had wanted the government to sell off 70 percent of its stake in the big banks, but his boss, Premier Zhu Rongji, the top economic policy maker, had Zhou water down the proposal to get approval from the more conservative top leadership. The state retained majority ownership.[11] Even with stocks listed outside mainland China and adopting all the trappings of modern corporate governance, top executives at state banks are still chosen directly by the party and double as high-level officials in the party's *nomenklatura*.[12]

Naturally, state-owned banks run by bureaucrats answerable to Chinese Communist Party committees preferred lending to the government or to state-owned companies.

Financial repression left huge demand for more investment options and credit that the banks could not meet but fintech would. The government channeled people's savings into the banks as deposits by effectively banning many other investment options such as bonds and many types of funds. Deposits paid an interest rate often set artificially low by the government, frequently less than inflation. The banks thus had cheap funds they could then lend cheaply to the state and state companies. As for the stock market, it was such a den of insider trading and market manipulation that prominent economist Wu Jinglian quipped that it was unfair to casinos to compare it to a casino.[13] Meanwhile, if investors wanted to take their hard-earned savings out of the repressive system, they would run into strict capital controls.

By the late 2000s, however, cracks began to emerge in the repression. Those who could afford the legal minimum investment of 50,000 RMB (7,500 USD), 1.5 times the average yearly salary in Chinese cities, could buy wealth-management products (WMPs) that paid better than deposits. At the end of 2009, a three-month wealth-management product returned 2.8 percent, a full percentage point higher than deposits.[14] Investors snapped them up, demonstrating the pent-up demand for better returns and the willingness to try new products. Investors held at least nine trillion RMB of WMPs in 2012, triple the number from only two years earlier.[15] In comparison, WMPs were about a tenth as large as the 94.3 trillion RMB in bank deposits.[16] In a double-edged sword for fintech investments to come, many Chinese investors were later willing to try new investments because of their experience getting better returns with WMPs. Unfortunately, WMPs contributed to what economists call "moral hazard" because investors learned to expect a free lunch of higher returns without risk.

Just as Chinese savers could not rely on banks to give them a good return, neither could those without enough savings rely on banks to finance a move to the big city for a new job or to help entrepreneurs hoping to start a business. The World Bank found in 2012 that the most-cited obstacle to small businesses in China was access to finance—only 4 percent of small firms used bank credit to finance investment.[17]

By the end of 2012, 57 percent of outstanding business loans were to state-controlled companies, compared to 36 percent for private firms, even though private firms produced far more economic value than the state sector. Larger private companies in many countries could turn to the bond market to raise finance directly, but not in China. In 2012, only 7 percent of bond issuance from nonfinancial companies came from private enterprises.[18] Mainland China's stock markets were also not a good option, in part because government approvals gummed up the initial public offering (IPO) pipeline. China's most promising companies, such as Tencent and Alibaba, listed shares in Hong Kong or New York, not in Shanghai or Shenzhen.

Households also had to look beyond the banks for loans. At the beginning of 2013, only a quarter of loans from Chinese banks went to households, and most of that was for mortgages.[19] Only 15.8 percent of Chinese had a credit card, and even fewer, 5.8 percent of the poorest 40 percent of the population, had one by 2014.[20] Although China UnionPay had been operating for a decade by 2012, most of China was still using cash instead of cards for payments. Only one out of ten payment cards was in active use in 2008.[21] One reason was the low acceptance. At the end of 2012, in a country of 1.3 billion people only 4.8 million merchants accepted payment cards, and only 415,000 ATMs could dispense cash.[22] These shortcomings became a key ingredient in fintech's ability to leapfrog. The potential market for a more convenient, tech-enabled financial-services provider in China was much larger than fintech companies in advanced markets, where traditional financial institutions left less of the potential market unserved.

When I moved to China in 2013, everyone paid mostly with cash. Even though hundreds of millions of Chinese had China UnionPay debit cards, they would rarely use them except to get cash at ATMs. Only upscale establishments seemed to accept cards. Cash's ubiquity would become a big opportunity for Alipay and Tencent because fintech made buying and selling vastly easier. Alipay and Tencent's improvements in China were much greater than anything Google, Amazon, Apple, or Facebook have done to make payments in the United States work better.

Moving a country to a new payment method, whether from cash to cards, cards to mobile payments, or cash to mobile, is a complex endeavor. Payment is a two-sided market in which both consumers and merchants must adopt a new method to build a successful network. Without consumers clamoring to pay with a new method, there is no reason for merchants to incur the cost and effort to support it, and no consumer will bother opening a new payment account unless merchants already support it. China's attempt to push electronic payments by card only partially succeeded because it ran into roadblocks with both consumers and merchants.

On the consumer side, less than a tenth of cards issued were credit cards. It is easier to ask a consumer to change cash habits when they can get thirty days of interest-free credit, flexible credit, and rewards points. Instead, cards in China cost more: some merchants tacked on surcharges for card users, and banks sometimes hit some debit-card users with hidden fees, which scared consumers off.[23]

On the merchant side, fees were a deal breaker. Government regulators set the transaction fees that merchants paid, which initially maxed out at 2 percent of the transaction.[24] The fees were a bit lower than the up to 2.5 percent merchants paid on average to accept Visa or Mastercard, and regulators cut fees in later years, but any fee is higher than free cash. It is also harder to hide revenue and underpay taxes with traceable card sales. With credit cards, at least merchants know that customers might be buying things they could not afford without credit. China's focus on debit limited the number of merchants willing to bother.

China's experience contrasts with the situation in the US, where payment cards caught on quickly after being introduced in the 1950s. Small merchants there jumped at the chance to accept credit cards even though the fees charged were 6 percent of the sale. Credit cards replaced store credit, rather than cash. US consumers were already used to credit, often carrying a pile of charge cards for various stores or having multiple store-credit accounts to keep track of. Credit cards made all this easier for consumers and merchants through one simple account, where banks doing the card business took on the credit risk, back-office billing, and collections that businesses previously managed themselves.[25]

Bureaucracy and lack of competition also held back UnionPay, a quasi-governmental organization. The heads of UnionPay have tended to be former central-bank officials, not businesspeople. It was protected from competition by government orders. Any organization granted this kind of monopoly will focus on maintaining it by pleasing the government rather than satisfying customers or investing in innovation. This attitude led it to downplay online payments and rebuff Jack Ma's overtures to build online payments together.

It is easy to imagine a Chinese payment market today that would look more like that in the United States. If foreign credit-card and other payment companies had been allowed to enter and compete in China by late 2006, as China promised, they could have leveraged their experience and technical advantages to carve out a large share of China's payment market. UnionPay would have had to compete for banks' business, which would be able to choose from a variety of options for their cards. Exposing

UnionPay to competition surely would have sped up credit- and debit-card issuance and acceptance.

If card payments were widely adopted, there would have been less need for online companies like Alipay and Tencent to build their own payment systems. The protectionism that delayed development of China's card market was certainly not beneficial for its payment market in the early years. But this backwardness became a critical ingredient in the leapfrogging that began in 2013. Countless small merchants still only accepting cash and others unhappy with UnionPay's fees were an unaddressed market waiting to jump to something better.

The Limits of Control

The party took a two-handed approach to the financial system. On the one hand, it exercised control. On the other, it always allowed financial activity of unclear legality under minimal supervision as long as no serious problems popped up. Policy makers recognized that private companies and consumers needed finance not provided by the state sector, so they turned a blind eye to informal finance. Yan Qingmin, then vice chairman of the banking regulator, said in 2014 that "it is necessary for financial regulation to both encourage a variety of shadow banking businesses and strictly control the formal credit system to maintain financial stability. Constrained commercial banking systems will inevitably breed shadow banking systems."[26]

A 2012 survey found that nearly 60 percent of small and medium-sized enterprises (SMEs) in China were involved in informal financial markets, well over double the share that had bank loans.[27] In Wenzhou, a city famed for its entrepreneurship culture, small firms banded together to lend, borrow, and mutually guarantee networks of at best quasi-legal intercompany lending. More than one in ten people lent out money through informal channels, and a third had informal loans—at exorbitant interest rates two to three times what banks charged.[28] "Old lady banks," usually run by elderly women, pooled money from people in their community to make large loans.[29] A government effort to measure private lending activity in 2008 estimated it at 2.5 trillion RMB, or 8 percent of the total lent by financial institutions. Nevertheless, the importance of informal loans was much larger than this figure suggests because these were crucial forms of funding for small business and consumers who had few other options.[30] Informal lenders relied on knowledge of the local economy and the character of people they knew well.[31] Without a strong legal system and market mechanisms like credit bureaus to enforce lending contracts, some lenders relied on social pressure to repay loans, and loan sharks could "hire a killer who will chase you down, beat you up and maybe even kill" borrowers unable to repay.[32]

Local officials often supported these quasi-legal activities because they depended on rapid economic growth to get promoted, and everyone knew that the banks could not cover the private sector's needs for financial services. In her seminal study on Chinese informal finance, Kellee Tsai found that informal financiers "exhibited an ability to cultivate political ties that not only enabled them to continue operating . . . but also enlisted highly publicized support among the highest officials."[33] Local governments even ignored orders from the central government to crack down on risks.

It was a dangerous game. Many poorly supervised informal financial institutions collapsed or turned into frauds, which the government refused to bail out because they were not part of the state system. When the Three Star Holding Company fell into trouble in the mid-1990s, it had promised 20–30 percent annual returns to "honorary employees" who invested in the company. It attracted nearly 900 million RMB (110 million USD) from tens of thousands of investors before a government investigation in 1998 led the scheme to collapse as panicked depositors withdrew their money. The aftermath foreshadowed how later online peer-to-peer lender collapses would play out. Tens of thousands of investors took to the streets, not to protest Three Star but to express their anger at the government for shutting it down before they could pull their money out, while keeping afloat state banks in just as shaky financial shape.

This is the fascinating paradox at the center of China's way of managing the economy: the government cannot control everything. In some cases it looks the other way to avoid any implication to the public that the state would bail out a new form of investment. The traditional financial system remained tightly controlled. But new activity, with little or no regulation, could thrive on the margins as long as it did not cause too many problems. This pattern for informal finance would hold for fintech: rapid growth and exuberance, followed by a period of retrenchment and crackdown once risks emerged.

Political Breakthroughs

China's repressive financial system underserved Chinese savers, borrowers, and consumers. But the government's grip on and protection of state-company monopolies started to loosen. Authorities were willing to lessen financial repression if doing so helped their other policy goals. A door was opening for private firms to build financial businesses in areas previously reserved for state companies or kept in the shadows as informal finance. A need to maintain growth by rebalancing the economy required more lending to consumers and small, innovative companies, which state banks were ill-prepared to provide. Allowing more private firms into finance could thus be viewed not as competing with banks but filling out an area they did not prioritize.

• • •

The last big changes to China's financial system were made in response to a crisis in the early 1990s. In 2012 reformers such as Governor Zhou had to convince the leadership that changes were needed to avert a potential crisis in economic growth. China's long-standing exports and investment-led growth model was losing steam by 2012. Therefore, finance would need to change to support new sources of growth for the future. Demand from abroad for Chinese exports slowed because of the sluggish global growth after the financial crisis of 2008, while a flood of credit used for government-led investment produced much more debt than economic growth every year.

As a result, Chinese policy makers faced an alarming situation in 2012. Growth fell sharply to under 8 percent while debt ballooned to 190 percent of GDP. If growth kept declining, the ever-larger debt would be harder to repay, raising risks for China's banks and its economy. The divergence between growth and credit also suggested that credit was being poorly allocated, wasted on projects and companies that were not contributing to growth.

Taking some of the advice offered by economists, the government signaled that it would control debt and maintain growth by "rebalancing," although in practice this would be a challenge akin to steering the *Titanic*. The objective would be to encourage strong domestic consumption, innovation, and efficiency gains to drive growth that investment and exports could not. The government wrote these goals into its five-year plan for 2011–2015.[34]

Financial repression that benefited state banks would need to be revised. Squeezing depositors depressed consumption, and government-directed lending starved innovative companies and households of the loans they needed to innovate and consume. Chinese banks had advantages in lending to large, especially state-owned companies, but they neglected consumer credit and were not set up for the newly favored lending to smaller companies. Premier Wen Jiabao, China's top-ranking economic official, gave a biting criticism of the banks in early 2012: "Frankly, our banks make profits far too easily. Why? Because a small number of major banks occupy a monopoly position, meaning one can only go to

them for loans and capital. . . . That's why right now, as we're dealing with the issue of getting private capital into the finance sector,
essentially, that means we have to break up their monopoly."[35] This
remarkably frank statement was a signal to the bureaucracy that
it should remove barriers to entry for private firms in financial
services, even if this step would threaten state-owned incumbents.
A few months later, the central bank's plan for financial reform
announced that it would open up finance more to private capital.

• • •

Premier Wen's frustrated comments about bank monopolies were
reinforced by the central bank's veiled criticism in 2012 about
the lack of competition in payments.[36] UnionPay's monopoly was
under fire. Bankers grumbled privately that even though they
were shareholders, UnionPay's fees and distribution of its profits were benefiting it rather than serving their interests. Unlike
banks in the United States, which can negotiate with competing
card networks, Chinese banks had no choice at home. Frustration
with the monopolists grew on the merchant side as well, with a
prominent businessman calling at the National People's Congress
to "establish a second UnionPay as quickly as possible" to coun-
terbalance UnionPay's power.[37]

What's more, UnionPay's monopoly position led China to international embarrassment and US frictions. Frustrated by years
of foot-dragging on letting American card companies such as Visa
and Mastercard into the Chinese market for RMB payments, the
United States brought a case against China to the World Trade
Organization, alleging that UnionPay's monopoly violated China's commitments to allow foreign competition. The WTO ruled
against China, and the case became an embarrassment that underscored the international costs of UnionPay's monopoly.[38]

UnionPay's problems were an opportunity for Alipay, which
was still too small to appear as a threat. Politically, it would be
harder to rally authorities to block domestic competition from

REPRESSION RIPE FOR A REVOLUTION

a popular company than it would be to keep foreigners out, and the banks were still making money from Alipay even if Union-Pay was not.

Pro-technology Signals from New Leadership

When the once-in-a-decade party leadership transition was completed in 2012, the economic policy agenda was up in the air, and China's new most powerful man almost immediately singled out technology companies for favor. Less than a month after triumphantly strolling out on a plush red carpet as the general secretary of the Chinese Communist Party, Xi Jinping left for his first trip.* His destination would send a signal of priorities for his expected ten-year rule, now one sure to last much longer. Rather than visit "red" sites associated with Mao's communist revolution, he journeyed to Shenzhen, a hub of tech innovation. There he paid a visit to Tencent, a sign that it was in the new leadership's good graces.

Xi heaped praise on Pony Ma and hinted at a partnership between the company and the government: "How do we adapt the Internet to manage society? We see that your work is all very important . . . you hold the most abundant data, so you can do the most objective, precise analysis. . . . Giving the government this sort of suggestion would be very valuable."[39] Xi's remark implied that big tech would be asked to assist in monitoring the population but left the specifics vague. If they were willing to offer such assistance, Chinese internet companies would gain friends in high places, and it was an offer they could not refuse. They would need powerful friends in the political battles to come once fintech disrupted powerful incumbents.

---

* The top-ranking official in China is the party's general secretary, who leads the standing committee of the Politburo. The second is the premier, who is both a Politburo member and head of the government through the State Council.

The March 2013 annual meeting of China's legislature, the National People's Congress (NPC), continued the positive signals. Such prominent tech executives as Tencent's Pony Ma, Robin Li of Baidu (search engine), Lei Jun of Xiaomi (consumer electronics), and Chen Tianqiao of Shanda (gaming and investment) were all delegates to the NPC, giving them access to top officials.* Pony Ma advocated for more government investment in mobile internet and lower data fees, calling it a "once in a lifetime chance" for China to leap ahead because "many top Internet companies worldwide have not prepared for the wave."[40] His ideas soon became part of China's official goals.[41]

Jack Ma's status as a Communist Party member was not yet public, but he also enjoyed access at the highest levels. He was invited earlier that year to the party's leadership compound in Zhongnanhai to advise outgoing Premier Wen on his government work report, which would include "encouraging business start-ups" in the final version. His favor and high-level access would continue with the new premier, Li Keqiang, who invited him to discuss the economy.[42] General Secretary Xi would also have been familiar with Ma and Alibaba. As party secretary of Zhejiang province from 2002 to 2007, he lived in its capital, Hangzhou, where Alibaba, one of the most important companies under his jurisdiction, was headquartered.

Another positive signal for fintech in 2013 was pro-innovation PBOC governor Zhou's unexpected reappointment to a third five-year term. He was past the mandatory retirement age, but his stature internationally, his reputation for competence, and a desire to show continuity in economic policy led the new leadership to keep him on. At a press conference at the NPC, he reaffirmed his staunch support for fintech: "I personally always support the newcomer, especially when it is using technology to advance finance

---

* Baidu is China's leading search engine, Xiaomi is most known for phones but produces all sorts of electronics, and Shanda started as a gaming company.

. . . this kind of challenge is good, improving the traditional financial system's development through competition . . . and keep[ing]
up with the times and technology."[43]

Zhou was frustrated by stalled progress on reforms that would
make the financial system more effective and commercially focused, and he saw that fintech could help achieve his goal through
the power of competition. Alibaba and Jack Ma had the green
light from the head of the country's most powerful regulator not
only to enter niches that the banks ignored but also to make good
on a threat Ma made back in 2008 to "change the banks." Thanks
to the political breakthroughs, two types of opportunity for fintech followed. The first was that the government granted fintech
companies new licenses that removed explicit barriers to entry in
finance. The second was a relaxation of implicit barriers to entry,
which allowed fintech firms to do more with their existing legal
authority. The decision by Alipay and Tencent's WeChat Pay to
make it possible to use their online-payment tools offline, in person at restaurants and stores, is a powerful example of this opening. Peer-to-peer lenders (covered in Chapters 4, 5, and 7) also
stretched rules meant for individual interpersonal lending to create gigantic nationwide online lending operations.

The opening was not limited to Chinese tech companies. But
they had unmatched data, with user bases now exceeding that
of individual banks, and the technology to take advantage of
the open door more than anyone else. Premier Wen might have
been envisioning their potential impact when he said in 2012 that
China should "use technological methods to advance innovation
in financial services and management [and] raise the level of informatization in finance."[44]

• • •

Tencent and Alibaba's users, data, and technology would make
a big difference throughout a financial system dominated by
state-owned, -controlled, and -protected monopolies. A political

breakthrough in 2012 enabled Alibaba and Tencent to take on incumbents without being crushed. The government, reacting to slowing growth following the 2008 financial crisis, increasingly emphasized small businesses, domestic consumption, technology, and efficiency, areas that technology companies were more capable of serving than slow-moving state banks. For the first time, the Chinese Communist Party opened large swaths of finance to private capital, bringing competition that would spark a boom, disrupt cozy state monopolies and financial repression, and remake Chinese finance mostly for the better.

PART II

The Cambrian Explosion of Fintech

3

Fintech Brings Financial Freedom (2013–2017)

"It blurs the line between your life and the internet"

In September 2014, Jack Ma's Alibaba set a world record for the most money raised in an initial public offering (IPO). A metaphor for technology's rise over traditional finance and China's rise relative to the United States, the $25 billion of the IPO, far beyond what any US tech company had raised, eclipsed a record previously held by one of the Chinese state banks. Fintech was crucial to this rise of Chinese e-commerce by removing the payment impediment. And one reason that Alibaba was so valuable was its remaining shares in and partnership with Alipay's booming fintech business.

Although Alibaba raised the money in New York, it was an event of national pride for China, proving its newfound technological competitiveness on the world stage. At the time, Alibaba's valuation of nearly $230 billion was more than Facebook or JP

71

Morgan Chase and exceeded that of Amazon and eBay combined. The IPO made Jack Ma the richest man in China and cemented his role as an inspiration for young Chinese who, in increasing numbers, decided to start businesses rather than seek the safety of government jobs. However, anyone who is too wealthy and powerful in China rings alarm bells within the Communist Party, over which General Secretary Xi Jinping was consolidating his power.

What neither the investors nor Xi Jinping knew yet was that Alibaba and its archrival, Tencent, were about to demonstrate big tech's latent power to transform finance. Alipay, in competition with Tencent's WeChat mobile app, launched a new model that would represent a turning point in the flow of ideas between China and Silicon Valley. This new model was the super-app, initially unique to China, which leveraged the mobile internet revolution that over the span of a few brief years transformed Chinese finance from a low-tech backwater to the world's largest and most advanced market for digital finance. The transformation came faster than anyone anticipated, thanks to an arms race between Alibaba and Tencent to become China's dominant mobile platform. The payment systems they built into their mobile apps became the foundation for fusing social media, e-commerce, services like ride hailing and food delivery, travel, and finance into a single, powerful app. To other countries looking for inspiration, Chinese super-apps would soon look more like the future of finance than anything coming out of Silicon Valley or Wall Street.

In fact, the super-apps are in many ways more like operating systems than regular apps. Just as developers create apps for Google's Android and Apple's iOS, China's large tech firms signed on partners, from big retailers to small start-ups, to create new services and products distributed through the super-apps. Each super-app thus became an immense, unbeatable bundle of services. Even though US firms continued to dominate as providers of the world's smartphone operating systems, the Chinese were not ceding control. They were in effect creating their own back-door operating systems accessible on both iPhones and Android devices.

Inviting big tech into finance brought unprecedented financial modernity and freedom to a billion Chinese people who had been financially repressed for a very long time, an experience we can learn from. At the end of 2017 the Chinese became the world's number-one adopters of financial technology. Nearly 70 percent of digitally active people in the country used fintech, more than double the world average or the US's middling 33 percent.[1] Thanks to super-apps, cash disappeared, and people left their wallets at home, knowing that their smartphone would be enough. Borrowers no longer needed to schlep mounds of paper documents to the bank and wait weeks to hear if they were approved for a loan. Instead, online companies vied to lend them money, approving and sending the funds within minutes. People accustomed to shopping online began investing through tech platforms, apps, and websites that offered perhaps overabundant choices of investments, some full of dubious promises of high returns.

• • •

The technology and many of the ideas employed to build super-apps were not "made in China." They came primarily from Silicon Valley and Japan, and they were recombined through "second-generation innovation" in ever-more-successful ways.[2] Perhaps the best example is the QR (quick-response) code scanned for payments. It is a technology that was developed in Japan but then used to more revolutionary effect in China. China adopted many technologies later than other countries, but a second-mover advantage helped compensate for its later start. Second movers and second-generation innovators do not have to go as far into the unknown as the pioneers, and they can learn from pioneers' experience, as Alibaba and Tencent learned from mistakes that hampered the earlier rollout of digital wallets from Google and Apple.

This rapid revolution in Chinese finance is a testament to the power of technology, but possibly more so to competition. The internet companies had strong technological advantages that compensated for the experience and explicit state backing enjoyed by the incumbent banks. The cozy norms and repressive rules did not apply to these new players. They had to dust off the playbook that scrappy Americans had used to disrupt the financial repression that reigned in the United States a few decades ago. For example, money-market funds got around interest-rate controls that the Federal Reserve placed on bank deposits by finding and exploiting loopholes in financial rules.

The fintech revolution would thus be a rude awakening for state firms not accustomed to competition. Tencent and Alibaba competed fiercely with each other to accelerate the digital transformation of finance, shelling out enormous subsidies to get consumers and merchants to adopt digital payments. Their relentless focus on consumer needs contrasted positively with the state-dominated financial sector's poor customer service, which even the party's official mouthpieces criticized.

The new financial products on super-apps disrupted not only the banks but also the system of financial repression by introducing real competition for loans and investments. Once incumbents woke up to the threat, their instinct was to marshal their political influence to lobby the government for a ban on the disruptive products or to regulate them into oblivion. Crucially, the government continued to protect fintech. Technology companies had emerged as political powerhouses and were well aligned with government objectives. Lumbering banks were forced to shape up and give savers and borrowers a better deal. Savers gained hundreds of billions, if not trillions, of RMB in extra earnings as banks paid them more in order to compete with tech companies for money that previously had nowhere else to go.

Eventually, around the world the image of big-tech companies would take a hit as issues of privacy, misinformation, monopoly, and others emerged. However, China's fintech revolution came before the global backlash against big tech. At that point in 2013, the government saw these homegrown technology titans as the perfect lever to leapfrog the West's financial system, which was more developed but still slow to embrace fintech. The strategy largely worked as planned. At least at first.

Jack Ma Disrupts Financial Repression

Alipay was riding high in February of 2013. Its mobile-payment volume had risen by 546 percent in 2012, and its market share in online payments was well over 80 percent.[3] Yet Alipay's impact was limited to Alibaba's core online business, especially payments for goods purchased through its e-commerce platforms. That was about to change. The political opening was not lost on Jack Ma, who ordered Alipay's leadership team to think big: "Do not always think about the payments business. Room for improvement in China's financial services is extremely large."[4]

The decision to start with investment funds would be a shot across the bow for banks and the state's financial repression. Ma and his team renamed Alipay "Small Financial Services Group" to reflect its expanded ambition but still ostensible focus on the little guy poorly served by the banking system. A second renaming— Ant Financial—followed in 2014, with a valuation soon reaching $150 billion, about twice that of Goldman Sachs at the time. The new money made in China from tech and finance together was already outpacing the venerable traditional model of America's established financial players. Jack Ma's ambition was not limited to enhancing his e-commerce empire. It was something grander, a push to remake China's financial system: "We are not doing finance to make money, what we care about more is 10, 20 years from now establishing in China a more open, transparent financial system."[5]

Ant launched Yu'E Bao, which translates to "leftover treasure," on June 13, 2013, the first fintech product in China to threaten incumbent banks. At a time when banks paid almost zero interest on regular deposits and about 5 percent for wealth-management products (WMPs) that locked up their funds for three months, the Yu'E Bao money-market fund (MMF) paid over 6 percent interest on funds, available immediately.* Alipay users could test the waters by investing as little as 1 yuan (about 15 cents), which opened a huge potential market: the vast majority of Chinese people who could not afford the steep minimum investment for WMPs from financial institutions. The combination of high interest, inclusion, and flexibility was wildly successful. It took only a week to reach one million investors, and within a year more people invested in Yu'E Bao than invested in the entire stock market.[6] A quarter of a billion investors had put money in by the end of 2015.

It was a testament to the open attitudes in China that people who were accustomed to parking their savings in state banks with government guarantees would trust their money to a private technology company. Alibaba had earned users' trust through years of financial relationships. Meanwhile, WMPs from banks and other investment firms had familiarized millions of investors with new financial products. Another reason investors trusted Ant was that China's state broadcaster CCTV featured Yu'E Bao in a report that for many Chinese amounted to a government endorsement. As Zhuang Chengzhan, a retail investor in Shanghai, said, "I will pick products sold by whichever big-name companies have the highest returns, as long as they've reached a scale that's too big to fail."[7] Chinese retail investors were happy to get higher returns, and many would think they could do so without taking any risk—an issue that would become a serious problem.

---

*Demand deposits can be withdrawn without penalty whenever a saver wants to use them. At the time, Chinese rules limited interest on demand deposits to 0.35 percent.

Previously, government rules barred just about anyone but banks from selling money-market funds, but banks were not interested in promoting them. Those who profited most from restricting people's investment options to cheap or free deposits had no incentive to sell products that raised their funding costs. Yu'E Bao was possible only because the China Securities Regulatory Commission removed what it later admitted were "excessively high entry barriers"[8] and granted new licenses to Ant to market and process payments for MMFs.

Money-market funds were actually a loophole in China's financial repression. The government capped bank deposit rates, but it did not set any limit on the interest that MMFs could offer. Yu'E Bao could thus pay higher interest than banks. In fact, MMFs were invented in the United States for this exact purpose back in the 1970s. When inflation exceeded deposit-rate caps set by the Federal Reserve at the time, US financial innovators sold these new MMFs, which were not subject to rate caps and pooled money from small investors to buy bonds and certificates of deposit in bulk at market prices.[9] Yu'E Bao did the same, pooling money from small investors to put into China's interbank market at higher, more market-determined interest rates.

Yu'E Bao's success also came in part from lucky timing. The PBOC tightened liquidity in mid-2013 to check the excessive growth of shadow banks, which made funds scarce and expensive.[10] Yu'E Bao could thus extract high interest, which it could pass on to its investors. The fund grew spectacularly, from zero to 190 billion RMB (32 billion USD) in its first six months. After one year, it controlled nearly 600 billion RMB (96 billion USD), making it the fourth-largest money-market fund in the world and more than the entire MMF industry before Yu'E Bao.[11] Tencent and other internet companies then jumped on the bandwagon with their own funds. Although none would rival Yu'E Bao's scale, Tencent's Licaitong attracted 800 million RMB in its first day by offering even better returns—nearly 7.4 percent annual interest.[12] Banks would need to respond to this threat to their bottom lines.

Political Protection for Disruption

Yu'E Bao marked a new era. Private tech companies could threaten state-owned bank profits, so controversy was sure to follow. Yu'E Bao's total assets added up to a miniscule 1.3 percent of banks' household deposit base of 46 trillion RMB in early 2014. But Yu'E Bao's first year of growth was about a third of household bank deposits' growth—hundreds of billions of RMB that otherwise would have been in bank deposits at nearly zero return. People started to transfer their entire paychecks from bank accounts into Yu'E Bao and then buy online with Alipay. Even though most of the money made it back into the banks, it came back in a more expensive form. As people in the hundreds of millions poured their money into Yu'E Bao, banks feared that fintech would raise their funding costs, cut into their profits, and weaken their customer relationships. They were right to fear disruption. Central-bank data show that after growing 17 percent in 2012, household bank deposit growth fell to 12 percent in 2013 and 9 percent in 2014.[13] Although Yu'E Bao was only part of this trend, the loss was painfully noticeable for China's banks. In the 2013 annual report of the Industrial and Commercial Bank of China (ICBC), one of China's largest, the chairman signaled that it was waking up to a new world, saying that internet finance and "big data" were driving a "fundamental revolution of banking."[14]

Jack Ma feared that banks would find a way to quash Yu'E Bao with their political influence. A few days after the launch, he published an op-ed in the *People's Daily*, the same state paper that carried Governor Zhou's bank-reform plan over a decade earlier, to make the case for disrupting the banks. He argued that finance would change only when driven by outsiders. He claimed that banks at the time served only 20 percent of the customers, leaving the other 80 percent hung out to dry. Most Chinese had bank accounts by then, but few had access to bank credit or to market-rate investments. Ma also railed against excessive regulation.[15] Such a statement about banks exploiting customers would have been controversial a few years earlier. And his second sentiment about regulations would land him in hot water years later in a very different political environment.

At the time, though, everyone from former premier Wen Jiabao to Governor Zhou had already expressed frustration with the monopolies that banks held and the poor service that they provided to most people. They were also implicitly criticizing the regulations that protected the monopolies of the banks. However, savvy readers knew that only highly influential individuals expressing views agreeable to powerful party insiders could get a piece published in the *People's Daily*, meaning that Ma had serious political backing. Alibaba counted investors like the son of then-premier Wen Jiabao and the grandson of previous president Jiang Zemin.[16] Amid calls from conservative commentators to ban Yu'E Bao to protect the banks, the China Securities Regulatory Commission (CSRC) declared that it supported Yu'E Bao "providing more investment and wealth management choice for investors" as "a positive exploration of market innovation."[17]

For Ma and other financial disrupters, political developments were encouraging. In July 2013 the State Council called for "the establishment of privately-operated banks launched by private capital" to help finance adapt to the new economy.[18] In August an official PBOC report gave a ringing endorsement of big data and internet finance, jabbing at the banks by writing that "innovative methods in financial products and methods of service complement what traditional finance does inadequately." It even noted that Alibaba's bad loan rate was below the average for banks.[19] Governor Zhou's PBOC had Alibaba and Yu'E Bao's back.

Then, in September 2013, the entire Politburo, consisting of China's most-powerful officials, boarded buses for a study session on "using innovation to drive development strategy." Rather than having bureaucrats and government experts make the usual pilgrimage to the party's leadership compound, China's leadership went to Zhongguancun, a small area of Beijing trying to imitate the success of Silicon Valley by attracting elements of the start-up ecosystem.[20] Private entrepreneurs gave lectures on their products and visions of technology's future, showing that one could gain the ear of the most powerful people in a communist country as a successful capitalist entrepreneur—which not many years earlier would have made one a dangerous "class enemy." At the Zhongguancun meeting, General Secretary Xi advocated for government support and help for innovation and entrepreneurship.[21] China's ambition was—without ceding control—to encourage entrepreneurship that would make innovation a driver of growth, and those entrepreneurs would need innovative financing. Fintech thus fit perfectly with Xi's grand vision of China as the world leader in key technology areas, and thanks in part to governmental favor, China would become a global leader in fintech.

That was followed in November by the party's first major blueprint for economic policy under Xi. The Third Plenum report called for markets to play a "decisive role" in resource allocation and added crucial party support for the idea of private firms establishing banks.[22] It became official party policy to "develop inclusive finance" and "encourage financial innovation."[23] Reading the political winds, local governments pulled out all the stops to attract fintech companies. Shanghai was one of the first local governments to issue policies to support internet finance, including offering subsidized office space.[24] Supportive policies then spread across China.

With tech enjoying such strong political backing, the banks realized that they had to shape up and compete, just as reformers like Governor Zhou intended. In an interview he explicitly outlined the flexible and supportive approach that Chinese regulators would follow to the application of new technology in finance and why it was pursued:

> Technological innovation drives economic growth. We should start by welcoming technological development. When they first come out, we can't always make these things clear, nor do we know the next step in its dynamic development, so we first want as much as possible to take a positive attitude and give them some space. Some new products may not fit our conventions, but if the size is small, regulators should give them a warning, not necessarily prohibit it right away.
>
> Second, under current regulatory conditions, there are two scenarios: on the one hand, financial institutions use the Internet, cell phones, technology to do their business. Most of the time, probably we just need to make a few changes to existing rules, and then they can develop the business. On the other hand, if businesses that did not have a financial license use new Internet technology to do business that required a financial license, we need to think of ways to research these new business models to give them some type of license and a certain amount of space.[25]

Zhou saw fintech as an experiment, with leeway to evolve while the government still retained control over the traditional financial system. His policies tilted the playing field in favor of fintech entrepreneurs, which would not be forced to comply with rules designed for the old institutions. Instead, they were in what might be the world's largest regulatory pilot program, or sandbox. The government would eventually decide the rules and handle the risks once the market grew large enough to merit real regulation. However, the new reality was that the uneven playing field tilted toward private companies rather than state-owned banks. Zhou wanted to achieve through competition what government orders could never accomplish on their own.[26]

The extent of political and regulatory authorities' support of fintech became clear in the negative reaction to an influential state broadcaster who spoke for the banks. In early 2014 he called the new internet funds "financial parasites" that "profit from raising economic costs for the entire society." The *People's Daily* retorted that if banks were worried, they should improve their customer service.[27] They did, and millions of Chinese savers were rewarded with better returns.

Analysts at the time framed it as a stark choice: "To defend their customer base, banks have no choice but to launch their own MMF products and cannibalize their own deposit base."[28] Many banks raised their deposit rates to be more competitive with Yu'E Bao, and some issued money-market funds.[29] Once the banks had hiked their rates and offered better options, Yu'E Bao's rise in terms of assets halted for a while. Yet it was still adding hundreds of millions of users, and its positive effects on China's financial markets remained. It was a major win for average people and fintech, but it was only the first battle in a longer war.

Mobile Disrupts State Payment Monopoly

With Yu'E Bao booming, the battle shifted to payments, where technology instead of policy opened a state-backed monopoly to disruption. In early 2014 Alipay dominated the 9 trillion RMB (1.5 trillion USD) nonbank online-payment market, with Tencent in a distant second place with about 10 percent of the market. Yet most payments were still offline, where people paid only in cash or with UnionPay's cards. In fact, many still paid for online orders on Alibaba e-commerce platforms in person, giving the courier cash or cards on delivery—not Alipay.[30] UnionPay debit cards processed nearly 32 trillion RMB (5.2 trillion USD) of consumption payments in 2013, three times more than online payments from upstarts like Alipay. It would be illegal to challenge UnionPay's monopoly on card payments, but mobile phones and QR codes made cards and thus the monopoly obsolete.

Online payments and e-commerce had developed symbiotically in the mid-2000s. Similarly, by 2014 there was a new need for mobile payments thanks to so-called online-to-offline business models such as Uber, which allow people to order and pay for in-person services with a smartphone. In the United States such businesses could just have users input their credit-card information into the app, so the move online did not challenge credit cards. In China, however, although credit cards were still rare, these new online businesses could easily accept Alipay or Tencent payments.

Smartphones became the key to revolutionizing Chinese payments. At the end of 2013, China's mobile internet users topped half a billion, many of whom were on fast 4G internet, and over 40 percent of internet users already used online payments. If you could pay for purchases on Taobao with a smartphone during dinner, why not pay for the dinner and the cab ride home with a phone too? Soon you could, as Chinese leapfrogged right from cash to mobile payments. A potent combination of competition between Alipay and Tencent, freely available foreign technology, and mobile phones would achieve in a few years what UnionPay could not do over a decade despite full government backing.

China's now much-vaunted mobile-payment system followed the earlier pattern, integrating technology pioneered abroad. Here China had a second-mover advantage, learning for free from the costly mistakes and false starts of pioneers, including Silicon Valley innovators whose digital-wallet ideas have barely dented plastic card use. Chinese tech giants had well over a decade of experience and technology from around the world to incorporate into what is now the world's largest mobile-payment market.

From a technological standpoint, it is deceptively simple to set up in-person payments. A bank card used for in-person payments needs to store only a small amount of data about the cardholder's account, which the merchant's point-of-sale (POS) machine reads. It then contacts the payment network to verify that the account is valid and has enough money, and if so, it then notifies the machine that the transaction is approved and records it. Smartphones can do all of that, rendering both plastic cards and POS machines obsolete.

Telecommunications companies from Korea to Kenya have often been innovators in this space. Their large user bases, existing branch networks to handle cashing in and out of the system, and control over SIM cards that can securely store payment data create a strong foundation to offer payment for other merchants. Mobile carriers in Korea were some of the first to experiment with a mobile wallet, starting in 2002, long before smartphones, and the phone-based payment system of Japan's largest telecom provider, NTT DoCoMo's FeliCa, was launched in 2004. Thanks to NTT's dominant market share, it had the users to attract merchants, and competing telecom providers even threw in the towel on payments and joined their competitor's system.[31] In Kenya, Safaricom, the dominant telecom provider, launched M-PESA in 2007, which built payments into SIM cards. Today it processes about half of Kenya's GDP. Alongside China, Kenya is one of the world's most impressive success stories about digital payments and finance. Except for M-PESA, however, none of these systems were successful enough to put a dent in cash or card use.

Regarding the US situation, in 2009 the head of innovation for Visa said, "Where there's a paper system, it's not that difficult to beat cash with an electronic payment. . . . But in [the US], we have yet to find the unique value proposition that's vastly superior to the existing ways that consumers are paying."[32] He was right. There was not as great a need for mobile payments in the United States when compared to China or other countries still primarily using cash.

Most high-profile US attempts to launch mobile payments preceded Alipay, although none ever represented a serious alternative to credit cards. Square launched in 2010 with a simple add-on to turn phones into a POS machine. It has become a mainstay of small business, but on the consumer end it retained plastic cards rather than mobile payments. For all its positive impact on e-commerce and peer-to-peer payments, PayPal has not caught on for offline payments. US big tech also preceded Alipay, but Google Wallet, launched in 2011, and Apple Wallet, launched in 2012, could not leverage their technical prowess and massive user base into payment success on par with Alipay or WeChat Pay. Partially this is because of ingrained habits and lock-in, such as rewards, on credit cards, which were not an issue in China, but another problem is that their choice of technology required the cooperation of too many parties.

Both Apple and Google relied on near-field communications (NFC), which embroiled them in a battle of competing standards among telecom carriers, merchants, phone manufacturers, and tech firms that wanted to build a better payment system. Unfortunately, instead of cooperating, tech firms, large merchants, and telecom carriers each tried to control the future of payments by launching their own system. A founding Google Wallet engineer blamed its lack of progress on the telecom companies, which tried to block Google Wallet use.[33] Carriers like Verizon, AT&T, and T-Mobile did not cooperate and give SIM access because they wanted to develop their own systems. (In their case the joint-venture system had the unfortunate name of ISIS pay.) Phone manufacturers like Apple refused to let apps other than Apple Pay access the iPhone's NFC capabilities, so third-party payment apps could not offer NFC-based wallets to the millions of potential users who had iPhones. Large US retailers, which have long complained about credit-card fees, created their own ill-fated system called MCX. The result was fragmentation.

Another downside of NFC is that it required most retailers to pay for new POS machines in every one of their stores. None of the new mobile-payment methods were catching on enough among consumers for merchants to undergo the major cost and hassle necessary to support them. This divided, competing set of players failed to reach the scale required to put a dent in plastic card use. US big tech was also far less ambitious than Chinese big tech, often just adding a technology veneer to the existing card-based payment system. Smartphones thus did not live up to their potential to create a fintech revolution in the United States.

The problem with US payments is not plastic cards, which are not that inconvenient compared to phone-based payments. The problem is that our payment system costs multiple times more than China's and is especially costly for small online transactions, for which it was not designed. Alipay and WeChat Pay charge merchants 0.38 to 0.6 percent, compared to 1.5 to 3 percent *plus* 20 to 30 cents that US merchants pay to accept credit cards.[34] A US merchant selling a three-dollar cup of coffee to a holder of a high-end credit card could end up paying 39 cents in fees to take that credit card, more than the cost of coffee beans that went into it. The payment fee would eat up 13 percent, or 22 times more than the percentage paid by a Chinese coffee shop using Alipay.

Unfortunately, there is little ability or pressure to change the situation. Banks will fight tooth and nail to preserve their cash cow, and merchants bear the cost of all the free credit and rich rewards for big spenders but have limited ability to steer consumers to cheaper payment methods. In any case, the subsidies required to get consumers to switch to a new payment method would be prohibitively high for any new entrant like Alipay, for it would have to outbid the rewards cards, even if it could cut down significantly on payment costs for merchants. Higher costs across the board are thus borne by people paying with cash, debit, or non-rewards cards, making our payment system a hidden mechanism entrenching inequality.[35]

What would turn out to be the most revolutionary technology for Chinese payments was in fact nearly two decades old when it caught on in China. A Toyota subsidiary invented QR codes in 1994 for supply-chain tracking, but they have come to be used for so much more. QR codes can encode far more data than barcodes, necessary for large alphabets like the thousands of characters in Japanese and Chinese, and are easier to read for smartphones. They came to China in 2006, but the technology was not ready. Back then, it took phones around seventeen seconds to generate one on the screen—too slow for payments.[36]

QR code use surged in the US and Canada in the early 2010s, but the fad faded. Smartphone cameras at the time lacked the quality to read the codes well, mobile internet was slow, and fewer people carried smartphones. Security was also an issue. Unlike entering a website's URL, you never knew if you were scanning a virus-laden QR code. Surprisingly, the earliest US example that I found of QR codes for payments was not by a payment or tech company but by Starbucks. The 2009 test version of its card app generated a QR code that the cashier scanned to pay for "coffee from the future."[37]

The move in China to take online payments for in-person purchases started in January 2013, when an Alipay app update introduced a "wallet-like experience" that incorporated payments with QR codes. The wallet tool also aimed to turn Alipay into more of a full-fledged financial management platform than a payment app, including bill pay, tracking spending, digital coupons, and ever more features.[38] For payments, QR codes are simple and flexible. Small shops do not even need a POS machine to accept payments; instead, they print a QR code on paper or display one on their phone for the customer to scan. The customer then enters how much they want to pay, and the merchant verifies on their smartphone that the money was received. Other stores have the user pull up a QR code on their phone's screen that the merchant scans to withdraw the money the buyer owes from her Alipay wallet.

The scan can be done either with the shop owner's own smartphone or with a POS device that costs about $50.[39]

Still, Alipay's mobile app did not catch on right away. In Beijing at the time, most people I knew used Alipay only for online Taobao purchases or (no differently than Venmo in the United States) to split restaurant bills. QR codes for payments were nowhere. Meanwhile, just about everyone was glued to Weixin, later known internationally as WeChat, Tencent's new chat and social mobile app. Alipay put its workers on a grueling "9-9-6" schedule of work from 9 a.m. to 9 p.m., 6 days per week, to catch up, but Tencent was beating Alipay on mobile by an even wider margin than Alipay was beating Tencent in payments.[40]

Although Alibaba's e-commerce and financial focus seemed distinct from Tencent's world of social media and games, they were bitter rivals. Alipay had left Tencent payments and the Q coin in the dust, but WeChat's success on mobile gave it a chance to catch up in fintech. The January 2011 launch of "Weixin," which has become essential for daily life in China, received almost no attention outside China. The only article in English about it at the time of launch noted that much of its functionality was just like Kik, a Canadian app, hinting that Tencent had continued its earlier copycatting.[41] Weixin was initially so focused on the Chinese market that Tencent did not even bother giving it an English name (WeChat) until it was more than a year old and began to have more international users.[42]

Tencent smartly chose to develop WeChat from the ground up for mobile, rather than trying to migrate its PC-based QQ chat product to mobile. The mobile-first strategy made it quick to pick up on possibilities for the new medium that would not have worked on a PC, like sending quick voice messages that the Chinese found more personal than text-based chats. It was a smash hit, reaching 300 million users in January 2013, just as Alipay introduced its wallet.[43] Alibaba had long tried and failed to compete with Tencent on chat and social media, and it was about to find out that weakness in social caused a weakness in payments. Alipay had only a few million daily active mobile users in late 2013, compared to more than a hundred million for WeChat.[44] Alipay users who wanted to make payments would switch out of the Alipay app and use WeChat to communicate payment information and amounts, and confirm receipt. For many, it would be easier to forget Alipay and use WeChat for payments.

Tencent added payments to WeChat in August 2013 to start turning its chat app into a platform with many other functions. Initially, it was slow to catch on because WeChat users saw no reason to trust their bank information to a chat provider. As Ge Fei, a Beijinger, told the *Global Times*, "I'm not comfortable having my WeChat account, which is primarily a social tool, linked to my bank card. . . . I have safety concerns."[45] Alibaba's advantage was that everyone knew they needed to share financial information to buy its goods, but the Alipay wallet's slow start meant the mobile-payment market was up for grabs. Alipay underestimated the threat.[46]

Tencent's opportunity came during Chinese New Year in early 2014, when social customs aligned with the need of people to move money. Hundreds of millions of people travel to join family in their hometowns. Whirlwind visits to relatives and family friends include exchanges of red envelopes stuffed with cash. China's massive urbanization complicated the red-envelope ritual by spreading givers and recipients across the country. It was hard to give the gift in person and a perfect use for digital payments.

Starting in January 2014, WeChat users could send virtual red envelopes with digital cash. It went viral. Users could receive money in the app they already used, but they needed to supply bank details to send or withdraw money. It was a smart way to get a few early adopters to recruit contacts to link social and banking accounts to receive the cash, overcoming some of the early safety concerns. Tencent also gamified red envelopes, which enhanced the virality to the point of addiction. Users could send money to a group chat that would distribute the funds randomly between the first few people to click the link.[47] People were glued to their phones, not wanting to miss out on the money sloshing around their group chats. WeChat also enlarged the tradition's scope. A physical red envelope with a few RMB previously seemed stingy and strange, but people now sent small amounts to informal groups. Red envelopes became the foundation for WeChat Pay. In the first ten days, eight million users sent more than forty million red envelopes. The competition would get dirty—WeChat helped stack the deck in its favor by refusing to let users send Alipay's red envelopes over WeChat.[48]

Alipay's leadership was stunned. Jack Ma cut short his New Year's vacation to hatch a response to what he dramatically called a "Pearl Harbor attack" on his territory. The second-mover advantage showed up again: observers said that Tencent had achieved in a day what had taken Alipay eight years. Alipay offered red envelopes as well, but instead of Tencent's fun gamification feature, they offered a slightly rude, Venmo-like way to request money from contacts.

The race was on to build out mobile payments offline, one that neither company could afford to lose because it would give an advantage to its rival's tech ecosystem in the booming online-to-offline market. The first battleground was ride hailing, in which Uber's model had been adapted to China. Payment speed was of the essence: trying to pay for a ride traditionally meant hurriedly counting out cash while cars behind honked and then occasionally finding out that the driver had slipped a counterfeit bill into the change.* It took even longer if you could convince the driver to swipe a card because they had to dig in the glove department to find a dusty, slow POS machine.

---

*Although it is not a common occurrence, I personally fell victim a few times to the counterfeit-bill scam when it was dark or I was in a rush.

Alipay was the first mover, partnering with taxis to display its QR codes for payments in cabs. It then inked a deal with ride-hailing app Kuaidi to allow payment with Alipay either with QR codes or in the Kuaidi app. Tencent then one-upped Alipay by integrating hailing and paying for a ride all within the WeChat app, gaining tens of millions of users for its payment service thanks to four hundred million RMB in subsidies to drivers and riders. Alipay followed Tencent in pouring half a billion RMB into subsidies for ride hailing and taxis as a spearhead for mobile-payment adoption.[49] The giveaways were a major draw, covering a significant portion of a short ride's cost.

Taxi payment was an important early step toward the rapid adoption of super-apps, an arms race to add new functions to outdo rivals. The money given to riders shows that subsidies can be crucial in the early days of a new payment method to get it off the ground and break ingrained habits. Suddenly, the fintech space was competitive, or at least had switched from a near monopoly to a duopoly. WeChat Pay's market share in mobile payments quadrupled in only three years from 10 percent to 40 percent. Alipay was still the leader, but it went from controlling nearly 83 percent of the mobile-payment market in late 2014 to only 55 percent in 2017.[50]

Tencent soon after invested in and gave JingDong (JD), Alibaba's main rival in e-commerce, access to sell products on WeChat. The move made WeChat more of a substitute for Alibaba's ecosystem. Just as with Yu'E Bao, imitators of a successful product entered in droves. JD launched a finance arm, and search engine Baidu, micro-blog service Sina, device manufacturer Xiaomi, and super-app contender Meituan-Dianping all launched payment services. None wanted to be beholden to UnionPay or to the big-tech platforms for their revenue.

The race between Alipay and Tencent to sign up users and merchants for online payments provided the competitive drive that incentivized quickly building a market, a stark contrast to the lack of competition in card payments. One of Ant's vice presidents later cast the competition in a positive light: "Actually, [Tencent] and us, we have long had a romantic relationship in which we copy from each other. . . . It's through such innovation and learning from each other and this competitive environment that we can all improve."[51] Their efforts drove mobile-payment adoption in China with lightning speed. In the first six months of 2014 alone, eighty million Chinese people used mobile online payments for the first time.[52] Only one year after Tencent's entry, nonbanks like the tech firms processed nearly as much payment volume as people spent with debit cards, and by 2018, they were handling more than double the consumption volume of debit cards.

UnionPay's monopoly was eroding quickly as tech companies and their system absorbed a boom in consumer spending with 100 percent growth per year in 2015 and 2016. Mobile-payment adoption was not just for wealthy urbanites in China's coastal cities either, as the share of the poorest 40 percent of Chinese using mobile payments doubled between 2014 and 2017.[53]

Alipay and Tencent learned from the travails of Google and Apple, leaving NFC and its mess of stakeholders out of the Alipay wallet. Unlike NFC, QR code payments could be controlled entirely through a phone app with no need to access the SIM card or NFC receiver, meaning no need to coordinate with telecom companies or phone manufacturers. Alipay could thus focus on acquiring users and merchants. Alipay was easy and virtually free for merchants to add, so there was no need for new POS machines that could accept NFC, or even any POS machines at all.

The disadvantage that Alipay had earlier experienced compared to tech firms in the United States turned into an advantage. Alipay already had its own system to route payments between bank accounts, whereas US mobile wallets in the 2010s had to either build a network from scratch or secure cooperation from card networks. Both Apple and Google chose to build on top of credit cards and their high fees, so they couldn't offer merchants cheaper payment fees to sign them up. Most payments between personal Alipay accounts are free, and the fees that Alipay charges merchants are many times lower than what US merchants pay on credit-card transactions.

Chinese banks were less resistant to mobile-payment alternatives than were their US counterparts. They had long-standing partnerships with the tech companies to process their payments, and credit cards were less important as a profit driver. In 2017 JP Morgan Chase netted $4.4 billion in card-transaction fees, net of costs such as rewards. If all of that revenue went to the bottom line,[54] it would have constituted 18 percent of the bank's profits. ICBC, in contrast, garnered about 16 billion RMB from its card business, only 6 percent of its total profit.[55] Alipay also gave banks a more marketable alternative to UnionPay, whereas US banks always had some competition between networks like Visa and Mastercard for their credit cards.

The worrying implication for the United States is that a "good enough" mentality regarding the payment system, thus sticking with traditional ways of paying, means falling behind the cutting edge of technology innovation and the formulation of the best new business models. Meanwhile, China raised its competitiveness and scale in the most advanced methods of payments. And once the fintech giants succeeded so strongly in China, they were bound to bring their innovation abroad, where they would compete with the US firms accustomed to dominating global payments.

Digital payments were on the rise all over the world, but China's growth was among the fastest and by far the largest in overall volume. From 2014 to 2017 alone, the share of adult Chinese making digital payments rose by 24 percentage points to nearly 70 percent as hundreds of millions of people started scanning QR codes.

By 2017, the Chinese were 50 percent more likely to use digital payments than their counterparts in other middle-income countries. And a larger share of Chinese paid online for an internet purchase than even the average for high-income countries.[56]

China had gone from a backward, cash-dominated payment system to a leader in mobile-payment adoption thanks to big tech.

Monopolist Backlash and Regulation

The boom in QR code payments put UnionPay into fighting mode. It also made some more-neutral policy makers uneasy. No country had ever had a retail payment system based on QR code technology, so the risk was unclear. It is difficult to separate regulations designed to protect incumbents from those driven by real security concerns. But as mobile payments boomed, there was a real need for regulation to ensure that the tech companies' imperative to grow fast did not put the financial system at risk. Regulators were pulled in multiple directions. Banks, UnionPay, and their political patrons increased pressure to restrain the upstarts. Leaders such as Governor Zhou and patrons of the tech firms tried to ensure that rules did not go beyond what was necessary for safety, ensuring continued space for innovation.

The first attack came from UnionPay, which wanted to absorb the new payment methods into its network and end the disruption. Throughout 2013 it sent notices to banks demanding that all offline payments go through its networks and its fees.[57] Initially, it seemed to be winning the political battle against the challenger, for Alibaba was forced to back out of plans to launch its own POS machines.

Banks also fought back, coordinating to dam the flow of client funds into Alipay wallets and Yu'E Bao. They claimed that transfer limits were necessary to comply with old "know-your-customer" identification regulations, but Jack Ma saw it as an abuse of market power, using banks' control over customer accounts to restrict what Ma called "depositor's rights to allocate their own money." He vented his frustration in a furious Weibo post that accused banks of trying to "smother" Alipay, and he admonished the regulators: "Even more so, who will regulate the legality of these 'hands of the state' together shutting out [Alipay]?" He also called for fair competition: "What determines victory or defeat in the markets must not be monopolies or power, rather it should be clients!"[58] Unlike the carefully vetted *People's Daily* op-ed, this piece went too far. The post was quickly deleted.

UnionPay would have liked to unite with the banks to kill off Alipay, but it did not count on Alipay's political support and banks' dissatisfaction with UnionPay. Banks refused to side with UnionPay at the risk of severing their relationship with Alipay and the lucrative payment fees it still paid them.[59]

Alipay wanted to build out its QR code payments as quickly as possible to get a leg up on rivals, even though the first generation of QR codes that people displayed on their phones were far from secure. Thieves could sneak a photo of the code as the user waited to pay and then drain her account. Other scams— fraudulent codes, for example—also took people's money.[60] The worried PBOC ordered an emergency suspension of offline QR code payments and proposed other restrictions on online payments such as transaction-size limits to ensure that they could be secure before they got too large.[61] Projections at the time suggested that Alibaba and Tencent would quickly reach acceptance at one million offline stores, rivaling UnionPay's base of NFC-based POS machines for its mobile-payment system.[62]

There was more at stake than monopolies in the debate over what to do with online payments: the tension between risk and innovation from fast-scaling big tech that is at the core of fintech.

The proposed transaction limits set off controversy, illustrating the newfound power of big tech. Alipay users protested online, arguing that the transaction limits were too low—even a purchase of an iPhone would exceed the cap. Interestingly, very few stories from consumers who had lost money had appeared up to that point. If the media had reported on them more, it may have scared off people from adopting mobile payments and have put more pressure on the government to regulate or even ban the QR code payments that had proved so revolutionary. It may well be that Alibaba managed to suppress such negative coverage, thanks to its influence over Weibo, China's closest equivalent to Twitter. Later, cases of bad PR for Alibaba appeared to be censored on Weibo, in which Alibaba owned a large share. Chinese officials would later consider forcing Alibaba to divest its media holdings because of worries about its power over public discourse.

Jack Ma also went on a private lobbying tour. Multiple former PBOC officials informed me that Alibaba went above the PBOC to lodge protests with more-powerful political patrons. Jack prevailed—strict transaction caps were not in the PBOC's final rules—and most shocking of all was that the QR code payment ban was simply not enforced. Alipay and Tencent were powerful enough to build QR codes from a tiny share of payments to being everywhere by 2014–2016 even though, according to Chinese law, they were illegal. However, Jack Ma's successful override of the central-bank regulations soured relations between Ant and the PBOC.[63]

One regulatory red line that Ant and Tencent could not remove was consumer credit. The PBOC put a stop to their plans to issue virtual credit cards and online payments on credit that would have made Ant one of the largest consumer lenders in China overnight. Its 80 million eligible users came close to the total number of credit cards issued by ICBC by the end of 2013.[64] But the PBOC order banned the whole product category, presumably because the same security concerns it had about payments were even more important for credit. Unlike with QR codes, the rules stuck. The risk that an unsecure payment network poses is greater if the funds entering it are borrowed: users might find themselves on the hook for money they never intended to borrow.

Still, internet companies had achieved immense power, fighting off the central bank, UnionPay, and other banks. In this case it may have been beneficial to stop incumbents from cutting off innovation, but such power mixed with finance could become a serious problem. If regulation lagged too far behind the size and risk of these new financial players, it could bring down China's financial system, and Chinese tech's expansion into finance was only beginning.

From Payments to Super-apps

After 2014, though, the government continued allowing tech companies to become financial conglomerates, opening the door for them to go beyond payments and make Alipay and WeChat into super-apps, one-stop supermarkets for financial and nonfinancial products and services that became indispensable for convenient daily life in China, bringing the online world everywhere that people brought their smartphones. As Jonathan Lu, CEO of Alibaba in 2013, vividly described the age of new possibilities with mobile internet, "It blurs the line between your life and the Internet."[65] Tech firms in the United States would soon look on with envy at the achievements of their Chinese counterparts that once imitated them.

Hundreds of millions of Chinese already used Alipay or WeChat for payments and investments, but in January 2015 the Chinese government granted provisional licenses to provide credit evaluation, including credit scores. Now, algorithms based on tech companies' payment, shopping, and social data could determine access to credit, especially if banks would use those scores to grant loans. The central bank opened credit evaluation and scoring to companies like Tencent and Ant, disrupting its own monopoly. The PBOC hoped that tech companies could supplement its Credit Reference Center with new sources of data and advanced technology to help lenders better manage risk and expand credit access to the hundreds of millions of Chinese who lacked credit histories. It was an admission that the government could not drive innovation on its own. Jack Ma had aimed to improve the credit system for many years, saying, for example, that he hoped to "make credit equal to wealth." The PBOC was finally allowing it to happen.[66]

Technological advances in computing, data collection and storage, and machine learning made the credit-evaluation business ripe for innovative new approaches using "alternative data" beyond a borrower's credit history. This was especially important in China, where many hundreds of millions of people had never accessed formal credit. Some of the most valuable alternative data came from payments, investment, online shopping histories, and social ties, which Alibaba and Tencent had in droves. Data that seem totally unrelated to credit can also be useful. Lenders in the United States have, for example, found that people who purchase anti-scuff pads to protect their floors from furniture legs are more likely to pay back their loans.[67] Such data points pick up difficult-to-measure traits like planning ahead, caring for property, and having property worth caring about, especially useful in China, where few people had traditional credit histories.

Ant's Sesame Credit system was the first out of the gate. It began with application programming interfaces (APIs), which allowed third parties like banks to access its credit data and evaluations as part of loan evaluations.[68] Its chief data scientist defined its mission as "focused on those who may have little credit history at traditional credit agencies. They may have never obtained bank loans or applied for credit cards. However, they might be active internet users who shop online a lot, e-pay their utility bills on time, have a stable residential status and have been using their mobile-phone numbers for a long time. We will take these and other factors into consideration when assessing consumers' creditworthiness."[69]

Users opted in with the Alipay app to see where they stood on the 350–950-point scale. Unlike in the United States, where the FICO score most used for credit evaluation is based solely on financial information, Sesame scores used much broader criteria. Traditional factors like credit history, proof of financial resources, and the extent of identifying information that confirms one's identity are only a small part. Sesame also counts a user's hobbies and purchase history. For example, spending long hours on video games lowers your score, and diaper purchases raise scores by signaling responsibility. The final, most controversial factor involves interpersonal relationships, meaning that payments to and from people with poor credit can lower your score.[70]

Sesame was a hit because it solved a long-standing pain point for the Chinese that Americans with credit cards almost never think about. Credit for many of us is so easily available that it is nearly invisible, but in China there were no easy ways to evaluate creditworthiness and few credit cards. Because of lack of trust, the Chinese had to put large deposits down before the many transactions involving credit, from medical care to renting a home, renting a car, or staying in a hotel. In contrast, people in the West simply enter their credit-card information and can then move on. Sesame enabled users to have the convenience of Westerners with their cards as businesses partnered with Ant Financial to waive deposits for highly rated users. Some lenders—though not the big state-owned banks—also started using Sesame scores. It became the proxy for creditworthiness used in lending, tenant evaluation for landlords, job-applicant evaluation for employers, car and hotel rentals without deposits, and even screening the creditworthiness of potential matches on online dating sites.[71]

Sesame's growing influence was also evident in that its high-scoring users could easily get visas to countries such as Singapore and Luxembourg. Sesame then partnered with the Beijing Capital Airport to allow those with especially high scores to access a special expedited security-screening line. Sesame's "university student credit day" campaign reached 27 million students at 3,000 schools, aiming to make it easy for those with high scores to get a credit card. Sesame would even recommend those with high scores for jobs.[72] The success on campus raised alarm bells because regulators in China have always been suspicious of allowing college students, who normally lack a consistent income stream other than allowances from parents, to borrow money.

Tencent's credit-evaluation system, by contrast, worked behind the scenes, focusing on partnerships with lenders to leverage Tencent's abundant social data rather than developing its own scores. One peer-to-peer lender had used Tencent data to evaluate more than thirty million Chinese people and gave out three million loans based on it.[73] The system was a realization of a vision that Pony Ma had laid out years earlier: "In the future, perhaps there will be a ranking system for morality. It will determine how much you can borrow. If your friends have high morality, then your credit should be good too."[74] Such methods are deeply problematic, for they are sure to worsen inequality and violate privacy, and officials developing China's social credit system, discussed in Chapter 5, could well have been inspired by Ma's idea. These parameters could lead to friends ditching someone who has fallen on hard times out of fear that they would lose access to credit by being associated with a defaulter, as well as violating the defaulter's financial privacy by providing a way for their contacts to know about their deteriorating financial situation.

Similar views on collective responsibility have driven some of the most-abusive practices that collectors of online debts employ, such as using access to a phone's contacts to harass the borrower's friends and family and shame the borrower into repaying, a practice that would be illegal in the United States. The ethical challenge is that such data are not needed for people who already have easy access to credit, but it is hard to grant access to those formerly locked out of the financial system without these alternative data, the collection of which leads to the poor and excluded being surveilled more than the rich. Tencent also partnered with more-traditional financial institutions, but as was the case with Sesame, none of the more-conservative big banks signed on.[75]

Tencent was also "about to launch a consumer credit rating service based on an individual's online social networks," but it backed out, reportedly because Pony Ma spiked the project out of concern for user privacy.[76] Tencent credit scoring could have made users more uneasy than the system used by Ant Financial because Alipay did not have intimate personal data like private conversations to use as inputs to its credit scores. For this reason and perhaps because social data were less useful than Alibaba's and Ant's financial and e-commerce data for credit, Tencent sat on the sidelines as the Sesame score caught on.

The Sesame score seemed to be a game changer for credit in China, but it was unproven. Its data and its algorithms were becoming a key decision point for lenders across the financial system, not just for gimmicky uses like renting a cheap shared bike without a deposit. If it did not work as well as promised, it could lead lenders to make bad loans and spread risk throughout the financial system. The PBOC had concerns that Sesame might be growing faster than it should.

However, the government was still going full speed ahead with granting big tech new financial licenses. It approved banks backed by Tencent and Alibaba with great fanfare. Banks have unique advantages, including that they can raise deposits—the cheapest and most stable source of funding in most cases—and they have special access to the central bank's payment systems. Tencent-backed WeBank's first loan of 35,000 RMB in January 2015 was personally granted by Premier Li Keqiang. Premier Li even evoked the Moon landing to underscore the new move's importance: "It's one small step for WeBank, one giant step for financial reform."[77] Ant Financial–affiliated MyBank launched later with a focus on small-business loans.

Deposits combined with the users and technology of Alibaba and Tencent could have quickly turned the banks that they backed into large institutions. But PBOC restrictions around deposits kept them small. China always required anyone opening a bank-deposit account to sign up in person, but neither WeBank nor MyBank would have physical branches. Although the tech companies could use their online operations to provide loans, payment services, and money-market-fund investments, their new banks' deposit services could not be immediately pushed out to existing users of Alipay and WeChat apps.

Two years later, the private-banking pilot had made limited headway, with all of the private banks combined registering only 61 billion RMB (less than 10 billion USD) in outstanding loans at the end of 2016.[78] The reform trumpeted by Premier Li as a giant step turned out to be a timid tiptoe forward, making up less than one-tenth of the outstanding loans of the booming peer-to-peer lending industry. However, Ant and Tencent were about to find other ways to become massive credit providers.

Ant and Tencent's data, the trust they engendered, and their hundreds of millions of users made them well placed to become dominant consumer-credit providers once the government let them. The government relented on its earlier bans and in April 2015 allowed Ant to launch its Huabei, or "Just Spend," which worked like a virtual credit card. It accumulated more than ten million borrowers in its first twenty days. On the single day of the annual "Double Eleven" shopping event in November, sixty million purchases were made on credit with Huabei.[79] Initially, it was like a store credit and could be used only at Alibaba's online shopping sites. But as Alipay became accepted at millions of off-line retailers, stores could pay a fee to let their customers buy on credit with Huabei. Alipay claims that on average, stores signing on to accept Huabei saw their sales rise by over 41 percent between 2015 and 2016.[80]

Unlike Chinese banks, which often require paper documentation and in-person branch visits to apply for a credit card, the Huabei enrollment process might have been too easy. One of my Chinese friends was furious when he accidentally signed up for Huabei while distractedly making a quick payment. Ant calls the enrollment process "3-1-0": maximum of three minutes providing information to apply for the credit, one second to make a lending decision, and zero human involvement. This automation, plus the ability to push the product to Ant's existing half a billion users, kept loan origination costs low. By 2017, Huabei had a hundred million users.

Unlike US credit cards, which rarely adjust a credit limit, Huabei can adjust it anytime based on a dynamic risk assessment. That helped keep Ant's default rate around 1 percent, except during the financial stress of the early pandemic. (In December 2019 only 1.05 percent of Ant's loans were ninety days or more past due.) Another way that it keeps the product viable is through effective antifraud mechanisms. Ant's control of Alipay allows it to trace where its loans go, not only through the user's account but also through those of the merchants that the user ends up paying, allowing more complete visibility than most banks could achieve.

Huabei and other online lenders benefited from a loophole that allowed microlending companies, regulated by local governments only, to make loans across China and package them into asset-backed securities (ABS). This was a common practice—Alibaba's rival JD also packaged and sold its consumer loans rather than holding them on its balance sheets. All the data behind individual loans, the relationship with the customer, and the risk-management criteria were in Ant's hands, and banks gobbled up the securities. Government oversight was limited.

Tencent launched Weilidai, its own consumer-loan product, one month later. WeChat and QQ users who passed Tencent's credit check could get unsecured loans between 500 and 200,000 RMB (80 to 32,000 USD). Tencent's process was also fast and automated; the entire loan application and approval process took around 15 minutes. After a year in operation, it had given 20 billion RMB in loans to 30 million borrowers.[81]

One issue with these consumer-credit offerings from fintech companies was a lack of transparency. Even for public companies like JD, the financial statements do not disclose their total loans outstanding or their audited bad-loan numbers. Many loans are packaged up to sell to financial institutions, so the balance sheets of such companies or their banks tell us little about how important or risky they are to the financial system and how well their companies' algorithms work in controlling bad debt. It made sense to raise most of the capital from financial institutions with abundant cheap capital, for that allowed more lending and lower costs. Cheaper financing in turn meant more profits, cheaper loans, and less-risky borrowers.

The risks, however, were ultimately offloaded to banks. The US subprime crisis exposed that in many firms in a position analogous to Ant's, loan originators that knew the risk was offloaded to others relaxed their lending standards and ended up contributing to the financial crisis. There was clearly an incentive to quickly create loans, for consumer credit could become an advantage in the competition for customers. In the race to dominate e-commerce, platforms that offered credit could boost sales and attract new buyers and new sellers.

As WeChat expanded its offerings, people devoted more of their lives to it. By 2016, half of WeChat's 768 million daily logged-in users spent over 90 minutes per day on the app.[82]

• • •

Thanks to Jack Ma's ambition and Pony Ma's competition, the fintech boom improved the lives of hundreds of millions of Chinese in only a few short years. By 2017, China was no longer a backward, cash-dominated financial system with limited access to credit. China's financial system began to be admired around the world for its lightning-fast, cheap payments and abundant choices for investments and loans. Its market for fintech rapidly evolved from miniscule to the largest in the world by far.

Jack and Pony seized the opportunity that China in 2013 presented for fintech. It was in the sweet spot for leapfrogging because it had the largest addressable market, great infrastructure, world-class technology companies with hundreds of millions of users, and, critically, the political will to remove protections for incumbents. China's policy makers took a gamble on fintech by removing barriers that kept private firms out of most of finance, knowing that injecting new competition could force improvement in the state banks better than any government diktats or subsidy-laden five-year plans. For once, the playing field was tilted toward private companies.

Yet even with all the environmental factors helping them along, it is a testament to Alibaba and Tencent's capacity for product design and business acumen that so many consumers adopted their financial products so quickly. Trust is fundamental in finance, whether in payments or investments. Both Alibaba and Tencent earned the trust of users even though they lacked state guarantees. Their innovative products continued to take in lessons and technology from foreign sources, but as they developed, they combined foreign technologies in new ways to create innovative business models.

China was not the only country to have a thriving fintech sector, but its super-apps were unique, more like phone operating systems than regular apps. Although the apps became so large that they could be slow and quickly drain phone batteries, China's fintech model was more powerful and intuitive than any effort by US fintech and technology firms. It was a much easier experience to navigate one app than it would be to keep track of money and services across dozens of platforms.

In the United States and the West in general, however, fintech's approach was the opposite. Instead of new bundles, US fintech's buzzword was "unbundling," with a small fintech company that focused on one specific "pain point," an area that existing financial institutions did poorly or charged too much for. The US approach recognized that banks provide bundles of services, some of which generate profits that subsidize other, less profitable activities. Banks thus overcharge in some areas and undercharge in others, and fintech could take on the profit centers for which consumers were overcharged to give them a better deal. This narrow approach meant that its fintech companies tended to be scrappy start-ups because major tech companies that could have taken on the banks more directly with a new bundle took at best timid, nondisruptive steps into finance. The best picture of the US approach came from CB Insights, a consultancy, in 2015. It starts with Wells Fargo's homepage, showing all the services that the company provides. It then superimposes the logos of new fintech companies angling to compete with Wells Fargo for each narrow slice of service: some for consumer credit, others for business credit, payments, savings, investments, and more.[83]

Essentially, every element of Wells's business had been replicated by a specialized fintech company. However, the problem with unbundling was that it would take a mess of apps to match the functionality of one account at Wells Fargo, meaning that even if each one was better and cheaper than Wells at this niche, the consumer experience would be poor, with many log-in credentials to remember, the effort to find these apps, and the risk of data breaches. Fintech has thus far failed to live up to its potential to revolutionize finance in the United States, but it completely remade the way Chinese pay, borrow, lend, invest, and get around.

The West can learn valuable lessons from China's experience in this crucial early stage. Regulatory playing fields are often tilted toward incumbents, in part because of political influence over rule makers but also because new business models fall into the kind of legal gray zones that made Jack Ma consider facing prison. Even a one-party state can create the conditions necessary for innovation by being flexible and proactive when it comes to new rules and enforcement of old ones, rather than crushing a fledgling new product that could bring real benefits. However, the government must also be ready to act quickly when issues emerge but still not overreact.

China's experience also shows that the players best positioned to inject competition into cozy monopolies or oligopolies in payments have many people already using their service. These users provide new players with a head start in building a new network

and the political savvy and influence to fight off incumbents in cahoots with connections in government trying to nip their potential disruption in the bud. The same was true for Kenya, where its
successful M-PESA mobile-money system came from a dominant
telecom company with many users and was outside the banking
industry. Kenya's government took a flexible approach similar
to China's and persisted despite pressure from banks to impose
stricter rules on the new entrant.

Big tech—Alibaba and Tencent—elbowed its way into China's
financial system by daring to make significant improvements in
the way individuals and businesses made payments. That has yet
to happen in the United States and may not in fact be necessary.
The poor state of Chinese payments was an opportunity for Alibaba and Tencent to ambitiously build new online systems from
the ground up. Their US counterparts, such as Amazon and Apple, mainly accepted current payment systems, primarily credit
cards, sometimes issuing their own cards together with banks.
Systems like Apple Pay have not challenged the existing payment
networks because they are not as ambitious as Alipay. They add
a technology layer of digital cards on top of existing credit-card
networks that manage the money movements instead of creating
a whole new payment system. The United States has thus saved
itself some of the negative side effects of big tech in finance that
we will see later, but it is stuck with a payment system that is far
more expensive than China's, in large part because of the outsized
profits that banks make from credit-card payments. The system
has serious drawbacks, like high fixed fees, which stem in part
from the fact that it was not designed for an internet world of
small digital transactions.

The fundamental lesson of China's fintech story is the power
of competition. Protectionism also helped, although its main effect to boost fintech was not to protect any infant industry but
to keep Chinese payments backward for so long that the pressure
to build something better became large enough for a revolution to

break out. Protectionism thus cost China dearly. If US credit-card companies had been let in, which is only beginning to happen now, Chinese people might be doing their spending on cards with Visa and Mastercard logos instead of digital wallets, but there is no guarantee that these American firms would have edged out Alipay and Tencent. After all, Alibaba beat eBay in China despite the latter's deep pockets and experience. If anything, China's fintech revolution demonstrates the dangers of protectionism's restrictions on competition, which for a decade held back both Chinese payments and the businesses that rely on modern payments by giving a monopoly to a state firm. It was only after the Chinese government encouraged competition that payments modernized. Now with two big tech firms controlling nearly the entire market, more competition, including by truly letting foreign players in, would be useful.

Super-apps made Alipay and WeChat into serious competitors to banks and other financial institutions. Ma Mingzhe, CEO of Ping An, one of China's largest financial institutions, said that "as a traditional financial institution, Ping An's biggest competitor in the future is not other traditional financial companies, rather it is the modern technology sector."[84] Tech firms were among the few that could compete with banks. But as the tech competition with banks was even more effective than anticipated, pressure built to end the loose regulatory environment that helped them get off the ground. Policy makers also began to face questions about the long-term implications of tech firms' success in finance. Would the tech companies replace an uncompetitive banking oligopoly with a tech duopoly that no one else could compete with? What hidden risks lurked under all this growth of new finance? Were the tech firms getting too powerful?

4

A Fintech Wild West

*"We are not working
entirely within the rules of the law"*

On a sunny Shanghai day in May 2015, I sat down for tea with Ding Ning, the founder of one of the fastest-growing "fintech" companies in China. His online platform, Ezubao, was one of thousands that connected companies and individuals in need of credit with millions of investors looking for better returns than they could get from banks or even Yu'E Bao. His platform had gone viral after less than a year online and already reported seven billion RMB (about one billion USD) in loans thanks to his offers of up to 15 percent returns for investors.

Ding was part of a new digital gold rush, actively encouraged by the government's pro-financial innovation push. Everyone hoped that fintech would allow them to quickly get rich or powerful. Local officials encouraged fintech start-ups in their jurisdiction, young entrepreneurs hoped to become the next Jack Ma, and of course the fraudsters and loan sharks preyed on investors who believed they could get high returns with low risk. As Ding's effective marketing campaigns said, "Start with 1 RMB, take your money out anytime, high return, low risk." Glowing reviews of his business in state media and advertisements on CCTV convinced investors that it had top-level political backing, which to them meant it was a safe investment.

Ding struck me then as the most honest and frank of anyone in the industry I interviewed. Most touted their big data and AI risk algorithms, but he seemed clear-eyed about the challenges. He warned me not to believe any of the impressively low bad-loan numbers that online lending platforms reported because they were all fake. "Big data" for credit scoring in China, he thought, was useless because borrowers could have massive outstanding debts to loan sharks that did not show up in any digital data sets. My conversation with Ding helped me see the ugly reality underlying many of the fintech industry's public-facing statements about innovation.

Seven months later, I nearly spilled my morning coffee while reading the news. Ding and twenty of his executives had been arrested. An investigation found that Ezubao was a Ponzi scheme that defrauded nearly a million investors out of 50 billion RMB (7.6 billion USD). Authorities found it on the brink of collapse and shut it down, sparking a wave of protests across China that were immediately crushed. All news of the protests vanished at the order of internet censors.[1] For years, the specter of future Ezubaos would taint the image of fintech, and years later Jack Ma would find himself in hot water for a speech that included a plea not to treat Alipay like the failed peer-to-peer sector.

The fintech boom and the laissez-faire attitude that made it possible were fragile. Innovation always comes at a cost, and the Chinese fintech revolution had a dangerous dark side of which Ezubao was an important part. As Benoît Cœuré, a prominent central banker from France, said in 2018, "The history of financial innovation is littered with examples that led to early booms, growing unintended consequences, and eventual busts."[2] China would be no exception. Freedom to invest outside a carefully controlled and cultivated walled garden patrolled by the state opened Chinese investors to an unfamiliar, unruly financial market with new risks and rewards that they were not equipped to navigate. After all, their experience with financial products mostly involved products with explicit state backing, and the state-owned banks regularly bailed out wealth-management products to avoid angering investors. One of the questions that officials had to pose was where to draw the line, how to encourage fintech innovation and experimentation without leading investors to assume that the government also guaranteed their money—a recipe for more risk.

Large technology companies like Alipay and Tencent, mindful of their reputation and under the microscope of the public and the government, offered relatively safe investments and payment tools, but they were not the only players in the new game. This chapter explores the more dangerous and risky sides of China's fintech revolution embodied by Ding's rise and fall. It shows the origin of scandals that destabilized China's economy and bilked millions of investors out of their savings. It also covers China's love-hate relationship with cryptocurrencies such as Bitcoin, an important financial innovation that, in the party's eyes, created too much financial freedom by giving people the ability to invest and transact outside its surveillance and controls.

High-profile blowups of supposedly innovative companies and making boom-bust cycles worse damaged fintech's reputation and would force the party-state to act. This segment of China's cashless revolution is a cautionary tale illustrating the difficulty of knowing which future innovations will prove beneficial as well as the shortcomings of China's efforts to promote innovation.

Bitcoin Booms in China

The first area of financial technology to boom outside of big tech's online payments embodied a much more radical change to the nature of money and payments, a vision of money existing only in computers, unmoored from sovereign states and powerful gate-keepers like banks. Bitcoin, an innovative digital currency and payment system, began to catch on in China in mid-2013, around the same time as Yu'E Bao took off. However, the libertarian ideals of Bitcoin and other cryptocurrencies are utterly antithetical to those of Beijing. Bitcoin's main innovation is that unlike most currencies, it has no central authority that manages the money supply, no tax revenues to back its value, and no banks that keep track of who owns what. Instead, computer code and cryptography help it manage a decentralized network that processes payments and maintains its value by limiting the supply of Bitcoins.

Demand largely from Chinese speculators drove global Bitcoin prices from about $100 to $1,000 in only a few months in mid-2013. China would play its first leading role in international fintech developments with Bitcoin mining equipment and speculative demand to buy Bitcoin. Speculation led authorities to intervene more quickly than in past financial innovations. From the party's perspective, decentralization meant that Bitcoin was risky and impossible to control. The government was not blindly supportive of all apparent financial innovations, instead using a risk/reward calculation that looked to be all risk/no reward in Bitcoin's case. However, the response of Chinese investors to Bitcoin showed that an increasing share of the population was willing to embrace new financial technology if it might make them get rich quick or get their money outside the watchful eyes and carefully controlled financial borders.

China's first Bitcoin exchange, BTC China, opened in 2011. Digital-currency exchanges allow people to purchase and sell Bitcoin with traditional currencies such as RMB or dollars. Its founders ran it as a hobby, and it was so informal that they used their personal bank accounts to handle the few orders that trickled in.[3] Chinese began to notice Bitcoin only when a charity accepted Bitcoin donations for relief after an April 2013 earthquake. The software required to transact Bitcoin was downloaded by 72,000 people in China that month, about 13 percent of the global total.[4]

But China's most important early contribution to Bitcoin was becoming the Levi Strauss of a new digital gold rush. Chinese firms made the equipment needed to "mine" digital currency just as Strauss sold jeans to nineteenth-century gold prospectors, profiting from the boom whether miners found the mother lode or not. Bitcoin's network requires participants called miners to keep it secure, process its payments, and create new Bitcoins about every ten minutes. The first miner to correctly guess the solution to a mathematical, cryptographic puzzle earns a "block reward" of newly created Bitcoins, along with transaction fees. The shared ledger, a list of who owns which coins, is then updated across the entire Bitcoin network. The race then begins again. There is a strong element of chance, and the only way that miners can raise their chances of winning the race to solve the next block is by trying more guesses more quickly, usually by throwing more computing power (and thus electricity) at the cryptographic puzzle. In its early years, enthusiasts ran mining software on normal computers, but competition stiffened as Bitcoin became more valuable.

Avalon, a Chinese firm, shipped the first specialized Bitcoin mining rigs based on application-specific integrated circuits in January 2013. It started a trend that would see developments in China become crucial to the future of digital currency. Avalon's equipment could fire off more attempts to solve the cryptographic problem than previous mining rigs, and it was a more efficient energy user than any other mining equipment produced outside China.[5] Others in China followed suit, and the total computing power in the Bitcoin network doubled in only three months thanks to Chinese technology innovation.

From this point on, Chinese equipment manufacturers and miners would dominate the market. Meanwhile, US-based Butterfly Labs, an earlier contender in the mining-equipment market, faced problems that delayed its shipments, leaving its customers' digital wallets empty while those using cutting-edge Chinese mining equipment raked in money. In the end, Butterfly Labs failed to deliver and had to shut down, a sad signal for US leadership in technology.[6]

The rise in interest put Bitcoin on the radar of CCTV, which ran a long feature in early May 2013. Similar to the touting of Yu'E Bao, for many viewers it was tantamount to a state endorsement. The official state channel said that Bitcoin's use for charity had "brought it closer to the hearts of Chinese people" and that Bitcoin "increasingly looks like a real currency." CCTV also displayed charts of Bitcoin's price rocketing up. Hinting at its ability to get past regulations, CCTV interviewed a foreigner who noted how easy it was to get money in and out of China using Bitcoin—later one of the government's reasons for cracking down.[7] At the time of the documentary, you could buy a Bitcoin for $100, a price more than 1,100 times higher than five months earlier.

Pent-up speculative energy was released on October 14, 2013, when a small unit of Baidu, China's leading search engine, announced it would accept Bitcoin, the first signal that it could become a mainstream currency in China. One of the largest property developers then announced that it would accept Bitcoin for apartments. Suddenly, exchanges were flooded with orders. Bobby Lee, the cofounder of BTC China, emailed his colleagues that "the market will continue to be super hot, and our workload will be non-stop." For many buyers, Bitcoin was their first ever investment in a financial product, and they bought it mainly as a get-rich-quick scheme.[8]

The price climbed ever higher, doubling from mid-October to mid-November and then tripling to break $1,000. China by then made up just under half of global Bitcoin trading, as its mass of speculative money piled into Bitcoin. There is no good way to model Bitcoin prices based on economic fundamentals, but the run-up clearly outpaced the speed of its adoption as a currency. In mid-2013, only around forty-five Chinese merchants accepted it as payment.[9] The government saw the boom as a speculative bubble that could pop and endanger social stability.

Experience with financial innovations like the Q coin and Alipay suggested that Chinese regulators would take a wait-and-see approach, letting around seven years go by before imposing strict rules. But this time was different. On December 5 the hammer fell with a notice from regulators that restricted the legal uses—although they did not ban Bitcoin. Exchanges could continue to operate with regulation, and people could buy and sell Bitcoin at their own risk. However, authorities severed links between Bitcoin and the financial system because they did not want it to become a parallel currency, loosening their control over the economy.

The market reaction was the clearest indication yet of China's central role in Bitcoin's bubble. Seeing that China would not become a major Bitcoin adopter, the global price dropped by over 40 percent after the PBOC announcement, from nearly $1,200 on December 4 to under $700 on December 7. Online-payment companies and banks had also been warned to stop handling payments for Bitcoin exchanges. Yet, as always, there were limits to the authorities' control. People in China still found ways to get their hands on Bitcoins. Whereas trading fell in China in December, it fell *more* in the rest of the world. China's share of world trading rose to over 60 percent and would eventually exceed 90 percent.

The episode demonstrates what made China's environment uniquely suited to adoption of financial innovations, as well as the massive scale of money that could flood into an online financial product with even a tiny market share in China. An ever-larger, younger part of the population had bought Q coins and was used to online payments with Alipay, so trusting money to an unknown online network no longer seemed like such a stretch. A survey of early Bitcoin adopters in China found that many had never owned any financial assets before they bought Bitcoin.[10] Others bought it to get money out of the government's reach. Academic studies have found that prior to the PBOC's intervention, Bitcoin was used for capital flight.[11] It was thus yet another financial innovation contributing to financial freedom, but on the flip side, much of the money that escaped could certainly be ill-gotten gains from crime or corruption.

Brave entrepreneurs started businesses buying, selling, and mining Bitcoin despite the legal gray area. The PBOC, always on the lookout for new technology to apply to finance, would soon start exploring how to use the technology behind Bitcoin for its own purposes, antithetical to the decentralizing, libertarian ideals of Bitcoin.

The Peer-to-Peer (P2P) Lending Bubble

A US company with no stakes in China made waves in December 2014. It proved to be the spark that set off in China one of fintech's largest and most dangerous booms anywhere in the world. When Wall Street valued US-based LendingClub, then the global industry leader in online peer-to-peer (P2P) lending, at $8.5 billion after its IPO that December, P2P went from an unproven industry to an attractive inspiration for copycats worldwide, but especially in China.[12] It looked then like P2P could become the future of finance.

The idea was simple. Online technology platforms could "democratize" investing and lending by serving as a matchmaker connecting peers. People who needed to borrow money would be connected with those who had extra funds to invest, doing an end run around big faceless intermediaries such as banks. It was not as radical as Bitcoin's invention of decentralized money, but it was a step in the same disintermediating direction. Chinese big-tech firms like Alibaba and Tencent had revolutionized payments but still provided only a tiny fraction of the huge pent-up demand for loans and high-return investments. P2P would step in and fill both sides of that demand. The government followed yet again an experimental approach, giving broad encouragement for this new sector along with a "wait-and-see" attitude to regulation.

The ideal model of peer-to-peer lending has borrowers apply on a website or app. Without human intervention, an automated, data-driven model estimates a fair interest rate and credit score. Investors log in to the online "marketplace" and choose the loans they want to fund, based on their risk preferences, or have an algorithm do it for them. In theory, these matchmakers could save costs over banks and pass those back in the form of cheaper loans and better-returning investments, for they did not have the legacy costs of banking: physical branches and human loan officers. Best of all, they appeared less risky themselves than banks.* Investors in P2P loans had less protection than bank deposits, often having no guarantee, for example, that they would be paid back. But people could reduce their risk by "crowdfunding," where, say, one investor with $1,000 could fund dozens of different loans or a hundred investors who each invested $50 could fund a single borrower's $5,000 loan, thus diffusing the risk.

US regulators regarded this new model with suspicion. They took action to ensure that it complied with a host of financial regulations. Chinese officials not only took a hands-off approach; they also encouraged P2P to deliver capital to private firms and consumers starved of credit. In Shanghai, for example, the government arranged subsidized office space for P2P lenders trying to attract talent and capital from competing jurisdictions such

---

* Banks are on the hook to pay back depositors even if the loans they make go bad, making them a concentrated source of risk. P2P platforms, on the other hand, promised to pass on this risk to many diffuse investors, making the platform itself less risky. In theory, investors also cannot ask to be paid back until the loans come due, meaning that the platform itself does not face liquidity risk.

as Beijing and Shenzhen. In 2015, P2P lending in China created around $90 billion in credit, three times the US market and nearly twenty times as large as the UK share.[13] Outstanding loans tripled or quadrupled every year from 2011 to 2015 as thousands of platforms rushed into the market and competed to give out loans quickly. Money poured into Chinese companies that hoped to be the next LendingClub. Venture-capital investment in Chinese fintech companies sextupled from $500 million in 2014 to $3.1 billion in 2015 and then doubled to $6.4 billion in 2016.[14]

P2P lending initially looked especially promising in China, and it boomed like nowhere else. It was already a cutthroat market, with more than 1,500 competing platforms by late 2014, and an additional 2,000 entered over the following year. LendingClub's IPO legitimized P2P and helped convince average investors that unknown internet platforms were an innovative international trend in finance, unlike the investing scams always around to dupe the unsuspecting of their money. Bitcoin and Yu'E Bao had already opened the floodgates of investments outside interest-rate controls, but they could not fulfill all the pent-up demand, especially after Bitcoin lost its luster and Yu'E Bao's returns fell. As growth accelerated, P2P attracted over 40 billion RMB in a single month after the LendingClub IPO, for a total loan balance of 142 billion RMB.

P2P's growth fed a cycle that appeared virtuous at first blush. The larger the industry, the more legitimate and established it appeared, drawing in investors who funded yet more loans. In 2015, a year after LendingClub's IPO, it was 3.5 times as large, with 357 billion RMB (55 billion USD) in outstanding loans. P2P became the new investment craze by offering more interest than Yu'E Bao and more stability than Bitcoin. P2P platforms offered on average nearly three times the return of Yu'E Bao, around 14 percent per year.

As P2P boomed, people who previously had few options for credit were inundated with loan offers. Millions were so desperate for credit that they agreed to pay interest rates many times higher than those of banks. Most borrowers (84.28 percent) took out small loans of up to 10,000 RMB, or about 1,500 USD, the kind of money needed to put down a deposit for renting an apartment, buy an iPhone or refrigerator, or finance inventory at a small vendor. Nevertheless, some leading platforms—Hongling Capital, for example—gave massive loans, sometimes over 100 million RMB each, to real estate projects.

Young budding entrepreneurs, modeling themselves on the fresh graduates or dropouts making billions in Silicon Valley, hoped to ride the wave to riches, and employees bored with their jobs at state banks started P2P lenders. Even financial institutions themselves became P2P lenders. Lufax started as a peer-to-peer online lender affiliated with Ping An, one of the first large Chinese financial institutions (it has about 500 billion USD in assets) to get serious about technology.[15] In 2012 its chairman announced that it would "promote the tighter integration of modern technology and conventional finance." By mid-2014, Lufax was adding 300,000 users per month, becoming the third-largest P2P platform in the world and reaching a valuation of nearly $40 billion.[16] With a leg up on other P2P lenders thanks to Ping An's large customer base and sophisticated risk models, it had 5 million investors and 14 billion RMB in loans by 2014.[17]

Large companies launched their own platforms. Property developers hungry for funds used them to raise money for their own projects, a blatant conflict of interest. Dalian Wanda raised 500 million RMB at 12 percent interest to fund the construction of shopping malls because the government had ordered traditional lenders like banks and trusts to pull back from real estate projects. Offline interpersonal lenders, loan sharks, and other informal financiers also entered the market, suddenly able to raise money from all over the country with a simple website and big promises.

Unfortunately, the idea did not work in practice. The larger the P2P sector became, the larger the eventual fallout, devastating millions before the government shut it down. Investors lost family life savings; underwater borrowers were hounded by unscrupulous debt collectors. Some hapless borrowers supplied naked selfies as collateral for loans they could never repay, having to live with the threat that the photos would be shared with their contacts. Others, tragically, committed suicide to end the debt-collection calls or erase the shame of losing their savings. This time, the government's experimental approach would fail. How it happened and why the government let such a mess develop are a stinging indictment of China's regulatory system that raises questions about its ability to maintain financial stability in the long term. Simultaneously, the party's success in shutting P2P down without financial contagion inspires confidence in China's ability to manage its system's shortcomings.

From the start, the P2P boom in China was built on a dirty open secret. Much of the industry consisted of risky unlicensed banks with websites that made them look like financial innovators. Yet, other than using online payments to gather money, many had little to do with real financial technology, nor were they truly peer-to-peer loans, despite being called P2P. For the P2P market to work properly, the government would have needed to ensure that firms claiming to be P2Ps were actually operating as such, not just running a big slush fund or Ponzi scheme behind the scenes, and that disclosures to investors, like the purpose and risk of the loans and bad loan ratios, were honest. Otherwise, there was no way for regular people to weigh the risk of investing. None of this happened. Chinese authorities knew early on that the P2P sector was fraught with problems, but they treated it like payments and informal finance: a useful experiment that should be left alone until serious risks emerged.

The China Banking Regulatory Commission (CBRC) started warning investors about P2P in 2011, and a PBOC investigation in mid-2013 found rampant illegal practices.* Yet a meeting of regulators then concluded that "it would be premature to draw up a specific regulation because the size of P2P lending was too small."[18] It appeared then that they had a point. P2Ps had only a few billion RMB in outstanding loans—too tiny to justify the attention of regulators. But P2P would not be small for long. Informal finance, which has always operated on the margins of the law, interacted with exorbitant financial and technological promises, and took off.

At that time (2014–2015), opening a neighborhood dumpling shop would have required more regulation, such as health safety checks, than starting a P2P lending business entrusted with billions of RMB to invest. As one P2P entrepreneur told me at the time, "We are not working entirely within the rules of the law, but we are working hard to avoid causing problems." Legality was strictly optional. Although payments were clearly under the People's Bank of China's jurisdiction and Yu'E Bao was under the securities regulatory commission, P2P did not fit under the authority of any existing regulators. Direct lending between individuals in China is governed by China's contract law, with disputes overseen by courts. Because P2P companies usually registered as information-service providers, not financial companies, they could argue that they were not lenders at all, just matchmakers, and thus that none of the financial regulators had the right to supervise their business.

P2P thus became a dangerous blind spot for regulators, exposing serious shortcomings in China's fragmented regulatory model. Informal finance tended to be the responsibility of local governments, which could work for microlenders operating only in their

---

* The 2011 CBRC annual report, which made the first warning, confused the industry with the name of a P2P platform called Renrendai, which translates to "everyone lend" (人人贷). The CBRC meant to flag the risk, but it didn't even know what to call it yet, let alone what to do about it.

city, but the internet allowed these firms to create national-scale businesses with local regulation. One might expect this gap in regulation to lead to a turf battle, but P2P instead became a hot potato. One of the most-senior financial officials told me that no government institutions wanted responsibility over P2P because they knew that many of the platforms would fail. If they regulated these institutions, they would be held responsible for the inevitable protests—social instability that could sink an official's career.

Frauds and most platforms that overpromised were thus free to take over the market with fake projects and hidden bad loans built up behind the scenes—a ticking time bomb. Moral hazard and the legacy of financial repression played a crucial role in distorting the P2P market. A basic rule of finance is the trade-off between higher risk and higher returns, but the Chinese had not learned that lesson because of years of state guarantees and bailouts. Zhao Xijun, deputy dean of the prestigious Renmin University School of Finance, remarked that "people are eager to achieve high returns, but they do not have adequate knowledge of the financial risks or how to screen [products] for them."[19] Investors thought the biggest platforms and those close to the government would be bailed out, so they had little incentive to think about risk.

Meanwhile, the government kept its distance from P2P and had no intention of bailing out unregulated platforms. However, investors had learned from experience that much more of Chinese finance was guaranteed than the parts that carried legal government or bank guarantees. An organized protest from losing investors could get local officials worried about "social stability" to pressure investment companies to repay them and make the problem go away, even if there was no guarantee on a risky investment. This practice of bailouts and obsessing over financial and social stability led to long-run instability and more protests, as investors came to believe that the same tactic would work for P2P.

P2P was on the back burner also because regulators had limited bandwidth, and P2P was miniscule compared to other forms of shadow banking. It might seem serious that unregulated P2P was an issue of billions around 2015, but risky nonguaranteed bank wealth-management products, trusts, and entrusted loans were hundreds of times larger, an issue of many trillions. Each was also full of illegal activities and hidden risks more likely to cause systemic financial problems than P2P. At a time when China's growth was slowing, the credit that P2P created seemed to be a way to keep the economy humming along and boost financial inclusion, channeling credit to sectors previously starved of it. The lack of focus on P2P, however, while sensible considering regulators' limited resources, created a dangerous and growing blind spot.

Fintech's First Strike

The fintech boom had clear benefits to the economy, helped modernize finance, and brought high-quality financial services to hundreds of millions of Chinese who had been underserved by banks. But serious problems in the less regulated parts of fintech forced a rethinking of the big pro-innovation push. The first strike came in June 2015, when fintech exacerbated a stock market bubble and bust that threatened to take down the economy. It was the first indication that fintech risks were large enough to pose systemic risks. Then, in December, a default scandal at one of Ant Financial's units exposed regulatory arbitrage and murky chains of lending, the same kind of practices that led to the subprime crisis in the United States. The last straw came from the collapse of Ezubao, Ding Ning's fraudulent P2P platform. Regulators were unnerved by the massive scale of protests planned against the government for its role in the mess. Their response to the Ezubao debacle marked the beginning of the end of an incredibly free, almost entirely unregulated part of the fintech era. The damage to fintech's reputation would spread beyond P2P and lead the government on a new path, regulating and asserting control over the big-tech side of fintech that had little to do with P2P.

Fintech contributed to the stock market crash of June 2015, which rattled China's financial markets. It started with the same get-rich-quick mentality that fueled P2P and Bitcoin bubbles, the idea that government endorsement meant riskless profits. China's growth prospects were declining, but state media began cheerleading the market. Without any significant change in China's economic fundamentals, the benchmark stock index rose 150 percent in the twelve months from June 2014 to June 2015.[20] Much of the rise came from investments made with borrowed money. Regular investors like Zhang Minmin, a resident of Alibaba's hometown, Hangzhou, made leveraged bets on stocks that made so much money that he measured his gains in luxury cars instead of RMB. As Zhang said, "Sometimes when the market is good, I would make profits enough to buy an Audi in just a week or two. However, when the market is down, it's also possible to lose half an Audi very quickly."[21]

Borrowed money in stock markets worked like an accelerant that amplified investor returns. Each rise in stock prices raised the value of shares serving as collateral for loans, allowing investors to borrow more money to plow back into the market, thereby fueling more demand and more credit. In China the legal way to put money into stocks is with regulated margin loans that limit leverage and restrict margin trading to more wealthy, experienced investors. If stock market borrowing had occurred according to these rules, the bubble and crash could have been less severe. Unfortunately, those who did not qualify for margin loans or wanted to borrow more than the rules allowed found a friend in fintech. Sometimes, calls to democratize finance are beneficial, but often it really means using technology as an excuse to promote risky products to people who do not know any better.

Hundsun, a financial software company linked to Jack Ma, provided software called HOMS, which channeled money from wealth-management products and P2P lenders to people who wanted to make bets on the stock market. HOMS also helped brokerages combine sometimes dozens of accounts too small to qualify for margin loans into a single "umbrella" brokerage account that reached the thresholds, a clear case of regulatory arbitrage. The software allowed up to ten times more leverage than the official brokerage margin limits from the CSRC, enabling people to make huge bets on the stock market with only a small amount of their own money. They could make a fortune in no time if stock prices rose quickly and lose one even faster if stocks fell.[22] HOMS helped pump hundreds of billions of RMB of gray-market margin funding into the stock market.

Everyone hoped to get rich with borrowed money in stocks. A firefighter I met in Beijing in May 2015 had borrowed from multiple P2P lenders, claiming the loans were for buying consumer goods like a refrigerator. Instead, he poured this borrowed money into the market. P2P lenders supplied at least 200 billion RMB in loans for stock speculators, three times less than the credit that banks' wealth-management products lent to speculators, but still an important factor in stock prices' meteoric rise. Official margin lending reached 1.5 trillion RMB. Fintech firms were a key part of the shadow lenders that provided unauthorized credit that added approximately a trillion more to the market without protections like leverage limits and disclosures that would allow authorities to track whether stock loans had become excessive.[23]

When the market finally began to falter on June 12, all the buying on credit that boosted prices went into reverse and caused a crash.[24] Lenders, worried that prices would fall on the stock they had as collateral on loans, liquidated positions, leading to further price declines that in turn fueled further liquidations and lowered prices. The more highly leveraged gray-market financing from fintech made the crash more severe, forcing more shares to be liquidated more quickly to pay off the loans. The higher leverage on gray-market loans meant that even a small price decline could trigger a large quantity of sales to meet margin requirements, compared to the regulated loans. Newly made paper fortunes were wiped out in an instant, and defaults rose as speculators' stock fell in value faster than their brokers could sell it. About half of the major stocks in China suspended trading, and the market stabilized only after the government pumped money into the market and even prosecuted some who sold stocks.

CSRC pressure forced P2Ps to stop their stock-margin business, but the damage was done. The stock market stagnated for years, propped up by state-ordered buying that distorted prices. The debacle is indicative of the party's fundamentally uneasy relationship with markets, happy to cheerlead when they are going up but unwilling to stomach the implications of their going down.

China's market crash spooked global investors, and a decision the next month to devalue its currency was seen as another sign of economic weakness and drove down commodity prices and stock prices across the world. Once the dust had settled, there was plenty of blame to go around, but it was clear that fintech could be a force for instability. It took a stock market crash for the risks that fintech was hiding to emerge, and regulators wondered what other dangers could be growing in the shadows if they kept allowing fintech to be a free Wild West.

Rethinking P2P

The stock market mess led the party to finally put the banking regulator in charge of P2P and set out principles for regulation, but neither had much effect. Regulators were in a bind. The rules they proposed would eliminate most risk from P2P, turning them into true tech platforms rather than financial lenders. But they were so far from industry practice that strict implementation would have forced them to shut down most of the industry, bringing protests from investors to the regulators' doors and bringing down economic growth by cutting off needed credit. Instead, the authorities kicked the can down the road by tasking local officials, who had no hope of being able to handle these national-scale companies, with supervising them.

Although P2P continued to boom in China, the experience in the rest of the world suggested that the early hype was undeserved. The dream of a democratic "peer-to-peer" system in the United States and the United Kingdom faded early as LendingClub's stock price plummeted. Most "peer" lenders neither had the expertise to evaluate loans nor wanted to take the time to choose individual borrowers. Pressure to grow fast enough to justify high, tech-company-type of valuations led these new online lenders to cut corners and take outsized risks.

As P2P lenders in the US expanded into new borrower markets, their algorithms and big-data risk pricing proved inaccurate, leading to a rise in defaults and an exodus of investors in late 2015. Renaud Laplanche, LendingClub's cofounder and the global face of the industry, resigned the next year after a string of issues emerged, from loans to himself and family members to staff members doctoring loan documents.[25] LendingClub and other marketplace lenders are still in business but have failed to live up to their promise. The fallout was limited, thanks in part to careful regulation that helped limit their size in the United States.* But P2P in China would become much larger and much messier. In the West, regulations constrained the risks that P2P companies could take, but in China they still had free rein.

Another strike against fintech came from Ant Financial's marketplace for investments and loans. Zhaocaibao, launched in 2014, was more of a straightforward regulatory arbitrage that used

---

*The Securities and Exchange Commission imposed a cease-and-desist order on Prosper, then the industry leader in US P2P lending, until it complied with a litany of regulation around disclosures and investor protection. To comply with regulations, most P2P loans were actually issued by banks and then transferred to investors later, adding yet another layer of rules and oversight.

technology to get around sensible regulation. Chinese law limits loosely regulated fund-raisings, called private placement bonds, to two hundred investors. Each would have to put up a large amount of money, which limited such investments to institutions and high-net-worth individuals generally more experienced at managing financial risk. The United States has similar rules to limit risky securities to "qualified" investors. But Ant saw the rules as an impediment to good returns that financial engineering could fix. A single large loan was split into a series of smaller loans, each of which had fewer than two hundred investors and therefore did not break the letter of the law.

The financial engineering did not stop there. Zhaocaibao then let the loan investors borrow money with their investments as collateral, creating yet more credit based on that single loan. The problem with this kind of activity, which became clear in the global financial crisis, is that a single bad loan or bond, when it anchors a chain of credit, creates much larger cascades of losses and uncertainty.

Zhaocaibao was a hit. By July 2015, 260 billion RMB had been invested through the platform. The risk appeared minimal thanks to state-linked companies that guaranteed the bonds. Zhaocaibao head Yuan Leiming admitted that its customers had no chance of understanding the risks of their investments: "I don't think individual investors have the ability to evaluate the risks in the financial products, so it's up to the financial institutions to screen the risks."[26] Unfortunately, those institutions were not up to the task. The securities regulator, with similar concerns, began restricting the practice of splitting up large loans into pieces starting in September 2015, but it was too late.[27]

In December 2015 a scandal rocked the platform when Cosun Group, a phone maker in Guangdong province, defaulted on $45 million in bonds that it had issued through Zhaocaibao. Although this was a tiny share of the platform's business, investors who received peer-to-peer loans with those bonds as collateral then defaulted, creating even more losses. A game of finger pointing ensued, as the insurer that guaranteed the loans refused to pay, blaming a bank that had also guaranteed the loan.

Fintech could be revolutionary in distributing financial products to customers, but it had done little to restrict the still-rampant fraud and opacity in China's banking system. Eventually, the banking regulator found that the bank had colluded with Cosun, meaning that the Alipay platform had unknowingly packaged and sold a fraud to its investors. One investor, sharing a widely held opinion, said, "I trusted the Alipay brand."[28] Investors had put all their trust in Ant to put only safe products on its platform, but it in turn had relied too much on a convoluted chain of guarantees that is common in Chinese financial markets.

The Cosun dispute gave average investors a rude awakening about the fragile nature of guarantees they took for granted, and financial regulators had to reckon with new risk accumulating in the fintech space. A big question worried regulators: if Ant Financial, one of the most sophisticated players with the most valuable reputation to maintain, had these kinds of issues, what problems lurked in other corners of the online lending and investing industry?

Ezubao Taints Internet Finance

The final nail in the coffin of unmitigated support for fintech came with Ezubao and Ding Ning. It is one of the most fascinating and mysterious stories of the excesses of the fintech gold rush, involving tens of billions of vanished RMB, mistresses, smugglers, weapons, likely corruption, and luxury villas. It demonstrates just how quickly that the internet, big promises, and overt signs of political favor could combine into one of the world's largest frauds, issues that any country hoping to promote fintech must avoid.

Ding, a vocational school dropout, joined the family hardware business, called Yucheng group, in the relatively poor province of

Anhui. He quickly pivoted to more profitable informal finance. By late 2014, Yucheng controlled multiple financial companies with capital of more than half a billion dollars.[29] The origin of such massive funds was too sensitive a mystery for Yucheng, regulators, or the media to talk about safely because of the signs that the company had links to rich and powerful political families, but these connections likely did not come from selling nuts and bolts.

Ding saw his chance to turn the family firm into a nationwide financial giant by joining the fintech boom. Yucheng bought a tiny existing P2P platform in Beijing, which it rebranded as Ezubao in July 2014.[30] Having headquarters in Beijing was a shrewd move, placing it close to the political leadership and making it appear more serious than any business in Anhui. Within the first two months it claimed to have taken in 20 million RMB in investments from people buying up pieces of its financial leasing projects. (Instead of lending a business money to buy equipment, a leasing company buys the equipment and then leases it for a fee to the company, retaining ownership.)

Ezubao focused on attracting money by signaling state backing. In February 2015 Ezubao held its annual meeting in the Great Hall of the People in Beijing, a sign of high-level political connections, for the brand-new company celebrated in the same building where China's top Communist Party officials select their leaders. The former vice chairman of the National People's Congress Standing Committee kicked off the festivities, at which Premier Li's support of internet finance was repeatedly referenced. Mid-level officials from all over the government attended.[31] It was common practice at the time in China to include thick "red envelopes" full of cash in the conference materials for officials to make it worth their time to attend.

A state-owned paper gushed about Ding's "faith and foresightedness," and noted that "investors welcomed expected reliable annual returns of 13%."[32] Even more importantly, Ezubao's advertisements ran on CCTV. A steelworker from Inner Mongolia invested half of his annual salary in Ezubao, telling the *New York Times* that "I thought to myself, now that it's on CCTV, there should be a lot of credibility." A former banker working in tech bought in too, saying, "Not every company will receive complimentary articles on government websites," assuming that the ads "would require strict vetting" because the channel is "part of the state."[33] Another ploy to gain attention was to brand an Ezubao executive named Zhang Min the "number one beautiful female executive in the Internet Finance industry."[34] The state links paid off: hundreds of thousands of people trusted their money to Ezubao.

More-sophisticated observers looked past state ties to highlight red flags. Rong 360, a website that rated P2P platforms, gave Ezubao a C−, the lowest possible score. It found serious issues, from conflicts of interest to questionable ties to banks in Southeast Asia.[35] *Beijing Business News* then undertook its own investigation with Renmin University, which found that investors were putting their money into fabricated projects for companies that did not exist.[36] Unfortunately, the appearance of state banking outweighed the allegations as investors continued to pour in their savings. Less than a year after its founding, Ezubao claimed to have made around 7 billion RMB (1.1 billion USD) in loans.

Despite such serious allegations, investigators did not swoop in until six months later, when Ezubao was ten times larger, at more than 70 billion RMB. Political protection probably played a role, but local government officials who regulated firms like Ezubao told me they were powerless to intervene even if they saw an obvious Ponzi scheme. China's system set up regulators in a lose-lose situation that reveals how officials will often be forced to choose between their own career incentives or safeguarding investor money. Early intervention to wind down the fraud would prompt losing investors to blame the government for their lost money and then protest, the kind of disturbance to social stability that can end an official's career. Waiting as they did until the fraud became large enough to blow itself up meant a larger mess, more victims, and larger protests, but in a sort of perverse logic this was less damaging to an official's career because the protest was not directly caused by their actions.

When Ezubao ran out of cash and investors complained, an investigation ensued. Little would ever be recovered. One executive admitted that "over 95% of the projects were fake." Ezubao's real account books took twenty hours to excavate from their hiding place six meters underground. Ding Ning was found with cash, cars, and high-powered weapons, but tens of billions of RMB had disappeared. The Yucheng group had a bank in Myanmar located in an autonomous region ruled by an ethnic militia group that appears to have helped Yucheng smuggle money out of China. Even when Ezubao was dismantled and its executives locked up, Yucheng was still sending smugglers with 125 kilograms of gold over the border.[37]

The Ezubao case was a bombshell for people accustomed to the government bailing out politically connected investments and companies rather than letting them fail. Angry investors thought that the government shared the blame, and this perception led to the public events that frightened the party. A widely shared notice online called for 维权, or "supporting rights," saying, "If we don't protect our rights, make appeals and take other drastic action within three days, we will recover little." The government sprang into action when it saw a call for nationwide protests, including demonstrations of around a hundred thousand people planned for Beijing.[38] The situation was diffused with a dose of heavy-handed censorship and coercion.

For a government considering what to do with an industry already on thin ice for its role in the stock market crash six months earlier, the protests that followed Ezubao's failure sparked two frightening realizations: these platforms were large enough to affect social stability, and the government had no framework to contain the risk. The head of one of China's largest P2P lenders worried that regulators "would close every P2P firm" after the scandal.[39]

. . .

Contrary to conventional wisdom in the West about China being a well-controlled, well-oiled authoritarian machine, the experience with P2P lending demonstrates that it can be uncoordinated, chaotic, lawless, and even blind to risks. Its experimental approach allowed far more experimentation with new financial models than in the United States. In some cases, such as mobile payments, it made sense to let an industry get on its feet before imposing regulations. At the beginning stages of a new technology application, it is not clear how to design new regulations that properly balance innovation with risk and consumer protection.

The downside of waiting to impose rules until the industry had grown up was that the government was reactive, often blind to building risks until they exploded into the open. It was particularly problematic in the P2P case. The platforms were adept at hiding risk and blatantly violating the law. The risk became very large extremely quickly because of the internet. By the time that problems emerged, P2P was already too big to fail or regulate properly. The financial-freedom-bearing super-apps illustrated that some elements of a regulatory framework existed when the fintech revolution began in 2013. Applying this regulatory framework came too late for P2P, which by 2015 was already large and had developed in a direction very different from what the government had hoped.

If the government let too many of the new institutions fail too quickly, a snowball effect could undermine confidence in the financial system and risk a devastating collapse. On the other hand, continuing to bail out investors taking ever-riskier bets on financial products like P2P loans, debt, and risk would spiral out of control and eventually outgrow even the CCP's financial capabilities, perhaps leading to a financial crisis. The P2P issue led to a sort of paralysis, weighing the hit to growth and government policies like inclusion against the risk of more Ezubaos.

Conversely, with the Bitcoin situation authorities proved that they could respond quickly and decisively. Their restrictions on Bitcoin use in China, developed and implemented in at most a few short months, clamped down on capital flight and immediately neutered the potential threat to China's monetary sovereignty.

Changes of a single word in Chinese government documents can take months of complex negotiations to complete, and they can express more meaning than the endless pages of Communist Party-speak that constitute the rest. In 2014 Premier Li Keqiang's annual report on the work of the government to the National People's Congress, one of the most important documents outlining government priorities, first mentioned fintech as something to promote. After so many scandals, however, a change in 2016 was ominous for fintech. All talk of "promote" (促进) was eliminated, replaced with "We will regulate the development of Internet finance."[40] The era of laissez-faire had to end, but authorities faced a long-standing dilemma: "When you loosen, you get chaos, but trying to regulate it kills it." It would take years to crack down on the riskiest practices, but for most of fintech the boom would continue as before. Regulators hoped to preserve as much of the beneficial innovation, inclusion, growth, and competition that came from the boom without running excessive risk, yet whether they can do so remains to be seen.

PART III

Party Control and International Expansion

5

Social Credit
and Crackdown on Risk

"Jack Ma may have crossed an unspoken red line"

J ack Ma seemed on top of the world as he took the stage at the
Bund Summit in Shanghai on October 24, 2020. He told the audience of China's economic and financial elite, including the now
former governor Zhou, that Ant Group was on the cusp of the
"largest listing ever priced in the history of the entire human race."
The night before, he received news that Ant's IPO would value
the company at $313 billion, on par with top US financial giants
like Mastercard and JP Morgan Chase. Ma's personal stake alone
would be worth a staggering $27.4 billion, more than the entire net
worth of global media baron Rupert Murdoch.[1] His empire of Ant
and Alibaba would together be worth more than a trillion dollars.

International investors hoping to get a piece of this prized company poured so much money into Hong Kong that they nearly
destabilized its currency. Their billions would boost Ant's technology development and international expansion, turning a domestic empire into a global one. Ma reminded his audience of the

geopolitical stakes in the competition between the United States and China for technology and capital: this "miracle" "happened in a place other than New York City." In a big win for China's stock markets, long unattractive for even Chinese companies to list in, Ant would list its shares in Shanghai and Hong Kong, not in New York, as Alibaba had in 2014.

Yet danger lurked behind the triumphal facade. Introductions of conference speakers are usually boring boilerplate, but before calling up Ma, Wang Haiming, the conference organizer and my boss during my years at the China Finance 40 Forum, said that Ma "is coming to the Bund Summit today to throw a bomb." It was a not-so-subtle warning that seemed to shake the normally confident Ma, who responded, "There's no bomb, who would dare throw a bomb."* He threw one anyway. His remarks were full of criticism of officials who would dare to restrict his business with excessive regulation and of banks that he viewed as outdated pawnbrokers. He advocated for a renewed focus on financial development, instead of the party's relentless focus on risk, and warned that "when the richness and depth of innovation are far beyond the imagination of regulations . . . the world will be in chaos." With his usual colorful language, Ma likened China's financial system to a polio patient and said that authorities' monitoring capabilities in finance were "obviously insufficient." He also included two citations of President Xi Jinping's speeches. He must not have realized how explosive his speech would be and that the bomb would mostly damage *him*.

Like Icarus, Ma then tumbled from the heights of wealth and power. First, regulators called him and top Ant executives in for a dressing down, then came draconian new regulations on Ant's lending, and finally the government canceled the IPO just days

---

*Those watching through translation would have missed the clear signal to be careful, for the interpreter translated the first as "he says he will say something very surprising" and declined to translate Ma's prespeech remark.

before it was to take place. Ma abruptly disappeared from the public eye, sparking rumors that he had been placed under house arrest or worse, while the government ordered a forced restructuring of Ant. Then the backlash spread to the whole consumer-tech sector. Alibaba and Tencent's stock prices tumbled as the government launched a regulatory storm with new antimonopoly rules for platforms, privacy rules, and antitrust investigations. The Chinese government could now break the super-apps into pieces and force them to share ever more data with the government and state banks. The central bank would run new data clearinghouses that control and share the data riches jealously guarded today by the big tech platforms in their walled gardens.

• • •

By attacking one of its star firms, the government joined the global movement to reckon with the power of tech giants. Their role in finance was greater in China than anywhere else, but the age of swashbuckling Chinese entrepreneurs bringing disruptive fintech revolutions was coming to an end. At the same time, the ideas of China's fintech revolution with its reinvention of money continue to spread around the world, including to the United States. Despite its travails at home, Ant is a global company with investments in fintech wallets serving billions of people. Thousands of US merchants accept it for payments. WeChat's addition of money to social networking has directly inspired Mark Zuckerberg to re-shape Facebook in part in WeChat's image and prepare to launch a new global digital currency that would give a tech firm the kind of sovereign powers usually reserved for governments. As the pandemic has driven more economic activity online and scared people off cash, China's cashless example has also become more attractive around the world.

The fate of fintech reveals seismic changes in China that may portend a darker future for both innovation and freedom. Jack Ma was free to criticize the government and bring competition to state companies around 2013, but the space for both has shrunk as the state sector has grown and authoritarianism is ascendant. For years, Ant and Tencent fended off government requests to share data, but they are losing the power to do so. Instead of tech companies' digital money in their digital wallets, the government is creating a digital currency of its own that will give it a database of every transaction and everyone's holdings. Fintech was a force for financial freedom, but as tech companies become more tightly controlled by the state, they could help implement even tougher repression than was possible in the past.

But the future direction remains unclear. The big technology platforms had amassed market power and flouted regulations, and as they became bigger, more rules were necessary. The government's crackdown on monopolies could in fact prove beneficial by protecting smaller innovators that would be squashed or absorbed into Tencent or Alibaba's orbit before they threatened the tech giants. However, the main beneficiaries could be the far-from-innovative big state companies that were effectively exempt from antitrust scrutiny. Their power relative to the big tech companies has risen significantly.

The journey from the hopeful period of fintech innovation to its fall from grace with Jack Ma's speech starts with recalibration of financial risk as regulators grappled with Li Keqiang's 2016 call to regulate internet finance, a sector they largely did not understand and lacked the proper tools to handle. They hoped to cut down on risk without stifling innovation or cutting off needed credit. It shows how Xi Jinping's consolidation of power and focus on financial risk swept up fintech in a broader crackdown on powerful business elites and risky behavior in Chinese finance.

Even fintech's most consistent advocates, such as former governor Zhou, concluded that inviting big tech into finance had not turned out as they hoped. Worries arose that the government's attempts to break the monopoly of the banks had created an even more dangerous one in the super-apps. Regulators took over aspects of Alipay and Tencent's financial businesses, worried about private companies controlling not only financial products but also the financial infrastructure that China's digital economy depended on. Meanwhile, fintech continued to boom throughout the period of reregulation, and new issues like cryptocurrency speculation challenged authorities.

As it grew bigger, big tech turned from a financial David into a resented Goliath. It came into the crosshairs of government and populace alike because of privacy issues: frauds built on identity theft and a thriving black market in personal data proliferated. Their labor practices also earned them scorn, from forcing their workers to toil at the office "9-9-6" (9 a.m. to 9 p.m., six days per week) to their treatment of delivery drivers, who earned a pittance serving demanding algorithms. Formerly viewed as heroes of inclusive finance, big-tech firms became vilified as loan sharks peddling loans that borrowers could not afford.

Big tech's falling popularity made it vulnerable to critics. Regulators resented how the political influence of big tech limited their ability to do their jobs, as the PBOC found in 2014 when its payment rules were neutered. Thus, the deluge that followed Jack Ma's speech was not revenge against one person but the breaking of a dam of political support that had protected his empire and big fintech. The speed with which the government rushed out new regulations affecting trillions of dollars of activity and China's most innovative companies makes it clear that pressure in that direction had been building for a long time, just waiting for the right political moment to strike. Jack Ma's speech was their golden opportunity. Economics, politics, and technology are intertwined everywhere, but fintech has made them even more so in today's China. As our commerce and finance become more digital, heeding how China's regime developed can teach valuable lessons that we will explore in Chapter 9, with both cautionary tales such as P2P and positive examples of expanding financial freedom through tech-enabled competition.

Social "Credit"

As China's tech companies became global leaders, Chinese political leaders developed the social credit system, the world's most ambitious plan to leverage data for governance. The logic underlying financial credit systems, that of collecting and sharing data to shape incentives, would apply to nearly all areas of life, with all the surveillance supervised by the party. It would first compile what may be the world's largest data set, with public- and private-sector data related to "credit" or "credibility" in every sector of society. The goal is "interconnection and interactivity of . . . credit information systems and . . . networks that cover all information subjects, all credit information categories, and all regions nationwide."[2] Second, it is a system of carrots and sticks to punish those who the data tell the Chinese government are not "sincere" or "trustworthy."

China has had serious struggles enforcing its laws despite being authoritarian. People who have defaulted on loans often ignored court orders, continuing to live large on money improperly taken from customers or business partners. It led China's Supreme People's Court to join social credit with a public blacklist of people and companies that fail to comply with court judgments. This blacklist is now part of the social credit system's records.[3] Social credit helps courts disseminate "credit" information to pressure compliance, just as credit bureaus encourage people to pay off debts by sharing their credit histories with other creditors. The system publicly names those who refuse to comply with court judgments and subjects them to "credit punishments." Blacklisted individuals find it harder to receive social security, work for the government, obtain business licenses, or get anywhere near a position as an executive in the financial sector. However, most crucial and controversial was the restriction on "unnecessary consumption." Those blacklisted would be unable to take planes, ride on high-speed trains, stay in five-star hotels, or leave the country. By early 2017, 6.73 million people on the list had been banned from planes and high-speed trains. The government believes that these draconian measures are justified as an incentive to change the behavior that got the person or entity on the blacklist.[4] The system also worked with banks to allow asset freezes and fund deductions from bank accounts.[5] The fintech super-apps joined the system as enforcers in 2015, lowering Sesame scores for defaulters and limiting what people on the list could buy from Alibaba—reportedly leading a hundred thousand people to pay unpaid debts so they could get off the blacklist and remove the restrictions.[6] Contrary to much of the social credit media coverage in the West, there is no evidence yet that the government plans to release a single algorithmic "nightmarish citizens score"[7] determining every Chinese person's position. What exists so far is quite low-tech: shared databases recording people who have fallen afoul of some regulation and punishments like the travel bans enforced by multiple government departments.

The kind of morality and credit culture that elsewhere is organic in how people interact or rely on systems run by private firms is what China hopes to engineer with the technocratic social credit system. Social credit is plugged into a wider, ever growing surveillance net that can leave a dozen or more cameras for a single intersection, identifying jaywalkers with facial recognition or cars with license plate readers, instantly sending them fines payable with Alipay or WeChat Pay.[8]

In the West a government effort to collect so much personal data and engage in social engineering would stir anxiety, but Chinese views on the system tend to be positive.[9] Its leaders believe that social credit can build trust in the government and base regulation on data and well-defined code, instead of bureaucrats' personal judgments. Local governments scrambled to come up with their own versions of the social credit system, and some developed dystopian citizen scoring systems that rated their citizens according to criteria like whether they visited their parents often enough or kept their home's entrance nicely swept.

There is nothing scientific about social credit. A key difference between it and the most important credit-scoring systems like the Fair, Isaac and Co. (FICO) scores used in countries such as the United States is that FICO scores are based on statistical data to provide an objective rating of the probability that a borrower will repay a loan. The score shapes behavior, making people want to take actions that maximize their score and reduce risk for lenders. In most cases it is useful, encouraging people not to default on debts or pay bills late. But it can lead people to open up multiple credit-card accounts to boost credit scores, which may encourage excessive credit use.[10] However, social scores, like those of Uber and Airbnb, have no scientific backing and more resemble the scores in the "Nosedive" episode of the dystopian Netflix show *Black Mirror*, where the characters are obsessed with their peers' constant ranking of their behavior. These scores have real impact—for example, causing the loss of jobs for Uber drivers whose scores are too low.

A social credit system is far scarier because it can measure whether behavior is in accord with the government's prescription and regulations. In addition, the government can impose much harsher penalties with the might of the state than can private actors using scores in the United States. The Chinese government's plans reveal its desire to shape citizens' behavior much more overtly than what Western governments find politically acceptable. More worryingly for fintech, which had been a force for financial freedom in China since its inception, social credit suggested a long-term government ambition to absorb its data and use its reach to implement social control.

The Campaign Against Financial Risk

The government's campaign to assert more control over fintech began with a narrow focus on financial risk, spurred by Premier Li's 2016 speech calling for regulation. Yet regulators knew little about many of the rapidly growing fintech markets they were supposed to regulate, and only a tiny number of officials at regulators had the space and resources to devote to focusing on fintech. As the government tried to figure out how to regulate without crushing innovation, China's leading status in fintech became a challenge. Unlike in other areas of financial development, regulators could not look to advanced economies for a ready-made playbook. The challenge depended on the sector of fintech. Big tech's activities were largely already under regulations that included data provision to the government and a supervisory framework. Online "P2P" lending platforms were a glaring exception. In 2016 no one in China—not Xi Jinping, Zhou Xiaochuan, or Jack Ma—knew how large that online credit had grown or how many bad loans had piled up. There was not even a mechanism for the government to collect such statistics. Instead, the government and this analysis were forced to rely on private data providers using self-reported statistics that were heavily manipulated. Smaller P2P platforms had an incentive to inflate their numbers to look more established, while large platforms underreported to avoid regulator attention.

No one knew when the next Ezubao would blow up, where it would be, or how many angry investors would take to the streets in protest. Despite all the discussion in the West about China's all-seeing state apparatus, surveillance capabilities, and AI tools, a deeper look at financial regulation presents a picture of Chinese officials not as all-seeing sages but as normal bureaucrats operating under severe constraints in a flawed system. The government faced a dilemma: rushing out regulations could lead to more risk, causing viable fintech companies to fail and leading to bad loans and angry investors protesting at government offices. Regulating before understanding the financial activities in question would also repudiate the strategy that had worked so well to unleash innovation and financial inclusion, cutting off both needed credit and useful activities while missing risks. Yet every delay meant larger risks and fraud scenarios from unregulated fintech.

The government swiftly banned some emerging risks, such as initial coin offerings of cryptocurrency, but in most cases acted cautiously, proposing regulations with long implementation periods to allow industry time to adjust. The regulators' caution helped avoid upsetting the delicate balance between clamping down on risk and maintaining credit supply. Meanwhile, fintech entrepreneurs pushed at shifting boundaries and craftily moved their businesses into less regulated niches, presenting themselves as more "tech" than "fin."

Broader shifts in China's politics and economy also began to constrain fintech, which would be swept up in two of Xi Jinping's core initiatives: a campaign against financial risk and a focus on party control over the economy and society. After initially signaling a push for market reforms in 2013, Xi Jinping reversed course. A thriving online civil society that often criticized the government and called out corruption was one of the first to disappear in 2013, as bloggers with large social-media followings were detained, threatened, and humiliated.[11]

As the government reasserted control, nationalizing payments and credit infrastructure and limiting Ant and Tencent's ability to compete with the state-owned banks, these firms pivoted to profit from opening their platforms and technology to other financial institutions, only to see even these models come under attack from regulators as the government's discomfort grew with big tech and their super-apps' power.

Growth, Credit, and Risk

Even with scandals and increased regulation, the future of fintech looked bright in 2017. The backlash against big tech was still years in the future. Fintech remained tiny in Chinese terms: a few trillion in a financial system of hundreds of trillions of RMB. Meanwhile, a core concern of the authorities was addiction to debt, which threatened to both slow down the economy and raise the risk of a financial crisis. Debt levels rose much faster than economic growth from 2012 to 2016, which led debt to GDP to reach nearly 250 percent.[12] Economic growth fell over this period from 7.9 percent to 6.8 percent per year, meaning that payments to service the debt would weigh more heavily on the economy. Fintech still looked like part of the solution, bringing more market competition and helping with technology that made financial intermediation cheaper, more efficient, and more inclusive.

Using fintech as a lever to improve finance had come with a looser regulatory regime for the upstarts, which posed risks that became untenable after Xi wrested control of economic policy from Premier Li. Xi launched a multiyear campaign against debt and risk in December 2016. He overcame long-standing resistance to taking the punch bowl away from the credit party by clamping down on the shadow credit that benefited powerful interests who got rich or secured promotions thanks to easy money.[13] Xi then installed policy makers aligned with the new goals in key positions. Guo Shuqing, a reformer who had once complained about party committees interfering in banks, became head of the China Banking Regulatory Commission, where he leapt into action with a flurry of new regulations that forced banks to examine such practices as "inappropriate innovations."[14]

There is often a chasm between the rhetoric in party documents and the reality on the ground, but Xi meant business.

Credit growth plunged from around 12 percentage points per year higher than economic growth to about equal in 2017 and 2018, so overall debt to GDP stabilized.

The main targets of new rules were more the core of the financial system—banks and trust companies rather than fintech—so the shift to deleveraging started as a market opening for fintech. In fact, just as Xi launched his crackdown on risk, Jack Ma laid out his most ambitious plan yet for Ant. The company reached a $60 billion valuation in early 2016, becoming one of the world's most valuable unicorns, companies that had not yet gone public but were still worth more than a billion dollars. Ma proposed reorganizing finance around Alibaba and Ant Financial's strengths, giving his company a leg up on the still state-dominated core of the financial system. Ant would no longer be a fintech company, which "takes the original financial system and improves its technology," but a "techfin" company, which "is to rebuild the system with technology."[15] Ma and Ant could argue that their technology and data were helping to reduce risk and cost in China's financial system compared to the high-cost banks relying on old technology to evaluate borrowers.

Another way fintech could help the government was as a safety valve. Borrowers that relied on the type of credit targeted by authorities flooded in to borrow from fintech firms. If the government turned off all the risky financing channels at once, it would cause too much stress on the private-sector borrowers that still could not get credit from banks. Regulators had to be careful. Although the new, unregulated online credit intermediaries were miniscule in China's mammoth financial system, they were growing over 50 percent per year and created about a fifth as much new credit as banks in 2017. They were also important to the flow of credit to new borrowers like small businesses and consumers.[16]

Xi also reorganized China's regulatory system to cut down on arbitrage. The separate institutions to regulate banks, securities markets, insurance companies, and the central bank often did not know where one's jurisdiction ended and another began, leaving a mess of loopholes and tending toward turf wars. The prevailing structure was particularly ill-suited to regulating a complex institution like Ant, whose many areas of business were supervised by separate regulators that did not coordinate well, meaning that no one but the company itself understood the firm as a whole and the interconnections of its parts. One of the lessons learned from the global financial crisis was that this type of regulatory setup led to serious risk because solely "prudential" regulation focused on single institutions was not enough. Instead, "macroprudential" policy was needed to consider the systemic interactions between them.[17] Xi thus created the Financial Stability and Development Committee (FSDC), directly under the State Council, to improve coordination, which would gradually improve the government's capacity to act decisively. Eventually headed by Vice Premier Liu He, Xi's Harvard-educated economic confidant, it had the heft to knock heads.

Reining in Alipay and Tencent

As the momentum for risk reduction built, political protection for fintech weakened. In June 2016 Governor Zhou followed Premier Li's reversal by promising to unwind the uneven playing field he had tilted toward fintech. He promised to "create a fair competitive environment" because Alibaba, he said, was a shadow bank with excessive leverage.[18] Alipay and WeChat still faced light regulatory burdens, but the super-apps had become not just products but also financial infrastructure crucial to the economy. Regulation on infrastructure tends to be high to limit the ability to profit from and gain power from control of it, just as many US electricity utilities have natural monopolies and prices fixed by the local government. Big-tech operations in payments, credit reporting, and lending would face scrutiny as the government had second thoughts about opening up so much of finance to them.

The first move came in online payments, where Alipay and WeChat Pay controlled around 90 percent of the market. There were two problems with this concentration from the PBOC's point of view. The first was a lack of competition. Banks largely did not bother supporting online-payment companies other than Alipay, WeChat, and UnionPay because the costs of adding another payment partner were much higher than the scale of new business that marginal players could add. The cost/benefit ratio did not make sense even though the tech giants' size gave them a competitive moat and leverage to extract beneficial terms from banks. The second concern was financial stability. Alipay and Tencent Pay moved trillions of RMB between banks through their own network of accounts. If something went wrong, like an accounting error, cybersecurity event, or the mishandling of client money, it could cause a crisis.

The PBOC thus took over the movement of money between banks and payment companies. NetsUnion, a new quasi-governmental entity, would also help banks rebalance their relationship with big tech. Fees would be standardized, and data jealously guarded by Alipay and WeChat would now be opened up to the banks, reducing big tech's leverage. The politics had shifted away from big tech.[19] The big-tech firms once may have had the power to quietly block such a move, but Alipay and WeChat found themselves in the unenviable position of being enlisted to help with the technical design of the government system that would replace some of what they had built over many years.[20]

The PBOC's reassertion of control of payment infrastructure was not an unjust nationalization but an action well within the norm in most countries. Central banks around the world are key players in the payment systems that govern flows between banks, including often backstopping the system with promises to inject cash if needed to maintain liquidity.[21] PBOC Governor Yi Gang, who replaced Governor Zhou in 2018, later referred to Alipay and WeChat Pay's activity in moving money between banks as "wrongdoing" that made them into a "second central bank."[22]

The regulatory process was a game of whack-a-mole. Once regulators got a handle on one set of risky practices, fast-moving entrepreneurs were on to another. For example, Ant could side-step NetsUnion by encouraging its users to make purchases with its virtual-credit line Huabei. Most payments would be internal to Alipay's closed loop, except for one payment from a user's bank account each month when payment was due. Only that payment would incur fees and share data with NetsUnion. In doing so, however, Ant set itself on a collision course with a government uneasy with the idea of Chinese becoming like some Americans, who pay for everything on credit. Eventually, Ant had over $271 billion in outstanding loans to consumers.

At the same time, the PBOC hit online-payment companies' earnings on "float," interest accrued on customer funds entrusted to the payment company. Alipay and Tencent Pay earned billions of RMB this way, allowing them to reduce the direct fees they charged users. Although there had been no issues with Alipay or Tencent, smaller payment firms had misused customer money for risky investments or even embezzled it.[23] The PBOC phased out this revenue stream in January 2017, when it ordered payment companies to start putting customer funds into special accounts at the PBOC that initially paid no interest, costing the giants an estimated one billion USD every year.[24] NetsUnion and the special deposit rules would make fraud more difficult, but they also made Alipay and Tencent Pay easier to regulate as their activity could be traced to a single account rather than a complex web of bank accounts. The moves on payments were only the beginning of a wave of regulation that next turned to wealth management.

Yu'E Bao, like P2P, was initially a beneficiary of the campaign against risk. Higher interest rates led investors to pour money into Yu'E Bao, leading it to double in size in 2017 alone, from

800 billion to 1.6 trillion RMB. Nearly half a billion Chinese had invested in what was now the largest money-market fund in the world, beating out US giants such as JP Morgan Chase and Vanguard.[25] This unexpected consequence of trying to clamp down on risk unnerved regulators, who declared in November 2017 that a "certain" money-market fund had reached systemic proportions, meaning that any sudden sell-off could cause a system-wide panic and harm "social stability."[26] Such events had happened before—for example, in the United States during the subprime crisis, when the Federal Reserve had to intervene to halt panic in the money market. Regulators thus pressured Ant to limit its own product's popularity with ever-stricter limits on inflows to counter the strong demand, leading it to shrink by a third.

The PBOC was beginning to rethink its rush to invite big tech into finance, reversing some earlier policies and closing loopholes in fintech regulation.[27] There were two larger issues at stake. First, big-tech platforms were so powerful and had so many users that any product they provided could reach systemic proportions faster than regulators could follow, creating serious risks. One example was "cash loans," high-interest short-term credit similar to US payday loans. When Qudian, one of the most successful cash-loan providers, was listed on the New York Stock Exchange in late 2017, it unwittingly demonstrated the power of super-apps and invited a crackdown. Alipay partnered with Qudian to evaluate borrowers cheaply with Sesame scores and push its loans to the hundreds of millions of Alipay users, which enabled the three-year-old company to make around $9 billion in loans to 5.6 million borrowers.

Foreshadowing the risks of regulator attention associated with IPOs, authorities alarmed at the scale of these risky loans cracked down, cratering Qudian's share price. The scrutiny on cash loans exposed a loophole that Ant exploited in its own business, offloading hundreds of billions of RMB in loans to banks with little government oversight. Realizing that any issues with Ant loans could lead to serious bad loan problems at the banks that bought those loans, regulators forced major painful reforms to Ant's lending business as well.[28]

Second, regulators were concerned about market distortions and conflicts of interest. The classic Silicon Valley model of charging below cost either until sufficient scale is reached or making up the difference through profits elsewhere in the company's huge bundle of services distorted financial markets. How could, for example, an independent credit-rating agency that had to pay for data and charge customers compete with a big-tech firm that already had all the data and made enough money elsewhere to charge tiny rates that gained it market share? Tech platforms performing credit scoring could distort the market and create a conflict of interest by providing artificially high scores to boost credit that would allow them to profit from both loan origination and the sale of products on their platforms, while banks bore the risks. Or they could create scores based on activity on tech apps. The resulting scores might resemble loyalty points from app usage more than objective results. These concerns led the PBOC to reverse course on the credit-scoring pilot, forcing Sesame Credit to scale back its ambitions and giving the only full license to a state company instead. Savvy observers noticed regulators' newfound willingness to hit a company as powerful as Ant with such drastic measures, weakening its air of political invincibility and portending more serious regulatory woes to come.

Banishing Cryptocurrency

Digital currency took off again in 2016. Even after the authorities dampened Bitcoin speculation in 2013, trading volume at China's exchanges continued to dwarf those in the rest of the world, peaking at 98 percent of global Bitcoin trading in December 2016.[29] What made Bitcoin so appealing to Chinese people was the inability of any government to control it. That was untenable to Chinese leaders. In addition to domestic risks, Chinese policy makers were preoccupied with capital outflows. Investment outside of China by large companies and money fleeing a slowing economy depreciated the RMB and drained almost a trillion dollars of China's foreign-exchange reserves by December 2016.

There is little evidence that digital currencies were being used for capital flight in large enough quantities to make a difference. But the government, media, and investors in China were abuzz with rumors that it was, and in huge quantities. One could purchase Bitcoin or another cryptocurrency with RMB at a Chinese exchange and then transfer it to a digital wallet that could be cashed out on an exchange anywhere in the world, with no way for the Chinese government to track it. Intermediaries specializing in this capital flight proliferated on WeChat, illustrating the limits of surveillance and control.* Authorities responded by tightening their oversight of digital-currency exchanges in China, which could be regulated even if Bitcoin itself was outside the government's reach.

On January 6, 2017, regulators announced that they had conducted "an interview" with BTC China to "require it to operate strictly according to relevant rules and regulations" as a result of "unusual volatility."[30] Because of another possible Chinese regulatory wave against Bitcoin, its global price dropped by 12 percent. Investors were right to worry, for regulators discovered problems from illegal margin financing to poor controls on money laundering.[31] Under PBOC pressure, China's top three exchanges imposed fees of 0.2 percent on transactions, ended margin financing, and shut off the ability to "withdraw" Bitcoin outside the exchange, making it just about impossible to use for capital flight. Yet the

---

* Bitcoin could hardly have been a key driver of outflows. Bitcoin trading volumes were miniscule compared to the nearly $1 trillion decline in foreign-exchange reserves, and it would be hard to cash out large amounts of Bitcoin at foreign exchanges.

PBOC remained tolerant and permitted the exchanges to resume business once their controls had improved. The exchanges might have thought they were in the clear, but another speculative frenzy would get them kicked out of China once and for all.

In 2017 the government's desire for control was in full display when a new investing craze—initial coin offerings (ICOs)—swept the world. ICOs sold new digital currency or digital assets to the public to raise money for blockchain ideas, from decentralized networks for cloud file storage to tracking tuna supplies with blockchain (for some reason). An ICO was essentially a presale for digital products that did not yet exist. Bloomberg opinion columnist Matt Levine memorably described this as akin to the Wright brothers choosing to finance their first airplane by selling discounted frequent-flyer miles.[32] Investors were betting that once the idea took off, demand for the digital currency would drive its price into the stratosphere.

In another frenzy to get rich quick, investors rushed to invest in tokens based on nothing more than a white paper, hoping to make fortunes overnight like early investors in Bitcoin and Ethereum had. By June 2017, new ICOs globally raised well over half a billion dollars, dwarfing what internet firms were raising from venture capital.[33] No one knew how to value any of these coins, and no blockchain company had created a product that fully worked, but digital tokens were now worth billions based solely on speculation—much of it from China. By the end of the first half of 2017, China's National Association of Internet Finance (NIFA) reported that 105,000 investors and 2.6 billion RMB, around $400 million at the time, were involved in ICOs in China through 43 ICO platforms.[34] There were surely many times more that authorities did not know about.

The first significant ICO known as such was the DAO, or decentralized autonomous organization, a crowd-funded investment vehicle that people could buy into by purchasing "DAO tokens," which granted voting rights over investment allocation and a share of the venture's stakes. In 2015 all it took was one month to raise around $150 million worth of Ether, but an error in the code allowed a hacker to run off with a third of the DAO's digital currency. Investors eventually got their money back, but it was an embarrassing start to endeavors that were telling people it was better to trust code and cryptography than old financial intermediaries.

Despite the DAO's failure, ICOs took off, and prices of successful projects rocketed up. One Chinese project, PressOne, raked in $125 million worth of cryptocurrency without even providing a white paper explaining what the project was building, saying, "We don't provide that. Even if we did, few people would understand it, and not even a couple of people would look at the thing."[35] Its backing by one of the most famous figures in China's cryptocurrency world, with millions of online followers, was enough. A get-rich-quick mentality and a small number of new digital currencies for sale meant that a bit of upward momentum in a token could make prices rocket up. Stories circulated that "one [ICO investor] took a nap and woke up to find he had just achieved financial independence."[36] ICO behavior was a carryover from practices in China's traditional financial markets, where investors were used to large bumps in price on day one of the IPOs of Chinese stocks, which also had shortages of available shares.

China then led the world in ICO investment and launches, but this was not the fintech leadership that Chinese authorities hoped for. For over a year, they had been trying to contain risks from the internet finance companies already in existence, so they were not interested in facing down another bubble of cryptocurrency speculation. The more digital currencies were available, the easier it would be for money launderers, people smuggling capital out of the country, and corrupt officials to move their money around without touching the financial system. Fraudulent ICO projects were bound to fail, meaning that losing investors would eventually show up at their doorstep as protesters. Because the money would be stored in the cryptocurrency world, out of the reach of authorities, there would be little they could do to recover money for the victims.

In late August 2017, the state-run Xinhua news service published a damning article exposing the fact that to appear legitimate, many ICOs fabricated everything from their projects to the team members supposedly building the new coins, and then disappeared with the money.[37] The PBOC-backed NIFA went further with an article associating ICOs with illegal fund-raising, pyramid schemes, and money laundering.[38] Days later, regulators banned ICOs, the most negative response to ICOs by any country. By contrast, the United States and the United Kingdom both waffled on whether their financial regulators even had jurisdiction over ICOs.[39] Chinese ICOs that had already raised money were ordered to return it. Just as the PBOC had said about Tencent's Q coin over a decade earlier, ICOs caused "severe disruption of the financial order." Unlike in the earlier episode, the tolerance of the authorities for new, risky digital finance ideas had worn thin. They were ready with a decisive response.

Cryptocurrency exchanges, which had been permitted to reopen less than four months earlier, became collateral damage and were forced out of the country.[40] The old approach of allowing years of financial innovations with loose regulation could last only if political support was sustained, and the previous delays also came because regulators did not coordinate well with one another. However, the official statement banning ICOs demonstrated more effective coordination and diminished political support for disruptive financial innovation.

Still, regulators could not stamp out cryptocurrency trading, for exchanges outside China could easily serve Chinese customers over the internet. Authorities enlisted the Great Firewall, usually used to block forbidden political content, to block websites of offshore cryptocurrency exchanges, but determined investors could use virtual private networks (VPNs) to get around the firewall and

trade anyway.[41] People in China could also buy and sell cryptocurrencies over the counter, with decentralized tools to match individuals buying and selling crypto. And once people had Bitcoin,
Ether, or any other cryptocurrency, the Chinese government had
no way to stop them from buying into offshore ICOs. Yet authorities did not need to entirely eliminate cryptocurrency to achieve
their goal, just ensure that it would be out of the reach of the general public.

Leading Global Fintech Innovators

In April 2016, Ant, which stayed away from ICOs, set a record for
the largest private funding round in a tech company, $4.5 billion,
at a valuation of $60 billion. The only private tech company worth
more at that point was Uber. Those billions would fuel not only
new technology development but also a new push to invest and
expand Ant overseas.

Tencent also continued to make important innovations for
the domestic fintech market, expanding the usefulness of super-
apps in ways that would inspire Silicon Valley years later. Tencent launched "mini-programs" in January 2017. Just as Apple
and Google set the rules and provide the operating environment
for apps in iOS and Android, Tencent controls the ecosystem of
mini-programs accessible within WeChat. Developers can build
mini-programs for WeChat's platform as scaled-down versions of
regular apps or build mini-programs from scratch. For example,
upon arrival at a restaurant, diners can scan a QR code in WeChat
to quickly pull up the restaurant's mini-program to browse the
menu, order, and pay through WeChat Pay without needing to
download a full app for the restaurant. In the United States, by
contrast, restaurants still want users to pay with plastic cards
in person, order through a website, or download a stand-alone
app for every restaurant, and each option requires users to share

sensitive credit-card details with the provider (unless it accepts Apple Pay).

Another illustrative use case is parking. US parking still requires taking a paper ticket on entry and paying at a separate terminal or holding up cars behind while paying at the exit. In China, WeChat mini-program users scan a QR code when entering the garage and provide their license number. When they exit, the time is automatically calculated and charged through WeChat Pay, a far more convenient experience. In addition, whereas a charge of a few dollars for parking might result in credit- or debit-card fees eating up a large share of the charge, such WeChat payments have miniscule charges that improve the economics of especially small payments.[42]

As for financial services and the sharing economy, payments tie the platform together to enable more-convenient services. Mini-programs are also cheaper to develop because of their small scale and the need to make only one to cover almost the entire Chinese market. US app makers, as noted earlier, need to develop separate versions for Android and Apple users.

By mid-2018, WeChat mini-programs had nearly half a billion monthly active users, and in mid-2019 they had nearly 750 million people spending nearly an hour per month using them. Alibaba came later to the mini-program trend, launching its own in September 2018, but it gained half a billion users in only a few months.[43] A whole ecosystem combining social dynamics and e-commerce built up around super-apps became a multi-billion-dollar industry. Run by popular influencers who peddle and review products online with gamified features like those that made WeChat Pay take off, the live-streaming e-commerce industry reached a scale of 440 billion RMB (63 billion USD) in 2019.[44]

Online payments and loans continued to grow to proportions far beyond anything outside of China. PBOC data showed that online nonbank payments, about 90 percent of which are controlled by Alipay and Tencent, reached 143 trillion RMB in 2017, a 44 percent increase over 2016 despite all the new regulations. Chinese big-tech payments dwarf anything else in the world. The Bank for International Settlements estimated mobile payments in China through big tech, primarily Alipay and Tencent, at over 16 percent of GDP in 2017. In contrast, in the United States, the next highest, the total was 26 times less, at only 0.6 percent of GDP.

China was not as much of an outlier with lending by fintech companies as in payments. Still, the Bank for International Settlements estimated China's fintech credit at 372 USD per person, more than double the next highest, the United States at 126 USD.[45] Apple Pay, Google Wallet, and the rest had beaten Alipay to the digital-wallet starting line, but Alipay and Tencent left them in the dust. China looked more impressive than ever globally for its fintech achievements, yet a crackdown at home was gathering steam.

Taking Down Tycoons

Meanwhile, major problems with financial conglomerates led to pressure to add a new layer of regulation for firms like Ant. Conglomerates holding a multitude of financial licenses can rack up mountains of hidden debt, hiding losses by moving them around in a shell game of multilayered subsidiaries. When those firms and their executives or owners have political clout, their ability to resist scrutiny and regulation amplifies the risk.

Jack Ma's ability to block payment regulations in 2014 is emblematic, but countless other examples of blocked or unimplemented rules must have never reached the public eye. Regulators I spoke with around 2017 expressed frustration at the resistance to regulating firms like Ant because of Ma's real and perceived political clout. When PBOC finally issued rules in July 2019, it said that this type of financial holding company had undergone "blind business expansion over the past few years" that needed to be rethought.[46]

Financial holding companies came into the government's crosshairs mainly because of the missteps of nonfintech conglomerates. Such powerful tycoons as Wu Xiaohui and Xiao Jianhua, who controlled webs of financial and nonfinancial companies, were detained, the latter apparently abducted from the Four Seasons in Hong Kong. Other tycoons such as Wang Jianlin, once China's richest man, were pressured to sell off overseas assets to shrink domestic debts.[47] The government took over Wu Xiaohui's Anbang, a giant insurer, in February 2018 after a debt-fueled acquisition binge that included the famed Waldorf Astoria in New York. A maze of holdings in financial institutions hid risk and embezzlement by its chairman until it all came crashing down, leaving the government with an immense mess.[48] Even more worrisome, billionaire Xiao Jianhua's Tomorrow Group, which owned stakes in dozens of financial institutions, so thoroughly raided a bank it owned that the bank failed. Defaults are so rare that Baoshang Bank's financial worries created a near panic in the interbank market, forcing the PBOC to intervene to avoid destabilizing the market that financial institutions in China rely on for funding every day.

The crackdown on tycoons was not just about legitimate concerns of financial risk. It was also about eliminating alternative centers of power outside the party and its state-owned enterprises. Instead of markets and private firms, which drove real innovation in China, Xi favored state firms, over which the party exerted more direct control.[49] In a 180-degree turnaround from 2012, when Wen Jiabao invited private firms to eliminate state monopolies in finance, the State Council in 2016 pushed consolidation of state control in key industries with ever-larger state firms. In 2017 Xi called for supporting "state capital in becoming stronger, doing better, and growing bigger."[50]

Even private firms were to be placed further under the party's thumb, with increased roles for party cells placed within any significant firm in China. When I visited Tencent's offices, artisan espresso bars in massive towers coexisted with reading rooms on Xi Jinping Thought, and an indoor running track was punctuated with Tencent Communist Party Committee posters reminding joggers of the People's Liberation Army's glorious victories.

It has always been dangerous to be a high-profile rich person in the People's Republic of China. The Chinese even call the Hurun list of its wealthiest people the "fat pig killing list" because seventy-two Chinese billionaires died unnatural deaths from 2003 to 2011 alone and others have ended up in prison or under investigation. As the highest-profile individual in China, better known internationally than even President Xi, Jack Ma may have watched his fellow tycoons' downfalls with trepidation. Ma may have crossed an unspoken red line when he met US president-elect Donald Trump at Trump Tower and promised to create millions of jobs in the United States. Ma could be seen as jumping above Xi in precedence by arranging such a meeting before President Xi had met Trump, suspicions that would have been further amplified by the "Jack Ma for president" line that spread on China's internet.[51]

The clearest sign that Ma's position had become dangerous came when he announced in September 2018 that he would step down as chairman of Alibaba to focus on philanthropy, although he was only in his mid-fifties. Perhaps he believed that creating some separation between himself and his company would help protect it if he found himself on the wrong side of the political line. Of course, behind the scenes he retained strong influence. He never really retreated from the spotlight, and his flamboyant style of speaking would continue to grab headlines. The shift toward less risk and more control meant that the writing was on the wall for private fintech companies like Tencent and Ant Financial.

Another shift in the political fortune of fintech was that in March 2018 its main protector, PBOC Governor Zhou, retired from his record-setting fifteen-year stint as central-bank governor. In a sign of continuity, one of his closest protégés and a committed reformer, Yi Gang, succeeded him. Yi, who had studied and worked in the United States for about fifteen years, was a surprising pick for such a sensitive position. He graduated from Hamline University in 1982, earned his PhD from the University of Illinois, and served as professor of economics at Indiana University from 1986 to 1994. Yi was pointedly not named the PBOC's Communist Party secretary, meaning he was not in as strong a position as Zhou, who had been both governor and party secretary. Yi also lacked the strong political network that Zhou had enjoyed as a princeling plugged into the party apparatus for his whole career. Although Zhou would retain influence in retirement, fintech's top-level political support continued to wane. If Yu'E Bao had been launched in 2017 instead of 2013, it might have been immediately banned. Disruption and competition were no longer tenable strategies, so fintech would need a new one to survive in Xi Jinping's "New Era." One idea was to take the company's capital, know-how, and technology abroad to markets ripe for the kind of revolution that it had brought to China.

6

Chinese Fintech Goes Abroad

"No credit cards—we only take Alipay or Thai Baht"

The global implications of the China fintech story really hit home when I traveled to Thailand for my honeymoon in 2017. Convenience stores had Alipay acceptance signs plastered next to those from credit-card companies, but when I tried to pay with Visa, the clerk said, "Actually, we only take Alipay or Thai Baht." I wondered if Chinese fintech could manage to make a dent in the current dominance of US payment companies. Thanks to the large number of big-spending Chinese tourists taking super-apps abroad before the pandemic, merchants around the world are falling over each other to accept Alipay and WeChat Pay. An executive at payment giant Ingenico has likened being a merchant not accepting Alipay to "not offering air conditioning in a car."[1] Soon, just about anywhere you shop, online or offline, in emerging markets or industrial economies, could accept Alipay and WeChat Pay—even if they do not accept US credit cards.

Chinese fintech's fate abroad is crucial to understanding its implications for the United States. The key question is whether the dominance that the United States enjoys today in global finance is similar to Alipay's dominance of online payments before WeChat's red packets used a lead in new technology to disrupt the incumbent player faster than anyone anticipated. If it proves successful only in China, then it will not pose a real competitive threat to the US financial institutions and tech giants accustomed to global dominance. Others might not follow the lead of Chinese fintech if its innovations can take hold only in China's unique environment. However, if Alipay and Tencent manage to gain massive user bases abroad, they will have the basis for global payment and financial networks that could provide alternatives to the dollar and the institutions that transact in them—similar to WeChat's social advantage being the crucial foothold to attack Alipay in 2014. From a national security perspective, Chinese firms collecting sensitive financial data from foreigners could also be a serious concern if they cannot guarantee that these data will not find themselves in the hands of the Chinese state.

Jack Ma's vision was to use Ant's technology to transform finance globally. In Davos in 2017, Ant CEO Eric Jing said that "we envision Ant Financial to be a global company . . . my vision is that we want to serve 2 billion people in the next ten years. . . ."[2] Ant and Tencent would expand abroad through investments and partnerships with local fintech companies in other countries and by signing up payment processors and merchants that would accept its QR codes. In the years following Jing's Davos speech, Ant shelled out billions for stakes in fintech companies in Asia, South America, and Europe.

The domestic crackdown has so far done little to constrain Chinese fintech's global ambition. Alipay and WeChat Pay can be used to pay in fifty-six markets outside mainland China, and WeChat claims to have hundreds of millions of foreign users. The most promising frontier for fintech is outside China's borders, although there are still hundreds of millions of rural Chinese not yet plugged into the fintech ecosystem. Chinese fintech has much to contribute to the rest of the world: technology, talent, capital, and tacit know-how. Chinese fintech companies have achieved some initial successes in globalization, but they are also encountering trouble with localizing to foreign markets, national security concerns, and protectionism. It is too early to tell how successful they will be outside of China.

Ant and Tencent have expanded abroad with three strategies: agreements that enable foreign merchants to accept Alipay or WeChat Pay, exports of their Chinese brands/apps, and investments in local partners. The first and most successful allows people to leave China while remaining glued to super-apps. The acceptance of WeChat Pay and Alipay has grown rapidly, but these two are still far behind the US credit-card giants. Because the users making payments are Chinese, what looks like a global expansion basically still serves the domestic market. The second strategy has had limited success so far in attracting users outside China. WeChat Pay has set up local wallets under its own brand in such places as South Africa, Malaysia, and Hong Kong. However, the efforts have so far failed to gain many users. Both Ant and Tencent have also followed the third strategy: large investments and deep strategic partnerships with fintech companies around the world. Thus far, they have flown under the radar because Ant's investments began only in 2015 and tend to avoid acquisitions that would expand its own obviously Chinese brand to foreign consumers. Instead, Ant takes large minority stakes in local fintech firms. At the same time, its partnerships try to spread the Chinese super-app model to places such as India, Thailand, and Korea. Meanwhile, its affiliate Alibaba is buying up e-commerce and logistics firms around the world, which can then integrate with the financial side as it did in China.

Fintech giants and new companies are going abroad for three primary reasons. The first is that the regulatory crackdown and the privacy backlash in China have put up barriers to growth at home that would come at banks' expense. Second, new-user growth in China is slowing. Most digitally savvy Chinese are already using Alipay and WeChat. Both services have shelled out massive subsidies to gain users, often at the other's expense—sensible for a rapidly growing market but not a sustainable long-run business strategy. Each, though, has room to expand abroad without stepping on the other's toes. Fintech in Southeast Asia and elsewhere is growing, and there is much more room for new digitization in many of those financial systems that remain in China. The third reason for going abroad is that, at least pre-COVID, domestic customers were traveling widely. If one super-app is more internationally useful than another, it gains an advantage at home by ensuring users never leave their super-apps, even if they leave China. It also gains access to the data and transaction fees generated abroad, which feeds into better products and profits at home.

Accepted Everywhere

By signing up merchants abroad, Alipay and WeChat Pay can not only fulfill the needs of their customers but also gather more data and take a further step toward controlling a global payment network. The millions of Chinese traveling, studying, or working abroad do not want to go back in time to analog payments. The United Nations estimated that Chinese tourists spent nearly $260 billion abroad in 2017, almost as much as tourists from the United States, Germany, and France combined.[3] However, acceptance alone does not penetrate deeply into the financial systems of other countries, for they rely on local partners to process payments.

Alipay and WeChat Pay increased their rate of acceptance by partnering with companies which provide payment systems that merchants already use.* Unlike NFC-based tools like Google Wallet and Apple Pay, merchants can mostly use existing point-of-sale (POS) machines to scan or generate QR or bar codes. In August 2016 Alipay began partnering with Ingenico, the largest payment gateway in Europe, to allow Chinese tourists in Europe to use its app the same way as they would back home.[4] By 2017, Alipay had claimed acceptance by ten thousand European vendors. Alipay's entry into the United States began in November 2016 during a trial partnering with First Data. It started with luxury-goods stores in California and New York but quickly scaled up. First Data's four million merchants could accept Alipay's QR code payments with a few taps on an existing POS machine.

In one fell swoop, Alipay could be easily accepted in nearly as many US locations as Apple Pay, which despite years of head start was only in 4.5 million US merchant locations at the time.[5] Alipay was successfully replicating a key to its domestic expansion: easy, low-cost merchant acceptance. The question was whether it would use this position to take on US financial companies on their own turf. Alipay initially had this ambition but quickly scaled back after encountering unexpected resistance. For now, it has focused on Chinese people visiting or living in the United States. Alipay aims to be "the Chinese traveler's local guide to any foreign city."[6] The Chinese can plan much of their trip within Alipay, including Chinese-language maps that conveniently point out which stores accept Alipay.

Many countries in Southeast Asia accept Chinese super-apps, including Thailand, Vietnam, and Singapore. The super-apps are also active in Africa. Chinese companies are selling to Africans,

---

*Alipay transfers a user's RMB only as far as the payment processor's account, where it enters the foreign country's financial system and eventually makes it to the merchant's account.

starting large local operations, and serving Chinese laborers working there to construct the massive infrastructure projects funded by China's Belt and Road Initiative. M-PESA linked up with WeChat Pay in 2018 to allow its users to send money to China, presumably to enable payments to Chinese merchants for imported goods. By April 2019, another partner made both Alipay and WeChat Pay available in Kenya, Uganda, Tanzania, and Rwanda.[7]

Once payment becomes untethered from physical presence, such as cards and cash, it is nearly impossible to limit to one country, even if Alipay and WeChat Pay do not even officially operate where their payment systems are used. Both found themselves in trouble in Nepal when authorities found that merchants used QR codes linked to Chinese bank accounts to accept payments from Chinese tourists.[8] Although the tourist and merchant are physically in Nepal, the QR code scan has just moved RMB from one account in China to another with no capital inflow to Nepal's banking system or paper trail there—and surely no reporting to the tax authorities either. Both companies tried to comply with Nepal's central-bank ban on such payments in May 2019, mainly by deactivating payment functions if the app's geolocation shows the person in Nepal. They then initiated efforts to enter Nepal legally, but the incident illustrates how innovations in China, and internet-based services in general, are bound to bleed over into other countries, whether those countries want it or not.

Payment acceptance has limited impact now but could be a foundation for increasing the number of foreign users. Payment is a two-sided market, where any player needs both widespread merchant acceptance and users to compete. Alipay and WeChat Pay expected to start gaining users after they announced in November 2017 that they would allow foreign visitors to China to link super-apps to foreign credit cards, instead of requiring a Chinese bank account. The move may have been related to the 2022

Winter Olympics in Beijing and was designed to avoid stories about how difficult it was to pay for anything in Beijing without super-apps. However, in a sign of shifting priorities, Beijing later excluded both super-apps from payments at the Olympic Village, instead putting the international spotlight on the government's new digital currency, which is covered in Chapter 8. Beijing hopes that this new currency, along with the super-apps, will expand the renminbi's use abroad.

Investing in Local Partners

The second method of expansion is "collaborate with local partners through technology transfer," as Ant puts it.[9] Rather than recruiting foreign Alipay users, Ant links up with local fintech companies, to which it transfers its technology and know-how. Tencent has done the same, including investments in Brazilian and Argentine fintech companies. Ant chose local partners similar to Alipay's in the early days, fintech companies affiliated with larger businesses. Fintech's experience in China demonstrated the power of entering payments with a company that has an existing user base, political patrons, and capital.

Ant's first major foreign investment came in 2015, when it invested around half a billion dollars in an Indian telecommunications company, One97 Communications, the parent of the Indian mobile-payment and wallet provider PayTM.[10] India seemed a sensible beachhead market for Chinese investment: many Indian companies already used Alibaba platforms for their sales. Just as e-commerce was both a clear use case and a source of users for Alipay, PayTM could leverage the users who needed to pay for One97's phone services as first adopters and then offer them more financial services.

At least forty Ant employees flew to India every week to help PayTM upgrade its technology to reduce fraud and scale up more quickly.[11] Ant convinced PayTM to follow the Chinese model as a budding super-app based on QR codes. Indian PayTM users could then leave their wallet at home to pay with their phone at offline merchants, ride the metro, or get a loan. Ant's intervention has been beneficial for PayTM, which grew from 20 million users to 120 million in the twelve months after the Ant investment and went public at a nearly $20 billion valuation in late 2021. PayTM now has more than 300 million users.[12]

The partnership was not without hiccups, showing the cultural difficulties that Chinese fintech will have as it expands globally. Early in 2016, a team from PayTM visiting Hangzhou stormed out of one of Ant's special "sanbanfu" marathon problem-solving meetings designed to push employees to their limits. Such meetings go without breaks for three days and three nights. The breakdown helped Ant's team realize they were being too rigid in forcing their new Indian colleagues to "experience" its uniquely intense culture.[13] There was also initial PayTM resistance to QR codes, known worldwide as insecure. Ant overcame resistance only by taking PayTM executives to Hangzhou to see the QR code-based payment systems in action, showing how well they worked in China and how they could be made secure.

Armed with the $4.5 billion in funding raised in early 2016, Ant went on an investing spree in fintech companies in Thailand, the Philippines, Indonesia, Pakistan, Bangladesh, and even the United States. As the deep nature of the tech transfer and influence it had on PayTM demonstrates, Ant became a key strategic partner that contributed much more than capital.

To regulators and users, Ant's partner is a local company run by locals. But how local they are in practice is unclear. Much of the strategic vision as well as the back-end technology and systems are run or at least designed by Alibaba or Ant. In January 2019 an announcement on Alipay's official Weibo account stated that it had reached one billion users. That figure lumped together Chinese Alipay users with those using what it called "nine local versions of

Alipay."[14] If being a PayTM or Ascend Money user automatically also makes one count as a sort of Alipay user, how independent can these apps be over the long term? It would be natural for Ant to tie its investee apps into one global network for payments, even if political considerations make it impossible to merge those wallets into one global Alipay super-app.

Fintech Entrepreneurs (and P2P Fraudsters) Go Abroad

Both the good and bad sides of Chinese fintech are migrating to the rest of the world. For smaller fintech companies, tighter regulations combined with the domestic dominance of Ant Financial and WeChat are leading them to try their models elsewhere. Entrepreneurs like the Chinese founders of Ant-backed Indonesian fintech start-up Akulaku gained experience in China but started their company in Indonesia.

On the negative side, once peer-to-peer lending platforms learned how to reach users on the internet, they took their fraud to other countries, including India, Vietnam, and Indonesia, where it has become a real challenge to regulators, who have to resort to Chinese-style website blocking. P2P is symbolic of an important global shift: China is now too large and interconnected for its domestic issues to stay isolated there—they will eventually spill over. China's inability to manage supply in its domestic steel market led to oversupply that caused global prices to crash and distorted markets around the world. Similarly, its inability to handle illegal P2P lenders has led Chinese problems to affect others.

• • •

In April 2017, Ant Financial was engaged in a fierce bidding war with Euronet, a US payment company. The prize was Money-Gram, an American company with 350,000 agent locations in 200 countries for money transfers and cross-border payments. If it won, Ant would instantly turn into a global player with billions of clients and relationships with financial institutions outside China. Immigrants sending money from Florida to Venezuela and members of the US military sending money back home to Arkansas would be part of a Chinese payment network. It would also scoop up licenses that would allow it to offer payments all over the United States, potentially taking on Visa and Mastercard on their home turf. Ant won with a last-minute $1.2 billion offer, but it still faced a US national security review. Less than a year after the merger was announced, Ant gave up. The Committee on Foreign Investment in the United States (CFIUS) was convinced that the deal would impair US national security. Such a high-profile failure to complete a deal is a sign that going out may not be easy for Chinese fintech. Outside China, many of their home advantages either will not help or could be impediments.

WeChat tried to promote its domestic branded apps to users in overseas markets, but it lacked the user bases and ecosystems that served as anchors in China. Ant will face the same problem if it tries to promote Alipay for foreign users. Problems adapting to local markets are even harder to surmount when you need to start from scratch, before any network effects take hold. WeChat itself can attribute much of its success in China to QQ. People could easily add their existing QQ friends into the WeChat network, and users in turn helped lure in businesses as partners. To get off the ground, Chinese apps will need to wrest market share away from companies like Facebook, which is far ahead of WeChat in messaging and social networks around the world, and local e-commerce companies, which already have relationships with sellers, merchants, and logistics networks. So far, TikTok is the only Chinese contender that has managed to successfully take on Facebook in social media at a global scale, although it is primarily an entertainment short-video app with less of a clear path to becoming a super-app.

WeChat's India launch has become a cautionary tale. In 2012 more than twenty million Indian users joined WeChat in the early months of an advertising campaign that featured Indian celebrities. The advertising was adjusted to Indian culture and conditions, but the app was not. WeChat was not as easy to use as WhatsApp, and the "people nearby" feature turned on location sharing that confronted women with a "stalking problem" of unwelcome messages from men.[15] Indian smartphone users tended to have less advanced phones, as well as less reliable and more expensive data service than in China. The large memory requirements and costly data demands of a super-app thus made it less convenient than bare-bones WhatsApp, which dominates the Indian market today. WeChat's challenges echo the issues that foreign giants like eBay had competing against Alibaba, especially the lack of adjusting the app design for another country. In this case the US company adapted better to the Indian market.

In June 2013, though, a greater challenge came—users realized the app was Chinese when India's government leaked that it was considering banning the app on national security grounds. US companies such as WhatsApp were also suspect, but local media reported at the time that "the security agencies are more worried because it is a Chinese company."[16] Active users fell to 6–8 million by October 2015, and most of the local team disbanded. Tencent then invested in a local player called Hike, which has also not had much success against Facebook and WhatsApp. It was not an auspicious start for a company used to dominance in its home market, and the security concerns in India would only get more severe. Most Chinese apps that were once popular in India are banned today.

WeChat expanded in South Africa in 2013 but could not dent the market dominance of WhatsApp, which has been owned by Facebook since 2014. Nor was WeChat able to do so in Brazil. It succeeded in China by starting with a successful chat app and then gradually adding functions to turn it into a super-app, but abroad the strategy was reversed, with Tencent trying to pull users into a chat product with super-app functions. It did not work. Tencent's partner in South Africa admitted the difficulty: "Because there is so much competition for the chat product you need a certain audience engagement before any of those other products can become mainstream."[17]

Despite raising hundreds of millions of dollars, Tencent's India investee Hike learned this the hard way. In January 2019 it announced it would reverse course from the super-app model and instead release separate apps for its key functions. Hike will "undo some of our experiments away from the Core to bring more focus and much needed simplicity to the product."[18] Tencent's trouble abroad may be evidence that the super-app model can't be built from the ground up or that it is just less suited to other markets than it is in China. It seems the super-app model is an all-or-nothing phenomenon that works only if you have a platform that is already dominant in other key markets. Therefore, until Chinese firms prove able to build out such a dominant platform abroad, Chinese fintech will pose a minimal threat to US payment companies and the US dollar.

The super-app model is designed to plug in to as many parts of users' lives as possible, harvesting and using sensitive data from real-time location and contacts to financial health, while connecting to a country's critical financial infrastructure. If one Chinese app gains this much power over and information about its users, would it be in a position to refuse high-level Chinese government information requests for insights it is gleaning about the foreign country?

Ant also has many state-owned shareholders, making the Chinese government an indirect partial owner. Ant's multibillion-dollar fund-raising rounds in 2015 and 2016, which in part aimed to give it the capital to expand abroad, included China's sovereign wealth and social security funds, China Development Bank (one of the main funders of China's Belt and Road Initiative), one of its largest state banks—China Construction Bank—and major state-backed insurers. As the Chinese Communist Party extends its reach into private companies, giving party committees more influence and forcing the alignment of business with its priorities, Chinese companies may find it harder to pursue purely commercial interests. In 2018 Ant's record-setting $14 billion funding round for "globalization and technology innovation" listed fourteen foreign investors by name but said little about domestic participants downplayed as "mainly existing shareholders." However, many are state-owned, almost certainly a liability when the US national security review killed Ant's MoneyGram acquisition.[19]

On the other hand, the regulatory history of fintech shows that powerful companies like Alibaba and Tencent cannot be boiled down to pure tools of the Chinese state, even if their power has been curtailed significantly in the recent regulatory reset. They have neutered government regulations, and their thinking on technology has influenced government policy. Police officials say that companies like Alibaba push back on government requests for data they find unwarranted.[20] The party needs firms like them to thrive to achieve its economic goals and reach the frontiers of technology development. Alibaba and Tencent know that if they have a reputation of sharing foreign users' private data with the Chinese state, then regulators and users abroad may block them. This tension between a status as national champions symbolizing China's rise and the desire to be viewed as purely commercial entities abroad is becoming more difficult.

When China's fintech giants expand abroad, they cannot rely on government protection from foreign competition. Other countries are protecting their own local fintech companies from stronger foreign competition. China's experience has taught these nations not only the power of super-apps but also the value of ensuring that foreign giants cannot nip the progress of their local firms in the bud. In Indonesia, for example, a central-bank official said about Chinese fintech firms that "all global players can bring their payment instruments to Indonesia" but that Ant and WeChat are restricted to foreign users and the foreign-currency business, just as China has largely kept Visa, Mastercard, and American Express out of China's domestic market.[21]

Ant and China may get the same treatment in other countries that Yahoo! and SoftBank got in China in 2010. If Chinese regulators were unwilling to allow their online-payment market to be controlled by Alibaba because of its large US and Japanese equity holders, why should other countries allow theirs to be controlled by one with a major Chinese equity holder?

Protectionism may have also contributed to the failures in localization and international expansion that WeChat and Ant have faced. Companies like Facebook and Google are blocked in China, so Chinese tech has limited experience competing with them. The large, protected home market helped them reach an enormous scale, but they may have become like a species on an isolated island uniquely evolved to that environment. Just as WeChat has failed to attract foreign users for its chat products, many of Alibaba's efforts abroad in e-commerce have floundered. In India, Amazon and Flipkart, owned by Walmart, are far ahead of PayTM's Alibaba-invested e-commerce arm, which has struggled since its IPO despite all the help from Ant.[22]

Although Chinese fintech giants and tech players have been adept at adapting foreign technologies and models to fit China, they are struggling to adapt Chinese technologies and models to foreign markets. Chinese fintech might be coming to the rest of the world only in its ideas and inspiration, rather than as a direct competitor, as the world was about to find when Facebook proposed an audacious plan to turn itself into a WeChat for the world.

Facebook Brings Chinese Fintech to the World?

While China was questioning the wisdom of letting big tech into finance, Facebook founder and CEO Mark Zuckerberg came out with a plan to bring China's fintech model to the world through Facebook's global social network. On June 18, 2019, Facebook sparked panic in officials the world over when it released a white paper announcing plans to create a consortium to launch a "global currency and financial infrastructure" called Libra. The goal, in part, was building a payment network with Facebook's billions of users, and Libra's ambition was to make sending money anywhere in the world as cheap and easy as "sending a text message or sharing a photo." Libra would be a "stablecoin," a digital currency designed to have a stable value against a basket of major currencies like the US dollar, the euro, the pound, and the yen. Each Libra would be backed by a pool of assets in those currencies, and its value would fluctuate with those assets. Pushed out to Facebook's 2.4 billion users, Libra could potentially transform e-commerce and finance overnight.

Libra marked the culmination of a growing envy in Silicon Valley of WeChat's super-app power, an attempt to make Facebook play the role worldwide that WeChat played in China. Just as Chinese fintech bypassed the undeveloped existing financial infrastructure at home, Libra would create a tech-enabled alternative to the slow and costly cross-border payment infrastructure. Libra also represented a techno-utopian dream: as the internet erased borders between people in cyberspace, it could form a supernational money. A traveler from America with Libra in Europe or Japan, or e-commerce companies selling around the world, could just quote prices in, pay, and accept Libra, never needing to convert between currencies and thus never leaving Facebook's ecosystem.

Meanwhile, Facebook would be poised to gather and control the valuable data generated by the payments and commerce built on top of it. Such power would be unprecedented for a tech company, for WeChat had so far only done so domestically. Facebook knew no one would trust it alone to run Libra. Therefore, it designed Libra to function as a decentralized system in which Facebook would be just one of many stakeholders, but its attempts to convince the world's politicians that it would not be in control fell on deaf ears.

Regulators were not as prepared as they should have been to respond to the idea. Federal Reserve Chairman Jerome Powell told Congress that Libra "lit a fire," forcing the Fed to recognize that big tech in finance was "coming fast."[23] The rise of big tech in finance to this point was largely a Chinese phenomenon, with little impact in the West. Researchers and policy makers were interested in what happened there, but it was largely treated as a Chinese curiosity.

US officials had missed years of Facebook clearly telegraphing this direction. In 2014 Facebook had hired David Marcus, then the president of PayPal, to run Messenger. After landing at Facebook, Marcus called WeChat "inspiring" and began adding features to Messenger similar to those on Tencent's platforms. In March 2019, Zuckerberg announced a new direction for Facebook, a move away from the public news feeds to focus on private messaging and also merging commerce and finance into one platform for its billions of users worldwide.[24] This "new" direction for Facebook was similar to what WeChat had achieved in China, and he all but admitted that it was based on WeChat by saying "If only I'd listened to your advice four years ago" to a journalist who had highlighted her 2015 article urging Facebook to learn from WeChat.[25]

Thus, of all the world's officials who had to digest the implications of the Libra project, the most prepared was probably the PBOC, which had been grappling with big tech in finance for years. Immediately, the G20 group of nations called on the

Financial Stability Board (FSB) to report on the risks of such a "global stablecoin" and recommend what to do about it. US regulators worried about money laundering through Libra, whose association would be based in Switzerland. Without an ability to ensure that Libra could not "print" more digital currency than it had in assets to back it, they also worried about a systemic financial collapse if Libra became crucial to global commerce without proper regulation.

Just as the PBOC had expanded its area of concern to privacy and competition, the West, already deeply skeptical of Facebook in the wake of the Cambridge Analytica privacy scandal, zeroed in on those issues as crucial to whether Libra should be allowed to proceed. France's finance minister said the EU should block Libra and create a public digital currency instead.[26] Meanwhile, smaller countries and those with less stable currencies saw financial risks, worried that they would lose their monetary sovereignty and face financial ruin if their citizens dumped local currency for more-stable Libras. China's fintech model, applied at a global scale, was a terrifying prospect for most.

For good reason, the world was not willing to take China's approach of allowing big tech into finance without a ready-made regulatory apparatus. After a wave of criticism, Facebook was concerned enough about its reputation not to launch Libra until it could address these issues. One by one, major sponsors of the Libra initiative—PayPal, Visa, and Mastercard, among others—pulled out. It would take over a year and a half for the FSB to draft a final report solely on the financial-stability issues, leaving privacy, money laundering, cybersecurity, and competition/monopoly questions unanswered, with these issues, as of this writing, being explored at places like the Bank for International Settlements but still unresolved. Libra's goal of creating a new global currency has disappeared. Facebook has renamed its digital-currency wallet initiative "Novi" and has begun a pilot using another digital currency to handle payments between the United States and Guatemala as it works on a set of country-by-country coins that Facebook hopes will improve upon slow and expensive cross-border payments.

The Libra project hit resistance, but it still implies that Chinese fintech could come sooner to the rest of the world than is generally thought. It is also emblematic of a widely underestimated sea change in the flow of innovation and ideas, with worrying implications for US global leadership in finance and technology. For decades, a look at Silicon Valley was a look at the future coming to the rest of the world, inspiring copycats in places like China, but this trend is reversing for fintech. China's WeChat instead would provide a preview into the future for the United States as tech leaders like Zuckerberg aimed to replicate the super-apps' Chinese success. Studying China would become crucial for regulators hoping to update outdated paradigms for the twenty-first century as technology and finance became more intertwined.

7

Techlash

"As a non-state-owned institution in China,
Ant is not allowed to grow too big to manage"

The common destinies of Alibaba, Ant Group, and Tencent were a double-edged sword. The fintech super-apps meant unparalleled data, capital, technical skill, users, and privileged political position. Tech and fintech were untouchable when viewed as key contributors to innovation and growth. When the backlash against big technology firms came to China, fintech was hit along with ride hailing, online tutoring, and many more sectors. The campaign against financial risk, with pushes for privacy and antitrust, formed a pincer movement. Pressure for a crackdown had brewed at least since 2018 but did not lead to immediate change: regulators across China's sprawling bureaucracy needed to coordinate and have high-level sign-off before taking on companies with so much influence.

The techlash began with a demand for privacy. People in China were fed up with their most sensitive data being freely bought and sold, putting their finances and even their lives at risk. The next concern was competition: the PBOC worried that its invitation of big tech to disrupt state bank monopolies might lead instead to even-more-problematic tech monopolies. Then shady online lending platforms collapsed, leading to protests and enormous losses, which called into question the idea that fintech could be a force for progress in finance. As the political environment soured, Ant and other fintech firms adapted by becoming less disruptive, using their technology and users to help the traditional financial system. Then Facebook's proposal for a global digital currency accelerated PBOC plans for a state-backed digital currency that could take away the linchpin of the private fintech empires: their role in payments.

But when COVID hit China, the super-apps' reach and technical capacity became indispensable. Alipay was enlisted to create the codes literally determining the freedom of movement for millions of Chinese people during the reopening phase of the pandemic. WeChat Pay distributed stimulus for local governments hoping to get consumption restarted. Yet despite its clear utility, big tech's popularity—and that of Jack Ma personally—was on the decline. Workers at big-tech companies complained bitterly about long working hours, start-ups resented the giants' monopolistic practices, and big tech's grip on the information that people can see on the apps attracted unwanted attention.

Amid all these shifts was a revival of Marxist thinking amid frustrations with a society becoming ever more capitalistic, with soaring housing prices and seemingly diminished opportunity to get rich like Ma had done. New regulations continued to pop up, but mainly to close loopholes in the rules. Big tech still seemed unassailable, with strong political backing, but its position was weakening.

Demanding Privacy

In March 2018, Robin Li, the cofounder and CEO of Baidu, China's dominant search engine, took the stage at the China

Development Forum. What he thought would be an uncontroversial overview of China's advantages in technology set off a firestorm. "Chinese people," Li said, "are more open or are not that sensitive about privacy. If they are able to exchange privacy for safety, convenience, or efficiency, in many cases they are willing to do that. Then we can make more use of that data."[1] Li's comments reflected the dominant thinking at the time, but they hit a nerve. One study called willingness to share data "the social foundation for e-commerce and digital banking success" in China.[2] Yet although many appreciate the convenience, the Chinese people did not feel they had a choice when it came to giving up data. The state-run *People's Daily* published articles calling Li "under fire," and it cited Baidu users who called Li "despicable."[3] During this dustup I recalled the comment a fintech executive made to me a year earlier: "Privacy is a luxury for you Western people."

China's embrace of fintech and online life generated mountains of data on more than a billion people. Payment apps generated transaction data; lending apps raked in data on contacts, location, income, and more; e-commerce apps collected data on people's purchases and their addresses (and learned what they had had delivered to their mistresses' addresses); and social apps could re-create an individual's social network and their conversations. The easy availability of data aided fintech, for any new entrant could buy data to train AI algorithms. Blacklists of loan defaulters circulated that could help new lenders avoid losing money to bad credit risks.

A 2014 Boston Consulting Group survey found that only 50 percent of Chinese users agreed that they must be cautious about sharing personal information online, far below the global average of 76 percent.[4] This willingness to share data would come back to bite, leading to frustration with big tech. Firms harvested data to sell on the gray market. Even those companies that refused to do so had rogue employees making money on the side selling data or had to deal with hackers stealing it. The result was a barrage of fraud. By 2015, an Internet Society of China survey found that 76 percent of internet users had received fraudulent calls or text messages, and one-third had lost money as a result.[5] Another study found that Chinese were more worried about identity theft than were consumers in the United States, the United Kingdom, Germany, and India.[6]

In that era, China's laws provided little incentive for companies and the government to be more careful with data. Its data-protection regime relied on a patchwork of laws and standards with unclear applicability to new technology companies. Until 2014, the maximum fine that anyone could face for privacy violations was a paltry 10,000 RMB (1,500 USD), nothing for a major corporation.[7] In the fintech boom, the Chinese government faced tough trade-offs between loose regulations that allowed entrepreneurs to focus on innovation over compliance, and data protection posed a similar dilemma. On the one hand, loose data controls helped the government meet goals to create national champions in big data and artificial intelligence. Policy makers saw that most of the leading companies in these sectors were based in the United States, where privacy and data-protection laws were lax, rather than in Europe, which was stricter.

A continued data free-for-all, however, meant growing risks of identity theft and data leaks. Fraudsters became more effective when armed with data. It is hard to ignore a personalized text message that knows your national ID number and that knows you have a bank account at a specific bank branch. When a phone fraud convinced a young woman in Shandong province to wire away her family's savings for her college tuition to people posing as education officials offering financial aid, she became so distraught that she died of a heart issue.[8] The case sparked national outrage.

The more that sensitive information about people is available to criminals, the more vulnerable that *everyone* is to social-engineering attacks. In one case the chief accountant of a government development zone was tricked into transferring 117 million RMB to scammers who impersonated government and bank officials. Investigators were alarmed to find that the perpetrators had a hard drive with more than a hundred thousand pieces of information on senior financial and governmental officials.[9]

Vulnerability from data leaks was also a national security concern. If common criminals could obtain this sensitive information, foreign intelligence agencies certainly could too. Often forgotten in discussions on privacy in China is the fact that lax rules on data did not just lead to regular individuals having their data leaked but that this was also happening to powerful businesspeople and government officials with the power to do something about it. After all, most of them were using all the same online services as regular people.

China entered a heated global debate on how to deal with privacy and data protection in an increasingly data-driven economy. In June 2017, China's cybersecurity law took effect, the most significant step toward a unified framework for data protection and privacy. However, key details were left to future regulations and interpretations.[10]

China hopes to chart a middle ground between the US approach, which it views as too lax on data protection, and the European Union's far more restrictive rules enshrined in its General Data Protection Regulation (GDPR), which Chinese experts believe restricts European innovation. Chinese experts involved in formulating the policy said explicitly that they wanted it to be more "business friendly" than GDPR—for example, by allowing companies to argue that people using their services have given their implied consent for certain uses of data.[11] Government officials concerned about cybersecurity and sensitive to growing calls for privacy (at least from private firms) are in a debate with technology firms which oppose regulations that limit their data collection and use, and consumer groups are trying to hold those companies to account.

Inertia favored powerful companies, but a trickle of actions turned into a flood within three days in early 2018. The head of Beijing Normal University's Criminal Law Science Research Institute would later call 2018 "an important awakening for Chinese consumers on data privacy."[12] On January 1 a prominent businessman made headlines saying that Pony Ma "is watching us through WeChat every day because he can see whenever he wants."[13] Tencent denied that it is able to access user chat logs, but its statement seemed to contradict the cybersecurity law, which requires it to store key data for at least six months and to censor content for the government.[14] Denying itself access to chat histories, full of rich data, seemed unlikely.

The next day, a Chinese court accepted a lawsuit brought by a consumer group against Baidu for data-protection violations. The group found that Baidu's search app and mobile browser used "eavesdropping" to gain access to users' messages, phone calls, contacts, and other data without user knowledge. Baidu relented and modified its apps.[15] Then, on January 3, the backlash hit Ant. Many Alipay users had inadvertently signed up for Sesame Credit by quickly clicking through a window that enrolled them by default. An online furor ensued, leading to a contrite apology from Ant and an official warning from multiple regulators. Ant changed the default and "immediately initiated a comprehensive review of our privacy protection policy."[16]

A comparison with the United States shows just how extraordinary this case is. Americans never gave credit-reporting companies consent to gather, store, and crunch data on them, yet there is nothing they can do to stop it, even after a hacking incident revealed lax cybersecurity practices at Equifax that put millions of people's financial lives at risk. Most US websites opt people in by default, and clicking through too quickly can lead to a barrage of marketing emails. It would shock most Americans to find out that the Chinese have *more* control over how their data is used for credit scoring.

Throughout 2018 and 2019, consumer groups and the government cracked down with audits of apps' privacy practices, demands to change them, and even arrests of privacy violators. Big data and finance, the core of fintech, were a key part of the crackdown, which led to the landmark Personal Information Protection Law, passed in August 2021.[17] However, it will take years to hammer out and finalize how it will be implemented. After one egregious privacy-violation case involving a company that collects and prepares data for AI applications, Chinese experts had widely differing views of how to interpret the privacy standards in China and what they mean for its future competitiveness in AI.[18] A representative of China's National People's Congress noted in March 2019 that "the biggest challenge we are facing now is defining what personal information is and how much of the information can be disclosed."[19]

Just as in fintech, it would take years to deal with accumulated risks without choking off innovation. China's experience is part of a growing global awareness of the downsides of surveillance capitalism.[20] Chinese companies and the government realize that if they want their companies to be successful or be permitted to operate in foreign markets, China will need to establish a reputation for good stewardship of data.

The super-app model, which draws its power from free flows of data over online platforms, may fall afoul of stricter privacy protections down the road. The changing balance of power has seen fintech's riskier financial practices restricted despite its best efforts at lobbying, and the same could occur on the data side. Chinese who disagree with Robin Li's comments about trading privacy for convenience may be less willing to share data with fintech companies in the future, and if super-apps can no longer freely share data, they may lose some of their model's advantages.

However, privacy was only the beginning of a broader backlash against big tech.

The PBOC Becomes a Big-Tech Skeptic

The public pressure for privacy, Xi's push for state-owned companies to grow, and the push for reduction in financial risk turned the PBOC against the big-tech firms that it once invited into finance to compete with banks. A global awakening to the risks that powerful internet companies posed to competition and privacy was underway, recognizing powerful network effects that led some markets they entered to become "winner take all." The PBOC had constrained the tech giants' popular financial products and taken control of infrastructure like interbank payments, but it would start publicly reversing its positive stance on big tech in finance only in November 2018, with speeches from senior PBOC officials and former governor Zhou.

The officials, clearly with authorization from higher-level officials to announce a policy shift, warned about big tech's deleterious effects on competition. They noted that the playing field was tilted away from banks and toward big tech, with its data troves and massive user bases that banks could never match. It was a far cry from 2012, when the banks were the monopolists and big tech was only an upstart. One official called tech-platform lending a "trap" in which the tech companies abused their position in payments to make small firms borrow more.[21]

Zhou Xiaochuan, fintech's onetime protector, then gave a speech acknowledging that the entrenched dominance of two super-apps was not what he and the PBOC intended. Although he was retired, it is a hallmark of China's system that party elders and retired officials retain influence after their terms end. Deng Xiaoping remained China's most influential leader even when his top official title was "Most Honorary President of the Chinese Bridge Association," bridge being his favorite card game.

As the architect of the strategy that went all in on inviting big tech into finance, former governor Zhou and his comments made waves—Chinese officials rarely admit errors. It was a remarkable admission that the strategy he employed to bring more competition, which initially seemed to work wonders with Yu'E Bao, had instead brought a dangerous concentration of power. He further argued that only private firms with a "public spirit" should be allowed to build and operate financial infrastructure like payments, and he implied that Tencent and Alipay lacked it.[22]

The message for big tech was that space to go head-to-head with financial institutions would be limited. Instead, it was encouraged to collaborate with financial institutions, helping more-traditional financial players upgrade their technology, access the super-apps' clients, manage risks, and gather data. The PBOC and its bosses concluded that big-tech firms being financial conglomerates had become too risky. However, they did not yet know what to do about it.

The desire by the Chinese party-state to maintain financial dominance by banks controlled and owned by the state combined with legitimate concerns about big tech to block Ant's ambitions for further tech-style disruption in finance. Chinese media quoted an insider with the message, "As a non-bank, non-state-owned institution in China, [Ant is] not allowed to independently grow too big to manage."[23] The change is a reminder that in China, it is not the law that counts but the political line. Far from its story being over, however, fintech adapted to the new political reality. Both Ant and Tencent set up new partnerships with hundreds of China's financial institutions to provide cloud computing, risk management, data analytics, and much more.

Previously, big tech drove progress in Chinese finance by competing with banks and other incumbents, but it shifted to providing services which enabled the digital transformation that banks were making, a less controversial position focused more on their comparative advantage and less threatening to incumbents. Ant

declared that it would become more of a technology provider for
financial institutions than competing with them as a financial institution itself.[24] It aimed to double the share of its revenue coming
from technology services from 34 percent in 2017 to 65 percent
over the next five years instead of relying on payments and financial services, and it even dropped the word *financial* from its name
in advance of its IPO application, becoming simply Ant Group.
The declared focus on technology, though forced by political constraints, was far from a hindrance. Ant's valuation ballooned to
$150 billion in 2018, with pretax profits of around $2 billion in
2017, partially because technology companies can scale up more
quickly with less regulation than financial companies.

The shift between emphasis on finance or technology brings
up an important question: Is there a clear border between the "fin"
and the "tech" in fintech? In an ever-more-digitized financial system, tech firms' apps, data, and algorithms that steer where capital goes might be more important for the financial system than
the banks that provide the capital. Former governor Zhou would
probably agree; he has called finance "a type of IT industry."[25]

The PBOC's shift heralds a challenge that authorities in any
country with a fintech sector like China's would face, one that requires a rethinking and expansion of issues for financial regulators.
They would not only need to handle the already thorny problems
of pure financial regulation but also to make sense of the interplay
between these and issues of technology and data regulation.

The Peer-to-Peer Lending Collapse
Tarnishes Fintech's Reputation

Online peer-to-peer lending was once among fintech's most-
promising ideas. By late 2017, however, it looked like a ticking
time bomb. The failure of what authorities once promoted and left
unregulated helped catalyze a change of mind-set among officials
toward more onerous regulation of fintech, which would ratchet

up the pressure on Ant and Jack Ma. It also illustrates the dark side of China's experimental approach to fintech regulation and explains why other countries might not want to follow suit because of the high societal cost.

The peer-to-peer lending sector, which peaked in May 2018 at 1 trillion RMB (171 billion USD) in loans outstanding from more than 2,000 companies, was on the verge of collapse.[26] Authorities ordered lenders to freeze their size or shrink, and news of new platforms shutting down every day shook investor confidence. On June 14, China Banking and Insurance Regulatory Commission (CBIRC) head Guo Shuqing gave an unusually strong warning: any investment promising 6 percent annual returns should be questioned, and anything over 10 percent means you should report it to the police as fraud.[27] The speech shattered illusions of hoped-for bailouts, leading investors to pull out en masse to avoid being left holding the bag. So many firms failed in the wake of Guo's speech that the local government in Hangzhou had to set up two massive stadiums to process scared and angry investors who streamed in from all over China to track down the platforms that disappeared with their savings.[28] Guo later estimated that the fifty million people who had invested in Chinese P2P platforms were left with around $115 billion in losses.[29]

There was little to no contagion to the financial markets, but bilked investors threatened the all-important "social stability" with plans for massive protests to demand their money back. Investors organizing protests on WeChat suspected that local authorities were in cahoots with P2P platforms and could not be trusted to get their money back. However, they elicited little sympathy from officials in Beijing, who saw them as gamblers making trouble when the bet turned sour. Security forces defused the protests by snapping up demonstrators arriving at the planned demonstration sites in Beijing and whisking them onto 120 buses en route to "black" jails. Some investors lost all hope and committed suicide.[30] Authorities' heavy-handed tactics like censorship and suppression of protests came at a high cost, but they helped avoid panic and contagion. Beijing's refusal to bail out failed platforms also set a good precedent—that risky bets are not always guaranteed by the state.

Most importantly for the successful parts of fintech, the super-apps, the peer-to-peer lending collapse convinced the Chinese government that it needed much stricter rules for fintech. Beijing had dodged a bullet because the failed platforms were relatively small, but Ant and Tencent were operating businesses that were orders of magnitude larger, and they were more interconnected with the banks.

Jack Ma had largely kept Ant clear of involvement in P2P, but he knew that the debacle was an indirect threat to Ant. He tried to limit collateral damage by emphasizing the difference between Ant's fintech and the failed platforms, stating that "P2P lending was not internet finance from the start. It is just an industry of illegal financing businesses that have websites."[31] Ma was right that peer-to-peer lenders were mostly not really fintech at all. The problem for his position was that telling the difference between real and fake fintech was extremely difficult ex ante, and the mess they would have to clean up if there were problems at Ant would be immense.

9–9–6 Labor Protests and Antitrust

Even authoritarian regimes like China's need to take public opinion into consideration. Public support of Jack Ma helped him quash regulations in 2014. By 2019, however, public opinion was shifting against the tech giants as people in China came to grips with the human costs behind all the conveniences that super-apps had brought. In March of that year, a rare protest erupted online against Chinese tech firms' common practice of forcing workers to be in the office from 9 a.m. until 9 p.m. six days per week if not more—adding up to a 72-hour workweek, well in excess of what

Chinese law permits. The site was called 996.icu, referring to reports about tech workers pushed so hard that they ended up in an intensive-care unit or even dead in their twenties and thirties from stress and overwork. (Knowing that their activism against powerful big tech would be censored if posted on a domestic website, the 9-9-6 protesters posted it on GitHub, an essential resource for software developers around the world and thus costly to block.)

Debate raged across China's internet, and Jack Ma added fuel to the fire by saying it was an "opportunity" and "huge blessing" to work such long hours, although he later reversed his opinion after an online firestorm cut into his popularity.[32] Online commenters called him a "greedy capitalist," and one column said "the grassroots no longer supports Jack Ma, and even has begun to hate him . . . Jack Ma has more and more enemies."[33] He seemed to be losing touch with the shifts in public mood, a dangerous position. Meanwhile, little changed for tech workers trapped in a hypercompetitive environment. Big tech then came under fire for its treatment of a less privileged group: delivery workers.

A report on delivery workers' plight went viral on WeChat in September 2020. It focused on how the relentless drive for efficiency by algorithms managing drivers' schedules forced them to take mortal risks to make impossibly tight deadlines which enabled the quick deliveries that people increasingly took for granted.[34] The report included graphic photographs of injuries that drivers received during their work. Pay is docked when the drivers cannot meet the automated system's impossible demands, leading around half of surveyed drivers to say they make too little money for their daily needs. One online commenter summed up the mood: "While we enjoy the convenience [brought by the delivery apps], we are exploiting the safety of drivers."[35]

Tech companies also lost popularity as they became a more firmly entrenched duopoly. They no longer represented an underdog compared with giant state-owned banks, leaving start-ups dependent on one or the other tech giant for capital and distribution through super-apps. Alibaba's reputation for looking out for small business and helping less powerful people changed into a perception that it was abusing its market power.[36] Amazingly, despite their enormous size and acquisition sprees, big tech had faced no real constraints because China's competition and antitrust authorities had mostly gone after easier targets, such as foreign companies.[37]

China's antimonopoly law dated from 2008, before big technology companies had emerged as economic forces. Enforcement was hampered by a messy structure involving three ministries with higher priorities than monopoly.[38] Antitrust enforcement against big tech was thus extremely weak. In 2018 the combining of the patchwork of agencies into one more-powerful market regulator, the State Administration for Market Regulation (SAMR), was the first step to more effective regulation. It soon released a draft update to the antimonopoly law that for the first time would explicitly apply to big tech.[39] Still, the political situation of big tech would need to change more for such rules to have teeth.

Government Digital Currency

Globally, the Libra project created shock waves across the community of central banks, which had to wake up to a world in which their function could be usurped by big tech. China saw Facebook's plan for Libra as a threat, fearing that if the rest of the world adopted it, China would be forced to choose to let up on its ban and allow Facebook in or be isolated from the global digital economy.[40] A millennium ago, China was the first country to issue sovereign paper money, in 1024. Now, China is the first major economy to undergo trials of a central-bank digital currency (CBDC).[41] The initiative's aim is to shape the future of digital currency and blockchain rather than being forced to react to innovations like Bitcoin or Libra originating in societies with values different from those of China.

If the PBOC is the first major central bank to introduce a widely used digital currency, it would signal that China is in the lead in what the party considers to be critical technologies. It could also become a foundation to remake domestic payments, wresting control away from the Alipay/Tencent duopoly. Internationally, it will be more difficult to make a dent in the dollar's dominance anytime soon, but China hopes a network of CBDCs might reduce the need for the dollar and blunt US financial power in the long term. The push is also part of a global effort by central banks to protect "monetary sovereignty," ensuring that digital currencies, private or state-backed, do not disrupt the banks' authority over the economy and the monetary and financial system of their countries.

The PBOC began research on digital currency after the first Bitcoin bubble in 2014, and two years later it announced its intention to launch its own, a central-bank-backed digital-currency system that it calls DC/EP (digital currency/electronic payments), or the eCNY. The PBOC's direct superior, the State Council, called blockchain technology part of a "new wave of revolutionary technology" in 2016, and in recent years control over critical technologies has become ever more important in Chinese government goals.[42] The Libra initiative then turned this long-term aspiration into an urgent race between China and Facebook.

Soon after the Libra announcement, PBOC research director Wang Xin said that "we had an early start . . . but lots of work is needed to consolidate our lead," and he warned that Libra's success could mean "one boss, the Dollar, America."[43] He even suggested that China might even loosen its strict cryptocurrency regulations to avoid falling behind. China thus saw Libra as a plot to entrench US financial dominance, heading off Chinese fintech's potential disruption, even though US officials were pushing against Facebook's plan. A domestic digital currency would "mainly be used to compete with Libra." Xi himself called in October 2019 for blockchain to be a "core indigenous innovation technology" after devoting an entire Politburo study session to the subject.[44] Mu Changchun, now the head of the PBOC's digital-currency efforts, called for strict global regulation of Libra, writing that "we must prevent [currencies like Libra] from becoming monopolies."[45]

Tencent joined the chorus when it warned that Libra could deal a "crushing blow" to Chinese fintech's global ambitions.[46] A digital currency could allow Facebook to achieve the success that WeChat had in turning a social network into a payment and financial giant. Just as WhatsApp beat WeChat in most markets around the world, so could Facebook's Libra potentially head off the efforts by Chinese fintech to expand abroad. Chinese officials knew about the potent foundation that a digital currency like Libra would have for payments, given WeChat's success with red envelopes.

Facebook's Libra head David Marcus stoked this geopolitical competition angle when trying to sell the project to the US Congress, saying, "If America does not lead innovation in the digital currency and payments area, others will. If we fail to act, we could soon see a digital currency controlled by others whose values are dramatically different."[47] His view is correct, at least in the medium to long term, but his pitch was not successful. Even those in Congress who agree and have been pushing for the United States to be a friendlier place to innovate in digital currencies did not want to see Facebook become more powerful by driving that change. Big tech, and especially Facebook, had become nearly as much of a punching bag in Congress as it was in China.

China, positioning itself as a first mover in digital currency, wields a double-edged sword. It is gaining valuable experience, but it risks costly mistakes that could imperil its financial system. A stable currency is the foundation of both the economy and the financial system, and an error that, for example, allowed one person to spend the same digital currency twice could deal a severe blow to that stability and the central bank's reputation. Other risks include draining money from banks. If too many depositors were to take their money out of banks to park it in CBDC instead, and the central bank did not replace that money quickly enough through other means, this could cause a crisis. Cybersecurity would also be a serious challenge. The International Monetary Fund has cautioned that "it is too early to draw firm conclusions on the net benefits."[48] Yet if China can manage the risks, the benefits of the eCNY to China's government and the PBOC could be substantial. Consistent with the government's approach to data privacy, it could provide individuals with greater anonymity from tech giants and the people they transact with, while increasing government surveillance. The PBOC has had difficulty obtaining data from fintech giants, but the eCNY could change that by giving it a record of every transaction made with the eCNY, which it could force Alipay and WeChat Pay to use in their wallets.

The eCNY could also provide new tools for monetary policy, giving the PBOC more levers to fine-tune the economy. Although many of the currently financially excluded are not digitally savvy, financial inclusion could receive a boost if "unbanked" people in rural areas can transact with the new currency using just a smartphone. It could also help combat the Alipay and Tencent near-monopoly position in digital finance by providing an even cheaper government-backed alternative. Finally, authorities hope that a CBDC will reduce the demand for Bitcoin and help the RMB gain adoption abroad as an alternative to the dollar-dominated global financial system.

Many of the most important elements remain to be announced, but the eCNY will be both centralized and in the hands of the government, the antithesis of Bitcoin's ideals.[49] It would be like cash—a direct claim on the central bank—and people will be able to buy or sell the e-RMB at banks for one regular RMB. Each unit of digital currency will be "backed" by a unit of real currency deposited at the central bank. It is not a cryptocurrency because issuance will be under PBOC control rather than determined by a predetermined cryptographic algorithm or decentralized governance structure like Bitcoin. A partial replacement of physical cash is a sensible starting point for digital currency—it has attractive attributes, but a limited scope for disrupting the existing financial system. Private tech firms or banks cannot track it, those without internet access or a bank account can use it, and there are no fees to pay with cash.

Although economic activity and even in-person payments are increasingly digital, cash has been stuck in the physical world. The ecNY could provide a viable public option for payments that would compete with private systems like debit cards and the mobile-payment duopoly of Tencent and Alibaba. People could, for example, buy cigarettes or liquor with a digital RMB without losing points on their Ant Sesame score. Of course, regulators will still be watching, but watching for money laundering, corruption, or maybe donations to human rights lawyers. The PBOC is also working with Alipay and Tencent, which have added the ecNY as a payment option in their super-apps.

The ecNY will have what the PBOC calls "controllable anonymity." That sounds Orwellian but gets at a set of difficult trade-offs that governments around the world have to deal with for CBDCs. Governments severely limit the right to financial privacy, enlisting banks and other intermediaries to pass data to the government to reduce crime facilitated by the financial system. Fully anonymous digital currency would become a vehicle for money laundering, ransomware, and all sorts of illegal activity. Paper cash, if invented only today, probably would not be allowed to exist because of its role in facilitating crime. The PBOC considers paper cash too anonymous and electronic payments or bank cards as providing too much data to payment providers and big tech.

Alipay and WeChat Pay track all their payments, which they can then use for other purposes, like credit scoring and marketing. Transacting with them can also reveal the purchaser's identity to the retailer, just as US credit cards reveal the holder's name and account number to a merchant. (Apple Pay and the move to chip-card payments, which are encrypted and tokenized, solve these problems to some extent.) Part of the PBOC's motivation is to provide a solution that preserves some of the privacy of cash— at least from merchants, tech companies, and banks—while retaining visibility and control. It will thus allow privacy from the government only for small transactions, allowing individuals to register digital wallets with their phone numbers alone.[50]

The eCNY system, however, goes beyond the privacy limitations of most countries. All but the smallest digital wallets and accounts will have no apparent privacy from the central bank, a privacy nightmare.[51] The PBOC will directly control the ledger that records all balances and transactions in the system, so it will be able to use the eCNY in real time to see what people own and are buying without having to request payment data from big tech, which might delay and resist.

Most likely, the demand for a PBOC digital currency will come from government orders to use it rather than market demand. Other than slightly higher privacy from financial institutions and payment companies, the benefit for consumers of submitting to this increased monitoring of their transactions is questionable at best, and the consequences to civil liberties could be dire. Even the anonymity it promises from the tech giants is not necessarily a benefit for those who want Ant Group to have their data so they can easily access credit. Unlike a bank deposit or money in Yu'E Bao, the digital RMB will be like cash, bearing no interest. One possible attraction to an e-RMB over cash would be for larger payments because the PBOC purposely makes it difficult to move large sums of money with cash. The largest denomination is 100 RMB, worth only about 15 USD. Yet those trying to move these funds, such as corrupt officials with entire apartments stacked full of bills, are not likely to use a tracked eCNY.[52] Where it could make a difference is for people who currently do not have a bank account and are thus not Alipay or WeChat Pay users, but it will not be easy to reach that group of mostly poor, rural, and elderly people and convince them to use digital money, even a government-backed one.

If the first step of replacing cash works well, the PBOC is unlikely to stop there. A digital currency could, like Ethereum, add functions like ecosystems of smart contracts on top of the PBOC's infrastructure. Tax payments could be automatic, and transaction costs could be adjusted to shape where and how quickly money flows through the economy, a new tool for monetary policy. Transaction fees could vary according to whether the PBOC wanted to encourage money to flow into a certain sector. For example, it could raise fees on real estate transactions to discourage speculation when housing prices are rising too quickly. Individuals on the social credit blacklist, or human rights lawyers, could see the government directly shut down their wallets.

CBDC raises an important and fascinating question about the roles of the public and private sectors in payments and money. In theory, a CBDC could provide accounts at the central bank directly to individuals, without any need for bank accounts or private digital wallets. Then, instead of depositors' choice of bank to entrust their deposits determining how much funds that banks have to lend, the state would control all the money, as it did under the command economy. The PBOC has been at pains to say this will not be the case for the eCNY, which will use a "two-tiered" system that maintains the roles of financial intermediaries such as banks and digital wallets. Yet it is not yet clear where the boundaries between state and market, or state and state-backed banks, will be drawn. Banks and super-apps are likely to end up a much thinner front-end veneer over a system under much more government control than exists at the present.

The trial runs for the eCNY reached more than a quarter of a billion people by the end of 2021, and they look a great deal like how payments currently operate with Alipay or WeChat Pay. What is new are transactions between phones not connected to the internet, a bid to improve financial inclusion in areas that do not have consistent internet access.

Officials say that the eCNY is primarily a domestic initiative focused on providing a public payment option to serve as a backup for or competing system to big tech. A crucial question for the United States and the rest of the world is whether the eCNY could become an international currency that unseats the dollar as the dominant reserve currency or as a vehicle payment used in trade. Although Chinese officials have linked the eCNY to internationalization, in the short and medium term it is unlikely to make much of a difference. Just as Chinese big tech has struggled to go abroad, the eCNY cannot count on domestic success or technological prowess to beat the dollar. Simply because the money is digital is not a unique advantage in a world in which the vast majority of money that changes hands already does so digitally.[53] Experiments like the Multiple CBDC Bridge with the Bank for International Settlements, which includes the PBOC and a few other central banks like the Bank of Thailand, are building prototypes for cross-border payments based on CBDC that do not need the US dollar or the infrastructure around it. However, these initiatives that envision a reset for cross-border payments are still in early stages.

Becoming a reserve currency is not easy, nor is it a free lunch. China thus far has prioritized control of its currency through capital controls over making it easy for those around the world who want to use the RMB to trade, invest, or borrow to do so. Even though China is the world's second-largest economy, data from the IMF and the Society for Worldwide Interbank Financial Telecommunication (SWIFT) show it stuck in fifth place, at only about a 2 percent share of international reserves and payments.[54] The dollar benefits from strong network effects, with not only an established set of financial infrastructures but also the liquidity and hedging instruments that make it often cheaper and safer to trade between the US dollar and any other currency. China will have a difficult time matching the dollar's strengths.[55]

The eCNY will need to be cheaper and more efficient to trade if it is to gain on the US dollar, which goes beyond technological questions. In the long term, the PBOC sees the shift to digital currencies, including among central banks, as an opportunity to have a hand in creating a new set of global financial infrastructure in which the United States has less influence. For now, being a lonely leader in CBDCs means that there are no other major central banks to connect to, and thus less useful network effects for the eCNY than for the regular RMB. However, that may change as other countries launch their own CBDCs in the longer term.

Fintech and COVID

The party faced one of the greatest challenges of its seventy-year rule in early February 2020. COVID was raging across China, but the draconian lockdown could not be maintained without economic collapse. Desperate to reopen its economy safely, the government handed over unprecedented power to a private company: Ant. In partnership with the local government in Hangzhou, Alipay turned its data expertise from finance to health, crunching data with opaque algorithms to produce a "health code" that determined whether millions were to be confined to their homes.

Users with green code were clear, but the dreaded red code meant two weeks of quarantine, which for some included apartment doors welded shut to enforce compliance. The system went viral, adopted in hundreds of cities that used it to reopen without a second wave of infections. Tencent also got in on the action, creating codes used by three hundred towns and counties that generated codes for eight hundred million people.[56]

The action taken revealed a serious issue of the failure to include those who are not digitally savvy. Millions of elderly people in China do not have internet access, or super-apps, leaving them out of the programs that allowed those with green codes to resume life. When an elderly man unable to show any health code was booted from a bus in Liaoning province early in the pandemic, video of the event went viral and put pressure on the government to ensure that those without the apps could show paper documentation to get around.[57] For now, the fintech apps are common enough that the government and businesses often assume that people have them, designing must-have services to plug into those ecosystems. But those without the apps illustrate that there is a human cost of the migration to digital.

It first appeared that China's initial cover-up of the pandemic would prove a disaster to its economy and political system. Wilbur Ross, then US secretary of commerce, even said that COVID-19 would bring back jobs to the United States because of China's woes. Soon after, however, the tables turned as China's combination of strict lockdown and tech-enabled reopening allowed it to virtually eliminate the virus at home while it raged in the United States. Tech investors active in the US and China told me that watching the United States bungle its response to COVID only gave them greater confidence to invest in China and the tech firms that were playing such a pivotal role in its successful response.

The proactive response of China's apps to COVID-19 seemed to be yet another indicator of Silicon Valley's relative decline. The health codes were but the first steps of the response of the Chinese techs. They also coordinated supplies of personal protective equipment, linked to government data to provide tools to see if one was exposed, and directed people to places where they could safely seek medical care.[58] By contrast, it seems that the extent of US tech's innovative ideas to face the crisis was to put links up to official websites, which early on disastrously told people not to wear masks, and social-media networks proliferating mountains of misinformation. Apple and Google did try to develop a joint contact-tracing app, but it failed to catch on.

The Chinese tech companies saw their business and profits boom amid the suffering. The shift online created enormous wealth for Alibaba and Tencent, which together went from $944 billion in market cap from the start of the outbreak in Wuhan to nearly $1.6 trillion in October 2020, when Ant Group was about to bring its IPO to market. Their super-apps were essential for allowing mobility to resume, but they also allowed vital commerce to continue when many remained confined to their homes or afraid of infections from touching paper cash. Unable to go shopping or eat in person, people moved en masse to the apps to order food, groceries, and just about everything else they needed. On the other side of the platform, millions of merchants not yet online signed up to ensure they could still sell during pandemic lockdowns, naturally leading their payments to flow through Alipay and WeChat Pay. Mini-programs allowed fully contactless restaurant visits in China, whereas US restaurants added QR codes only for the menu, still forcing servers and diners to pass credit cards, receipts, and pens back and forth in order to pay.

Health codes on fintech apps helped authorities track Chinese people to an unprecedented degree, providing a window into what could become a terrifying totalitarian future. Albeit with a legitimate public health imperative, super-apps became the ideal tool for controlling the population. Going anywhere relied on having a code to scan, from boarding public transportation to leaving one's housing complex, and each scan would send the user's data right to the police thanks to a command in the Alipay health code literally called "reportInfoAndLocationToPolice."[59] Yet, attuned to citizens' demands for privacy, including those from the government, Alipay and WeChat, at least publicly, denied that their payment data was being used in the contact-tracing apps. However, the state-owned telecom companies shared individual location data to see who had been in high-risk areas.[60]

Local governments were loath to give up their newfound powers of observation. The government of Hangzhou proposed that once the health crisis was largely over, the health codes should be transformed into health scores used to surveil and evaluate people's habits. If it went forward, it would be a step toward the dystopian future that social credit critics warned about. Encouragingly, the Chinese populace fought back online rather than accepting permanent curtailment of their liberties. The groundswell of public opinion led influential state news providers like Xinhua to criticize the idea, calling the health code a "product of wartime" and suggesting that continuing such unprecedented government data collection raised "the risk of information leakage and abuse."[61] Hangzhou had to shelve the idea, an encouraging sign that demands for privacy extend not just to private tech companies but also to the state. Nevertheless, the pandemic reveals just how easy it would be for the super-apps, as ubiquitous and powerful tech tools, to become tools of social control. The continuing zero-COVID policy in China, requiring a massive response to any outbreaks, has made it unclear when, if ever, the health codes will be phased out.

· · ·

By 2020, the many fronts of backlash against big tech and its higher profile caused by COVID made a crackdown close to inevitable. The tech giants were victims of their own success, showing through their positive role keeping the economy running during the pandemic just how important they were. The party decided that institutions of such criticality needed more direct oversight. Though part of a global movement, the urgency in China to rein in big tech was much greater because of big tech's deeper penetration into Chinese daily lives and the financial system. Nevertheless, unlike in finance, the government had largely taken no actions to rein in big tech's business outside of ensuring that tech platforms banned content critical of the party.

The backlash started with privacy issues and a resentment toward big-tech companies that gave Chinese citizens little choice about how their privacy had been repeatedly violated. The government has gradually built out data protections yet is wary of taking actions like those in Europe, which it views as hobbling European firms' technology developments based on big data and artificial intelligence.

Then the PBOC walked back its support of fintech. Concern that the initially pro-competitive effects of big tech in finance were reducing market competition as big tech turned more markets into a duopoly was one factor. The PBOC's call for more rules and oversight to handle issues of privacy, data protection, and market distortions introduced by big tech added momentum. Then the collapse of P2P in mid-2018 meant that the utopian dream of a democratized technology-based financial system had vanished along with millions of people's savings. The Chinese government thus had to reconsider its financial liberalization, no longer so sure that the gamble to allow new firms to apply technology in finance was a good idea.

8

The Costliest Speech in History

"Prevent the disorderly expansion of capital"

On December 11, 2020, Xi Jinping gathered the Standing Committee of the Politburo for a meeting that would mark a sea change in China's tech policy. The meeting was top secret. But the agenda must have included what to do about one outspoken entrepreneur. Jack Ma had dared criticize the government publicly, and the big-tech sector now appeared to pose a political threat. Ant's planned IPO was already suspended, but the meeting summary released to the public demonstrated that the repercussions were only beginning. China's top leaders ordered the party-state to strengthen antimonopoly work and to "prevent the disorderly expansion of capital," code for a serious crackdown on companies that had become too powerful and dangerous to tolerate.[1]

The cancellation of Ant's IPO and its aftermath are a culmination of China's fintech story, a clash of forces, some pushing for Ant and others urging the government to restrain it. It is a story of inexorable forces of global and national reach, combined with the contingencies and consequences of one man's choice to speak out. Ma's criticism of the government crystallized the view in top

government circles that the big-tech founders were dangerous oli-
garchs not willing to abide by the party's decisions, so his speech
broke a dam of political influence that had held back regulation
for years.

When Ma's aura of untouchability crumbled, the pent-up pressure resulted in a flood of regulations ranging from competition
and privacy to financial risk. The speed and variety of government
actions made clear that the bureaucracy had long been waiting for
the right political moment to act. Much of the media coverage of
Jack Ma's speech and the aftermath implied a capricious decision
to take revenge against Ma for his criticism of regulators and Chinese finance. That element was part of the government's response.
Yet, if anything, the government's initial approval of the IPO was
even more surprising than its forced postponement.

Fintech Thrives, but Thunderclouds Loom

On July 20, 2020, Ant announced that it was filing for an IPO
at a target value of around $200 billion, up a third from its 2018
valuation of $150 billion.[2] The deal was set to raise tens of bil-
lions for Ant, more than Aramco, Saudi Arabia's oil company, had
gathered in its 2019 IPO. Ant and Alibaba would be the first- and
third-largest IPOs in history, respectively, a stunning achievement
for Jack Ma. The listing documents included the grandiose vision
to "build the future digital infrastructure of services," lasting 102
years, part of Jack Ma's goal for Alibaba to survive from the twen-
tieth century into the twenty-second. It also recognized that "as
we continue to grow in scale and significance, we expect to face
increased scrutiny."[3]

Still, new regulations had done little to dent the growth of fintech. Ant claimed nine hundred million annual active users in
China by mid-2019, most of whom signed on not only to payments but also to other services like credit, wealth management,
and insurance.[4] WeChat Pay was not far behind, claiming eight

hundred million active users making payments at more than fifty million merchants.[5] WeChat and Ant together controlled nearly 94 percent of the 250 trillion RMB (35 trillion USD) market for online payments made outside of banks in China, with Alipay comfortably in the lead at a 55 percent market share.[6] Government efforts to shrink Yu'E Bao did not stop hundreds of millions of new investors from piling in, including first-time Alipay users in rural areas and smaller cities. At the end of 2018, 588 million people, nearly 60 percent of adults in China, had invested in Yu'E Bao, making it probably the most popular investment product in history.[7] Meanwhile, even some former P2P lenders thrived, rebranded as loan brokers feeding data and customers for loans to China's financial institutions. Ant's blockbuster IPO filing was thus only one of many indicators that big fintech was doing better than ever and that Ant and Tencent had successfully adapted to the new political environment.

Banks could no longer openly be disrupted, but China's financial system was still moving toward bankers' worst nightmare, in which tech companies dominated finance through the power of their data, users, and technology. The enormous valuation of Ant's IPO reflected the belief that this would continue, redistributing bank profits into fintech company profits.

Regulators continued their moves to put the company under a more secure regulatory net even with the pending deal. Two days after the IPO was announced, the Supreme People's Court cut the interest cap on some loans from 24 percent to 15.4 percent. If applied to Ant, its ability to profitably lend to riskier borrowers would be compromised.[8] Then the PBOC demanded that banks report on their lending made through Ant's platforms, effectively admitting that supervisors had no clue* how large Ant's total

---

*Sources in China tell me that the CBIRC had these data but did not share them with the PBOC at the time, an indication that the regulatory system remained seriously fragmented.

lending was and which banks would be at risk if there were losses. Other rules in September tightened the net on microlending companies like Ant's subsidiaries.[9]

These rules, however, paled in comparison to new financial-holding-company regulation released in September 2020. It would submit the portion of Ant's businesses with financial licenses to group-wide regulation. The rules were on a collision course with Ant's nimble, aggressive culture that would chafe under a regime requiring that it not only hold costly capital at the group level but also ask the PBOC for permission before making crucial business decisions. It could, Ant feared, be held up for months before the PBOC gave it the green light.[10] These rules would have been planned long before Ant's IPO announcement, but pressure for new rules ratcheted up once the IPO prospectus lifted the veil of secrecy that hid Ant's scale, especially in lending, from the public and even most of the government.

Both the public and the government questioned the adequacy of existing regulation for a firm like Ant. In late September, PBOC Vice Governor Fan Yifei criticized the "nesting" of credit inside payment apps as difficult to effectively supervise, for all the financial and data flows rested in a closed loop understood only by the super-apps themselves.[11] Yet no consensus of what to do about this had been reached.

Lending was crucial to Ant's valuation; it made up 40 percent of the company's revenue. For the first time the huge scale of its lending operations, 2.1 trillion RMB outstanding, was made public, but the most explosive revelation was that Ant provided only 2 percent of the capital lent on its platforms. Ant could steer enormous loan volumes with minimal capital, keeping expenses down and shifting the risk of bad loans. However, regulators worried about misaligned incentives if 98 percent of the risk was borne by Ant's partners. Because Ant made money on every loan while taking little risk, the government worried it could overissue debt to profit and leave the consequences to others—as mortgage brokers had done before the 2008 financial crisis.

In a financial system awash in capital looking for good returns, the real comparative advantage is not money but Ant's control of the marketplace for loans, the customer relationship, the data, and the algorithms. Just like it had once been with Yu'E Bao, the banks collectively might see the growth of Huabei and Ant as a threat, but individually they could not resist partnering. None could match Ant's efficiency, data, or user base. Participating banks become almost dumb pipes, commoditized providers of capital: the customer does not even see which bank funded their loan. Such power breeds resentment.

Ma and his patrons seemed in a strong political position despite the techlash and Ma's diminished public popularity. Ant technology was helping banks make loans they could not manage on their own. And Ant's credit to groups like farmers and small businesses were in line with Beijing's policy priorities. Listing one of the world's hottest companies on Shanghai's STAR market (China's attempt to build its version of NASDAQ) would boost the attractiveness of China's underdeveloped equity markets. Both Shanghai officials and the securities regulator thus had a strong incentive to fast-track the deal. In addition, powerful people and institutions that had invested in Ant, from China's sovereign wealth fund and major banks to the relatives of former officials, stood to benefit financially from a successful IPO.

Ant's power was on display when reports leaked that the PBOC was considering investigating Alipay for antitrust violations in late July 2020, yet no Chinese media dared cover the story.[12] It seemed the top officials had determined to make the deal a success, ensuring that no government actions could get in the way. However, this success bred resentment from regulators who believed that they were unable to do their jobs because of political interference.[13] Ant's bankers kept raising its value, reportedly to $250 billion in late October, for investor demand was strong.

Yet there were signals that a backlash was brewing against Ant's credit expansion. State media brought attention that September to young people "trapped" in debt by Huabei.[14] Criticism of Jack Ma stepped up in early October, when an advertisement for Huabei hit a nerve with China's online public. It depicted a working-class father using a loan from Huabei to give his young daughter a "presentable" birthday celebration, which looks like a meal from McDonald's. One of the most liked online comments about the ad said that Huabei ads were "malicious" and "encouraging unrealistic consumption in every corner of every not-so-successful life."[15] By this point, people in urban areas had gone from having few options for credit to being inundated with advertisements for loans from seemingly every app they used. As one Weibo user wrote, "Weibo tells me it can lend me money; the delivery app tells me it can lend me money; and now even the photo editing app tells me it can lend me money."[16]

Credit can be freeing when used responsibly, but apps now seemed to be pushing people, especially the poor, into expensive debt to buy things they did not need. Big tech would then profit twice, once from the sale on the linked e-commerce platform and again from the loan origination. Chinese leaders and the public were deeply uncomfortable with a society that big tech was helping move toward US-style debt-fueled consumerism. From 2015 to 2019, Chinese households added nearly as much debt as US households accrued before the 2008 financial crisis, worrying authorities.[17] The PBOC would lean against this trend. The one signal that Ant was not invincible was a short IPO delay that amounted to a slap on the wrist. Regulators discovered a conflict of interest—that Alipay had helped sell mutual funds that would invest in the IPO to tens of millions of investors.[18]

Jack Ma Throws a Bomb

With the Ant IPO only a week and a half away, Jack Ma made his plea at the Bund Summit on October 24, 2020, against what he saw as outdated, innovation-strangling regulation. It was the ideal place for Ma to have the ear of China's financial and economic elite, who held the future of his empire in their hands. Revealing his position in China's hierarchy, his speech came after top-ranked officials like ministers and the former governor Zhou, but ahead of acting vice ministers. Major figures in companies about to go public generally enter a "quiet period," strictly limiting public statements during this sensitive time, knowing that a single stray remark could derail the deal, so giving any speech at all was bold. In retrospect, it was a sign of overconfidence. Little did he know, he was about to make the most financially costly speech in history.

Some signs suggested that Ma's confidence was not absolute. He put aside his usual extemporaneous style to read word for word from a script, said upfront that "I was quite torn about whether to speak here," and tried self-deprecation, saying his points might be "immature, incorrect, or laughable . . . if they make no sense, just forget about them."[19] Curiously for a speech of such import, it starts with a simple factual error, which suggests that he never had it vetted.*

---

*Early in his speech, Ma references a talk he gave at an event in 2013 called the "lujiazui financial summit," which does not exist—the kind of error that a team reviewing the speech would have easily caught. He seems to have mixed up the high-profile official Lujiazui Forum, at which he did not speak, and the Bund Global Financial Summit, at which he did speak that year.

Ma's argument was that the government was risking overreach in fintech regulation, to the detriment of growth and innovation. "To make innovation risk free," he said, "is to stifle innovation."[20] In that he was right, but authorities found much more in the speech objectionable. He insulted international banking regulators like the Basel Committee, which he called a "seniors club" dealing with Alzheimer's disease in tottering Western finance. He argued that China should follow its own path in financial regulation instead of adopting global standards that could not fit its vision of a financial future. He called out Chinese banks for being stuck in a "pawnshop" mentality, unable to handle credit without collateral, and he likened China's financial system to a polio patient. His standard for true fintech innovation was primarily based on big data, to distance Ant's activities from P2P and argue that "we cannot refuse all the innovations that internet technology brought finance because of P2P."

Much of Ma's speech was accurate, but it was dangerous. He contradicted Vice President Wang Qishan, who spoke first at the Bund Summit. Wang, who had led Xi's anticorruption campaign, said earlier that day that in finance "security always ranks first" above efficiency, and he warned of "heightened" risk from financial technology. Public criticism of the government's focus on risk put Ma on the other side of one of Xi Jinping's top personal priorities, which Xi viewed as crucial to the economy and to the survival of the regime. Ma's assertion that China did "not have a problem of systemic financial risk" seemed a direct contradiction of Xi's remarks a year before that "preventing the occurrence of systemic financial risks is the fundamental task of financial work."[21] Ma also crossed another line, infuriating regulators with the gambit of using two vague statements from Xi as a cudgel to imply that regulators' policies were not in line with the general secretary.

Ma was likely hoping to reprise his victories from 2014, when criticizing the government in public pressured the PBOC to loosen payment rules, but he underestimated his weakened political support and how much China had changed. The space for public debate on most issues in China has narrowed, and the only safe place for Ma to voice such criticism was behind closed doors. If the result was not to his liking, he would have to accept it, not criticize the government openly. The fact that he did so made him look like a political threat, someone who thinks they can do an end run around the party and its decision making to benefit their companies, perhaps to the detriment of China's "financial security." Unlike in 2014, when Chinese people online rallied to Jack Ma's defense against the big banks, the State Council canvassed public opinion, which was soundly negative about Ma's speech. Senior regulators were furious, telling Reuters they saw it as a "punch in their faces."[22]

Confident that a deal this important would go ahead anyway, two days later investors agreed to price Ant at a staggering $313 billion, on par at the time with global financial giants Mastercard and JP Morgan Chase. Four days later, on Halloween, Vice Premier Liu He called an emergency meeting of the Financial Stability and Development Committee, which issued a rebuttal to Ma and put in motion a new wave of harsher financial regulation, antitrust enforcement, and privacy rules.[23] Investors did not yet know a closely held secret, that the politically fraught decision of how to handle Ma and the deal appears to have been kicked up from the usual regulatory channels to the apex of the party, where Xi personally made the call to cancel the largest IPO in history.[24]

The guardrails constraining regulatory actions against Ant were off, and senior regulators were now free to directly attack Ant in public. Knowing that Ant and Ma still had powerful friends, most did so through pseudonymous articles. One probably authored by former governor Zhou and published on November 1 stated that when "a large Internet company conducts a large number of financial businesses but claims to be a technology company, it will not only evade supervision, but will also be more prone to disorderly expansion, causing hidden risks not conducive to fair competition."[25]

The next day, November 2, was the end of the IPO. It started with a storm of further criticism, including an article from a CBIRC official who criticized Ant's lending products, arguing that "financial technology companies use oligopoly status to charge excessive fees" and accusing them of predatory lending and misleading consumers.[26] Then regulators released a bombshell notice with a single sentence: Jack Ma, along with Ant's top executives, was summoned to a "supervisory discussion" with four regulators.[27] Xinhua issued a veiled verdict with an essay titled "You Can't Just Say Anything . . . People Can't Just Do as They Please." Ma showed up in the article metaphorically, as a painting with a white horse in the clouds alluding to his Chinese name, which translates to "horse cloud."[28]

Simultaneously, the PBOC obliterated Ant's capital-light lending model with a proposed regulation that would require it to put up 30 percent of the capital for its joint loans with banks. If all of its loans were subject to this regulation, Ant would have needed to raise far more than even its record-breaking IPO, by some estimates at least 100 billion RMB, to be able to fund even its current loans.[29] Further expansion of Ant lending would also become more costly, making it hard to live up to investor expectations. The abrupt shift in regulatory environment made it impossible to go ahead with the IPO: investors needed to reevaluate Ant's prospects. Just two days before the planned November 5 IPO, the Shanghai Stock Exchange delayed the deal indefinitely.[30]

Much of the world's attention was diverted by the US presidential election, but this shocking story needed explanation. A narrative quickly developed that attributed the move to "capricious and thin skinned" policy makers in Beijing and a "diminishing tolerance for big private businesses."[31] It seemed emblematic of Xi's China that it would be willing to destroy such a useful deal to punish anyone willing to criticize the party. The Chinese public and many Chinese investors, on the other hand, supported the government's decision, saw Ma's speech as a desperate attempt to block the coming regulation of his out-of-control empire, and did not see the action as punishment for speaking out.[32]

There is truth in both interpretations, but neither can tell the whole story. Some facts fit well with the first interpretation of Ma being punished: even if new regulations were needed to legitimately control financial risk, it does not explain why authorities did not introduce them before the IPO was approved instead of looking erratic or punitive by derailing the IPO so late. Other facts fit with the second interpretation: Ma's speech was an attempt to block rules the government already had in the works; important regulation in China goes through a long process of drafting, revision, and vetting before it is seen by the public. Therefore, it is impossible that the rules could have been created from scratch in the week or so between the speech and their release.

Investors assumed that Chinese regulators coordinated to settle on a regulatory environment before approving the IPO. That was not the case—this process failed. It would have taken months for the information in Ant's prospectus to filter through the bureaucracy and reach top leaders. However, the deal's time line was too compressed for this to happen in time and for a response to be formulated—until the speech led to decisive party action. The STAR market, for example, took only about a month to review the listing documents, whereas a more usual process would take about six months, and the CSRC gave the nod to the IPO a month later.[33]

Later the party would investigate how such a complex deal sailed so quickly through the process, scrutinizing the stock exchange, the securities regulator, Shanghai's municipal government, and the state companies invested in Ant that stood to gain enormously if the IPO was successful.[34] All had good reasons to boost the IPO even if there was no corruption involved, for a successful domestic listing would have benefited China's financial markets, Shanghai as a financial center, and the coffers of state firms. The investigation was sure to make any patrons hesitate to help Ant resist future regulation, lest they face scrutiny themselves. Alibaba's hometown party secretary was put under investigation for corruption in late 2021, in a case that soon after would be linked to Ant.

In a sense, the regulators got lucky. Had Jack Ma not created an opening for the deal's opponents with his speech, the IPO almost certainly would have gone ahead. Authorities would have then been in a bind. They could and did hit privately held Ant with regulations that cut its value without repercussions beyond elite politics and foreign institutions. After the deal, however, they would face the wrath of tens of millions of Chinese retail investors and international opprobrium as a dangerous place to do business if new rules directly caused financial losses to those who had just poured tens of billions into the company with the reasonable assumption that the government had determined a stable regulatory approach before approving the IPO.

Just as Ant's aggressive push with the Sesame score led to fallout for the whole industry, the campaign against big tech would not stop at Ant—another sign that it was not a personal vendetta against Ma. Tencent would be in the crosshairs too, even though it tried to position itself as the opposite of Jack Ma. Its president said soon after the Ant mess began that "we must collaborate intimately with regulators, as blind innovation can cause more risk."[35]

Rectification

A wave of regulations crashed over fintech and big tech in the months after Ma's speech. It started with the State Administration for Market Regulation (SAMR), which released draft antimonopoly guidelines for the "platform economy" on November 11. Many of big tech's anticompetitive practices, like exclusivity arrangements forcing merchants to choose to distribute through either Alipay or WeChat, would be scrutinized.[36] The rules wiped $280 billion off the market value of Chinese big tech.[37] One month later, on December 11, saw the Politburo meeting attacking the "disorderly expansion of capital" and promising more antitrust scrutiny. This was the political signal that both the SAMR and the PBOC needed to move forward.

The SAMR first started hitting Tencent, Alibaba, and other big-tech firms with fines for violation of rules long left unenforced, like the requirement to report acquisitions.[38] Then, at the end of the year, the SAMR announced an investigation into Alibaba's ex-clusivity requirements, and the PBOC served Ant with five demands for "rectification."[39] The close timing suggests that each regulator had to get clearance from higher-level party authorities. The SAMR investigation caused a 13 percent drop in Alibaba's share price, bringing the cumulative decline in its value to $240 billion since the Ant IPO was delayed.

The PBOC's demands asked for nothing less than a reinvention of Ant. First, it would need to halt "unfair competition" in payments, including nesting credit within Alipay and "inappropriate" links between Alipay and other financial services. Considering that the entire super-app model in fintech was to bundle financial services together with payments, strict implementation could mean breaking it apart into separate apps.

Second, its "information monopoly" would need to end, and better protection for data privacy and security needed to be offered. Compliance would be a challenge because there is often a trade-off between these two goals, in which the benefits of information sharing come at a cost to privacy.[40] If Ant opened its data to others, it could no longer keep any information that left its protected environment from being shared or hacked. One way the PBOC proposed to move forward was a reversal on credit reporting, seesawing back to the demand that Ant obtain the very credit-reporting licenses that the PBOC had denied it for five years. The PBOC was now more confident that it could use the licensing process to expand its jurisdiction beyond just Ant's purely financial data.

The third demand was a major blow. Ant had hoped to keep the parts of its business focused on technology—and without financial licenses—lightly regulated outside the new financial-holding-company regime. But the PBOC demanded that all of Ant Group become a financial holding company. Authorities reasoned that this would be the only way to prevent arbitrage that led risk to migrate outside the supervisory net. Fourth, the PBOC demanded more cooperation with regulators and reduced leverage. Finally, Ant would need to further shrink Yu'E Bao and reduce risk in its other investment products.

As with Sesame Credit, the blowback on Ant then expanded when an anonymous CBIRC official told local media that the issues with Ant were "universal" and urged all entirely internet platforms to examine their practices.[41] JD, Alibaba's e-commerce rival, had to cancel the IPO of its fintech unit, and the STAR market barred all fintech IPOs.[42] In 2021 authorities demanded that Tencent also form a financial holding company for its financial businesses. To top it all off, the PBOC acted to protect its turf by joining the antitrust wagon, declaring that Alipay and WeChat Pay had a "dominant market position"* in payments, paving the way for it to reduce their market share or even split them up if they did not engage in fair competition.[43]

After months of intense negotiations, Ant's rectification plan was accepted in April. It released few details, other than that its loans would come not from its microlending subsidiaries but from a new consumer-finance company that would involve it sharing the wealth with two state-owned shareholders. It also pledged fealty: "We will put our growth proactively within the national strategic context . . . [and] beef up our global competitiveness." Once

---

*The rules defined market dominance as one firm with more than one-half the market and/or two firms with two-thirds, which was the case for Alipay alone and Alipay and WeChat Pay together.

again, this occurred within two days of action from the SAMR, which levied a $2.75 billion fine on Alibaba for having "abused its dominant position in the market" and ordered it to halt the exclusivity agreements.[44] Investors, expecting worse, bid up Alibaba shares in a sign of relief that the punishment was not more severe.

Amid this alarm came another scandal for big tech. Baidu was found to be blocking an article from the respected business magazine *Caixin* on how tech companies enabled online gambling, probably to avoid further bad press. The move backfired, instead shining a light into tech companies' power over information. As one Chinese internet user commented, "The superpower of global internet monopolies has shown its face, but where is the supervision to keep them under control?"[45] Alibaba faced a similar episode when Weibo, in which it has a major equity stake, was found to be suppressing articles about an Alibaba executive's alleged affair. In the wake of the Jack Ma speech, the government would demand that Alibaba shed its media assets to reduce its ability to shape public opinion, power that the party would not share.[46]

Regulators underscored that the reorganization of Ant was not to negatively impact its services, which would cause financial disruption or incur the wrath of its billion users. The PBOC said Ant should "maintain business continuity and normal business operations."[47] Thus, even with severe regulatory demands, Alipay users would notice little difference—except for the younger users, who now faced lower credit limits. Yet the changes they demanded meant that Ant would face more compliance costs, less of a competitive moat, and less room to expand its profitable credit business. Ant investors halved the valuation, but Ant remained a nearly $150 billion company.

The Ant IPO was a debacle on many levels. International headlines about China's leadership in fintech, innovation, successful entrepreneurs, and new attractiveness of its equity markets transformed overnight into negative assessments of the environment for private businesses and the lack of free speech in China. Regulators looked both unpredictable and less competent than investors had given them credit for. The massive changes demanded of Ant after its IPO were the kind of serious decisions one would expect to be made *before* allowing such a landmark deal to go ahead. Jack Ma would see his fortune in Alibaba and Ant shares shrink substantially, as would his behind-the-scenes influence.

Ma's speech and its repercussions shifted the political ground underneath fintech and big technology companies in general. Once the party's top leaders set a new direction of curbing the influence of capital, regulators were free to set the rules now that big tech no longer enjoyed such strong political protection. Unlike with peer-to-peer lending, they were prepared and could act decisively. Surely many of their rules would have been imposed anyway if Jack Ma had not dared to give his speech, but the countervailing forces supporting Ant would have slowed what instead became a punitive flood of regulations, and those that came through would surely have been watered down.

Chinese Digital Paradise or Doom for Innovation?

What initially looked like trouble for only Jack Ma spread across the tech sector and beyond. Eventually, the campaign became more of a wholesale renegotiation of the role of the private sector and entrepreneurs, putting China's future growth and innovation at potential risk. In late 2021, General Secretary Xi Jinping made a call for China to achieve "common prosperity," a core part of his pitch to stay in power beyond the customary ten years.[48] In conjunction with stopping the "disorderly expansion of capital," Xi's campaign came to mean a series of crackdowns involving every major big-tech platform, live streamers, high earners, celebrities, gaming, fintech, and real estate, while most for-profit online tutoring and Bitcoin mining were banned outright.

Especially in the big-tech sector, Beijing eschewed the laissez-faire attitude that it had long used for consumer-tech, outside of censorship and more recently fintech. Instead, authorities introduced new rules around the use of algorithms, cyber-security, listing shares abroad, tech-firm acquisitions, data privacy, worker rights, and much more. Many of these rules went deep into detail to correct real societal problems caused or exacerbated by technology companies. In fact, many of these rules would be quite popular if they were introduced in Europe or the United States, but with due process instead of a campaign-style crackdown. Under the new rules, gig workers are gaining better rights, consumers are being granted better privacy protections, and anticompetitive acquisitions from big-tech platforms are being banned as a result. They demonstrate that the challenges confronting China are similar to those everywhere, with the glaring exception of ensuring that a one-party state cannot be challenged by businessmen.

Take privacy concerns, where the new political situation helped break years of logjam and allowed a sweeping new personal information protection law (PIPL) to be enacted. Meanwhile, the United States lacks a national-privacy or data-protection standard, leaving data collection, sharing, and processing subject to a mess of largely ineffective protections for different sectors in different US states.[49] China, on the other hand, now has a framework that, if effectively enforced, will give Chinese consumers many more rights than Americans have today in relation to how their data are collected and used, at least by entities outside government. For example, Chinese people will be able to refuse handling of their personal information by firms like Equifax, request that their data be deleted, and obtain copies of the data that firms have collected on them. Firms dealing in data now face serious risk of being punished for "excessive personal information collection."[50] The US is widely viewed around the world as lax on privacy, but in some respects China's data-protection regime sets a higher bar than even the famously strict General Data Protection Regulation (GDPR) in the European Union.[51] Of course, the state will face far less constraints, but China is perfectly capable of requiring serious privacy protections from private actors while also ratcheting up state surveillance.

The devil is in many details to be determined, but they will have a far-ranging impact on fintech and big-tech companies. Tech platforms will have to prove that their algorithms for purposes such as credit scoring are fair and transparent, opening up the black box to users (and competitors). The law will also force platforms to allow data portability, meaning that users can export their data from one platform and take it with them to another.[52] The walled gardens holding data in Alipay and WeChat will thus be dismantled, so the largest platforms will lose some of their unique data advantages and their ability to "lock in" users to their platforms. For example, an Ant user could share their payment history with another credit provider to shop around for credit. Some of the market segments that Alipay and WeChat have dominated will therefore become more competitive. Still, it would take a massive wave of users sharing data to fully level the playing field between the top platforms and their smaller competitors such as JD and Pinduoduo. In addition, the flows of data will not only be from the largest to the smallest: users of other services will have a new ability to share those data with Alibaba and Tencent, adding to their troves of data. Smaller firms with fewer resources may also have a harder time assimilating data generated by the top platforms.

More specifically on fintech, piecing together Politburo statements with the actions of financial regulators and the SAMR paints a picture of the market that China's government hopes to have. It is radically different from the model that made it the world's fintech leader. Authorities do not want a duopoly of private technology firms powerful enough to deviate from state priorities and turn China into a debt- and consumption-fueled economy like that of the United States. Americans have long fused credit and payments, just as Huabei did, which expands access to credit but induces others to overconsume and then face crippling debt. At every step of becoming a more consumerist society, a tech platform would profit, from the merchant payment fee, to the revenue from a purchase on Taobao, to the interest paid on and eventual sale of the loan. The PBOC vowed that China will not "rely on developing consumer finance to expand consumption," which it sees as unsustainable for both individuals and society.[53] Consumer lending will be viewed with more suspicion, whereas small-business lending will continue to be encouraged. Instead of encouraging consumerism with games and rapid delivery of food and coffee from algorithm-optimized delivery drivers, the government wants more of China's capital and talent to focus on hard technology, such as semiconductors, that can free it from technological dependence on the United States.

Policy makers also hope to have a much more competitive market, which could be both more vibrant and at less risk of producing powerful tycoons than today's duopoly. Instead of walled-off super-apps with closed flows of data and funds, authorities hope to open up big tech's data troves to the government and to competitors, leaning against the market's winner-take-all dynamics. Regulators issued a call to break payments away from the other financial offerings of super-apps and oppose what they call "abuse" of market power from payments. The competitive moats that super-apps' payment dominance gave them may soon be filled in.[54] Super-apps will need to have more barriers and checks, which will jeopardize the advantages that big-tech companies have gained from free flows of data inside their ecosystems. The eCNY project to develop a digital currency will reduce the data that big tech can garner from handling payments—which could, for example, not allow big tech to use data it collects from payments for other purposes such as marketing and credit scoring. The eCNY is also likely to put downward pressure on payment fees. In 2019, 43 percent of Ant's revenue came from payments, so lower fees could hit a valuation already pummeled by the new lending rules.

Ant has created a separate consumer-loan company that it will jointly own with other institutions. That entity faces much stricter regulation and will likely absorb Ant's Huabei and Jiebei lending.[55] It and Tencent will be required to create separate apps for credit and payments to ensure they are not able to use their privileged position as digital wallets to dominate the consumer-credit market. Thus, both in the apps themselves and in the back end that users do not see, some parts of the super-apps are being split into pieces.

This storm of regulation and pushback against some of China's national technology champions was necessary to some extent, but the way it is being pursued is at serious risk of going too far too quickly, harming innovation, growth, and China's future competitiveness—including with the United States. On the one hand, many abuses of market power and privacy could end, which would benefit consumers and smaller innovative companies. The digital-economy base of convenient mobile payments, cheap credit, plentiful investment options, online shopping, and a host of other digital services is not at risk. The year 2021 was a record one for venture-capital investment in China despite the crackdown—as entrepreneurs continued to found new promising companies, and investors doubled down—but the investment has come increasingly outside the government's crosshairs, such as in health care and manufacturing, not in fintech or consumer internet.[56] There are around twenty million private firms in China, many of which are intensively investing in research and development, and most of those have not been targeted by this new campaign.[57]

Innovative start-ups that could have never competed with Ant or Tencent's market dominance can get a chance now that the giants' power has been reduced. Start-ups long forced to choose between the two camps as part of investment and access deals may be freed to grow much larger now that exclusivity arrangements have been banned. However, smaller technology players will struggle to comply with the barrage of complex new regulations, something that today's giants did not have as a hurdle when their staffs and budgets were small. Thus, even if more rules were needed, one of the key ingredients of past waves of innovation can no longer contribute to the next rounds of it in China.

A group of firms largely absent from the crosshairs is made up of state-owned companies. The government, confident that state firms are a political base instead of a political threat, continues to merge its firms into gigantic conglomerates that reduce competition across China's economy, whereas the private sector bears the brunt. The power of the big banks relative to private-sector players like Tencent and Alibaba has grown, which will surely mean less disruption and less innovation in fintech.

The new risks of becoming too large or influential, especially of stepping on the toes of state incumbents, could also blunt the ambition of the next generation of tech entrepreneurs, who could fear growing too large or too important. Pony Ma is an increasingly rare exception to the growing group of founders or cofounders of Chinese tech companies who have stepped down from their companies amid the crackdown, including Richard Liu of JD.com and Colin Huang of Pinduoduo in e-commerce as well as Su Hua and Zhang Yiming of video-sharing apps Kuaishou and Bytedance (which runs TikTok). Thus, some of China's most successful entrepreneurs have taken a backseat, which is not a positive signal for future innovation in China.

The coming years will be risky for the original political supporters of fintech and especially Alibaba/Ant, whose hometown party secretary Zhou Jiangyong has been detained for corruption that "aided the disorderly expansion of capital." Ant Group has already been implicated, allegedly trading investments in Zhou's brother's companies for cheap land deals.[58] The party is only getting started: the feared anticorruption commission has vowed to end the "corruption behind platform monopolies" and "collusion between power and capital."[59] Corruption should never be excused, but it is important to note that the whole impetus for Xi Jinping's anticorruption drive was that it had become systemic. With the way that China worked for decades, just about everyone with major success in politics or business has skeletons in their closet that can be dragged out if they are on the wrong side of the political line.

The signals coming from the top of the party mean that voices of moderation in the debate over regulation in China know they may be putting themselves at personal risk. China's experimental policy record includes a long history of correcting its policy mistakes and stepping back from the brink, learning when its actions are self-defeating or costlier than expected, but China is not just regulating; it is also renegotiating the long, mutually beneficial partnership between its government and its firms, and quickly. It will be much harder to gain true insight into the cost of the current policies if one side of the debate is silenced, which raises the odds that this campaign will go too far and hurt innovation instead of settling into an acceptable balance.

In sum, beneficial effects on competition and privacy must be weighed against the compliance burdens, deep uncertainty, favoring of less innovative state firms, talent exit, and ominous political signals. The headwinds to growth and innovation seem most likely to predominate in the coming years. The change in regulatory environment will also make the already difficult process of expanding to countries outside China even more fraught, although the new regulations tend to mention increasing "international competitiveness of fintech" as a government goal. Activities abroad are harder for Chinese authorities to police, making them riskier for firms already under the microscope at home. A focus on reorganizing operations at home also takes away energy and resources needed for a strategic focus on expansion in foreign markets. Finally, the public pledging of fealty to the state and the clear imperative to hand over data mean that foreign regulators are not likely to believe any claims that Chinese big-tech firms make that they will keep the non-Chinese data they collect out of the party's hands.

9

From Liberator to Oppressor?

"Once the cat is out of the bag for big tech in finance ... the changes become irreversible"

In late 2020 authorities in southern China's Guangdong pioneered a new form of cruel punishment to deter criminals. Instead of the traditional methods of prison, labor camps, or fines, perpetrators would be free but would be subject to a five-year ban on digital payments—in one fell swoop making them outcasts excluded from the modern, convenient economy that financial technology brought into being.[1]

It is a testament to the rapid, revolutionary change in China that a tool leaping from the fringe to the mainstream just a few years ago is now so essential to daily life that being denied its use is deemed sufficient punishment for some crimes. The link between police action and digital payments also vividly illustrates how governments might leverage these tools as concentrated points of control over the population, separating people out into digital haves and have-nots. For better or for worse, as finance goes digital, more of it can be tracked and controlled by both big-tech firms and governments, and China is the world's laboratory for these changes. Mark Zuckerberg regrets not paying attention to WeChat before waking up in 2019 to the possibilities that the Chinese fintech revolution unleashed. Understanding the implications of changes in China that are the harbinger of the future remaking of finance around the world is essential to ensure that populations, businesses, and policy makers are ready to reap the potential benefits while controlling the dangers of an increasingly digital financial system.

The fintech story in China began not with state plans but with innovation and entrepreneurship that dared to take on incumbents firmly established in the Communist Party hierarchy. Flush with money, technology, and ideas from abroad and empowered by allies in government, visionary entrepreneurs fought for freedom from the constraints of the repressed financial system by creating their own payment tools. The importance of foreigners to China's fintech success has been quickly forgotten, but it is crucial to understanding how innovation can thrive, even in technological laggards, through cross-pollination that adapts existing technologies and ideas in exciting new ways.

Jack Ma and Pony Ma bided their time as they and their companies became richer, stronger, and more powerful. When the right moment arrived, they took on the banks and other powerful state companies in a direct clash that played out not only in the market but also behind the scenes at the highest levels of the Communist Party. At first, the entrepreneurs won, bringing competition, rapid modernization, convenience, and, most importantly, financial freedom to a billion people. Super-apps and China's digital finance revolution demonstrated the power of big-tech firms to upend industries, even the most regulated and protected sectors, and reflected the freewheeling economy and explosive growth of China in the 2000s and 2010s.

The successful encouragement by the authorities of innovation that disrupted even state companies is a striking example of how, contrary to wishful thinking in Washington, China has proven that innovation can thrive in authoritarian political systems. It thrived in fintech not because of industrial policies and subsidies that the US now seems keen on emulating but because the state created a stable, encouraging environment with good infrastructure; reasonable yet not excessive regulation; and market forces primarily determining the winners. China, despite being a one-party state obsessed with stability, has shown itself willing to take big risks for potentially big rewards, as with its invitation of big tech into finance with little regulation or precedent, or its pioneering efforts to launch a digital currency. Rules written for the finance of the past will never fit unambiguously with the finance of the future, and creators of pioneering innovations always create risks and rewards for society. China's experience shows how a nation can thread that needle effectively, providing cover to entrepreneurs taking sensible risks and ensuring that regulation is flexible enough to adapt to new challenges. Where China failed in this, as in the case of peer-to-peer lending, illustrates that encouraging risk-taking pays off only when the government makes clear who is responsible for supervising the new activity and then monitoring it effectively.

Chinese fintech has found imitators from India all the way to the companies that Chinese once copied in Silicon Valley—inspiring Facebook's controversial forays into launching its own digital currency that could help it become a global version of Tencent's super-app. US big-tech firms now regularly copy new business models and features from Chinese tech, and US banks send their people to China to see what the future of finance everywhere might look like.

The fintech story shows that the United States cannot sit back and presume that its primacy in technology and finance will continue indefinitely. The US financial system and the way of transacting have changed little, whereas China's digital remaking of its financial system has raised its ambitions to play a greater role in the world's financial system, including with a state-backed digital currency that is exploring interoperability with other central banks. The effects are not likely to be immediate, partly because of strong network effects that make the dollar's role hard to dislodge. The US system has not changed as much as China's, in part because it had far less room for improvement than theirs, but our financial system could also use a great deal more competition, innovation, inclusion, and lower cost.

China's pioneering efforts will pay dividends in the coming decades as central banks around the globe explore rebooting their currencies and cross-border payment tools for a digital era. Chinese fintech apps are already accepted in dozens of countries, and Ant Group and Tencent are important players, expanding China's footprint in finance and commerce around the world. China's growing weight in the world economy, from finance to trade, means that even if its digital currency is not the killer app against the dollar, the RMB will naturally gain ground against the dollar as a global currency.

Still, even those firms able to benefit from China's immense markets in terms of scale, capital, and technology have not yet succeeded, as US tech firms have, in building large user bases across the world. But complacency is dangerous. Betting that they will not learn from earlier mistakes and writing them off as competitors to Wall Street or Silicon Valley would be as foolish as Alipay's dismissive attitude about WeChat Pay before 2014: in the blink of an eye, WeChat Pay turned a market dominated by one player into a multipolar system of two strong competitors. The potential parallels between the US-China rivalry suggest that the United States might do well to see itself in Alipay's position back then and ensure that it does not miss the equivalent of the shift to mobile that gave Tencent a crucial advantage.

The United States does not need to follow in China's shoes or rush out its own central-bank digital currency. However, it does need a push to make payments with dollars easier and less costly, whether at home or across borders. One way China has shown this could be done is inviting more competition in payments that could put pressure on the system to innovate more and process payments at lower costs to merchants. Any improvements that the United States can make to its own financial system will reduce the ability for Chinese offerings to displace dollars by improving on what is available from the US.

Behind the fintech boom and its revolutionary positive change for a billion Chinese people, however, is a dark side that any country hoping to unleash the power of fintech will have to deal with. Some of the explorations enabled by the government's permissive attitude turned out to be dead ends, such as the peer-to-peer lenders posing as innovative firms to take loan sharking online or to bilk unsuspecting investors out of their savings. Learning from the regulatory models that have worked in China and elsewhere and avoiding what has failed, as this book has explored in depth, will allow other countries to avoid many of these costs that China has borne as a fintech pioneer while harnessing many of the benefits.

Even the successful parts of fintech gave authorities pause. The big-tech companies were the only players powerful enough to take on the banks and create sorely needed competition. But giving tech titans the ability to dominate both consumer tech and finance started to look like a recipe for a winner-take-all outcome with deleterious effects on competition across finance and beyond. What made the super-apps so revolutionary—the integration of data across so many services, the immense user bases, the bundling of finance and e-commerce or social media—was also a recipe for conflicts of interest that gave regulators deep disquiet, even those like Governor Zhou, who were crucial to big tech's permission to enter finance. What if a big-tech firm lowered its lending standards to sell more goods online, but banks were the ones that would take losses? What if it could push its own stock price up by steering trillions in client money? What if credit scores became more like loyalty scores, and tech companies even became the arbiters of who is a security threat at the airport? When complex financial institutions are already dangerously too big to fail, what would happen if a fintech giant with much larger complexity and scope collapsed, and how could any regulator hope to understand the risks?

For all their fears, regulators had to tread carefully. Tech entrepreneurs had powerful friends throughout the party, and there were good arguments to be made that excessive corrective regulation could have a damaging effect on the availability of credit and continued financial innovation that China needed to sustain growth and have strong companies that could compete with America's top firms outside China. Yet pressure for more privacy, competition, better labor rights, and more direct government control built up. President Xi's consolidation of power and focus on big state companies was destined to leave less space for big tech, and Jack Ma's disastrous 2020 speech criticizing the government broke the logjam.

Chinese authorities were fearful enough about big fintech's power and the risk it posed that they canceled the world's largest IPO and embarked on a crackdown that shaved over a trillion dollars from the market value of China's top internet companies, drawing the particular ire of foreign investors. Now the government is trying to rein in fintech's excesses without killing the goose that has laid many golden eggs. Xi Jinping's concentration of power has increased party control and coordination, but systemic issues with China's system of government are not going away anytime soon, and concentrated power risks overreaching and groupthink, a major risk in the crackdown on fintech and big tech.

A deep look at fintech in China has also shown the true nature of China, whose rise is one of the most serious strategic challenges confronting the United States. The image that most people in America have about the People's Republic—a perfectly ordered place run by an all-seeing government—is flat-out wrong. China, in fact, is extremely messy, with rampant lawbreaking and a government with massive blind spots about what is going on in its economy and financial system, with tacit permission often given to blatantly illegal activities. The government struggles to pass data between different silos. As is inevitable in a huge bureaucracy where changing policy can be like steering an oil tanker, it often fails to act decisively. It will be extremely challenging to China's state capacity to implement the complex new regimes of antitrust, privacy, financial risk, and much more.

One lesson from China is that once finance is shaped by big tech, with a billion users and millions of businesses relying on it, many changes become irreversible. Even with Jack Ma's fall, Alipay and WeChat Pay will remain key players in Chinese finance. This is positive, for the big banks cannot roll back the digital revolution that gave people so much more choice and convenience, but in another sense anyone following the China model should be aware that they need the proper rules in place in advance, especially robust competition policy. China's antimonopoly investigators were divided and asleep at the wheel so long that the government suddenly woke up to what it saw as a political threat, slamming on the brakes with harsh corrective action—to the private sector only, of course, for authorities have done little or nothing to stop monopolies of state firms. Other countries could ensure that their competition frameworks are ready before providing the green light and then address the issues in a fairer manner consistent with the rule of law and slower deliberation in democratic countries. Going first, China had no way to know beforehand where the revolution would lead and what rules were necessary. We now have the benefit of their experience.

The China fintech story is a cautionary tale for the rest of the world to tread carefully, recognizing that tech's tendency for explosive growth, network effects, and complexity unleashes great, useful productive forces but creates an unprecedented challenge for regulators. Considering that few countries have large, home-grown tech sectors like the US and China do, the considerations become even more complex because the big tech entering finance in most countries would be companies based outside their borders, potentially with very different values. China's experience is showing a trend we will see everywhere, in which regulation of finance requires parsing difficult financial issues, the technology, and the connections between the two.

The way that big tech enters finance can also be very different across countries and does not necessarily mean following a Chinese model. There is a large middle ground between the maximalist Chinese model, of allowing tech firms to become financial giants and own banks, and the US model, where tech firms have done far less. Technology companies can focus on their comparative advantages, like providing consumer interfaces, data analysis, cloud computing, and data-security expertise, whereas holding customer funds, making loans, and evaluating investments are performed by institutions designed and regulated for that purpose.

Facebook's Libra/Diem currency is now being dismantled, but this does not mean that US big tech is still not eagerly looking for a way to get into global finance. Facebook's ambition for its global digital currency went far beyond anything Alipay or WeChat Pay created in China, and Jack Ma probably would have been shipped off to jail if he had tried to launch such a product from China. Yet the US has different super-app contenders in fintech companies like Square and PayPal, often including cryptocurrencies that super-apps in China cannot touch. Even classic retail giants like Walmart are getting in on the action, buying up fintech companies that it could use to become much more than a store. Apple Pay is growing, and Google Pay aims to reset and become "the connective tissue for the entire consumer finance industry."[2]

Some of the crucial ingredients of China's response that deserve replication include serious rules around conflict of interest and monopolization to ensure that big tech's entry into finance enhances competition, not ultimately diminishes it. The United States already has a financial-holding-company regime for supervising financial conglomerates, which could be adapted to include the unique risks posed by fintech. China's system is still in the early stages, but it supervises the uniquely complicated and big fintech companies at the group level, limiting risk by imposing capital requirements and supervising related party transactions, and it could be worth emulating.

The story of fintech in China is crucially important to understanding the future of finance and technology. Many of the most-urgent issues revolve around the enormous promise and unintended consequences of new technologies and the firms that have developed and harnessed them. Governments are now struggling with how to protect cybersecurity and privacy, combat financial exclusion and scams, and reduce financial risk, but both tech and tech firms move so fast that authorities always seem to be lagging in their responses.

The uncomfortable conclusion for the West is that China has become a laboratory for consumer-technology innovation and how governments can deal with it. Looking at the super-app-centered daily life and advanced central-bank digital currency gives a preview of what life may look like as our money goes digital and where digital companies become more like providers of the essential infrastructure for our new world. The governmental and societal response to these trends that are further advanced in China are also worth studying as they play out, whether it is in data protection, cybersecurity, financial risk, or state-backed digital currency. They may inspire positive steps to take and pitfalls to avoid.

Where We Go from Here

Payments, finance, and commerce around the world have rapidly digitized in the wake of the COVID-19 pandemic as contactless transactions became a priority for billions of people used to in-person payments with cash. The US card habits seem impossible to kick, so the pandemic's impact on finance may not be that large here. Meanwhile, the rest of the world is likely to see the seeds of what has happened in China: payments first going online and then tech companies leveraging that data to create new eco-systems of financial and other services. At the same time, those new data trails could lead to more surveillance and a transformation of risk from physical theft of banknotes to cyber crime.

For now, the effects of Beijing's new campaign to rein in big tech and extend its control and regulatory prerogatives are unknown, with the exception of a reduction in the still-immense fortunes and power of tech giants and new suspicions by foreign investors that China's government is bent on control at all costs—including massive losses by those who put their capital to work at Chinese firms. Trillions of dollars of commerce and a large part of a billion Chinese people's lives are being remade through new rules that could either stifle innovation by tilting the playing field back toward unproductive state firms or improve it by allowing a new generation of start-ups to compete with the large players.

Of greater concern is the state pushing for control over the data of private firms. Ant Group is apparently being forced to create a joint venture with state firms, to which Ant will have to release not only credit histories, which would be in line with global norms, but also other sensitive user data that are inputs to its underwriting. This partially state-owned joint venture will then be responsible for ensuring that Ant's trove of credit is useful for credit evaluation.

Ensuring interoperability, protecting privacy, and curtailing monopolistic practices as a regulator of markets in which private players compete are positive steps, but having a party-state with no effective check on its power more directly gathering data and becoming the arbiter of what data are shared with whom, at what price, is dangerous. Such a step would lead back in the direction of the central planning that failed China so miserably before, and the government's track record of running a market itself—for example, with UnionPay—is not a positive one in terms of innovation.

Putting all these data directly into government hands, where the new privacy protections are much weaker, is also a recipe for an even worse environment for civil liberties and freedom from government surveillance than exists today.

On August 15, 2020, twenty-one-year-old Tang Mouhui had had it with Tencent, but he could not live without WeChat. Tencent had slapped him with a ban on using his WeChat account, a disaster for his small business, which relied on it to make sales and communicate with customers. The impact radiated out because people in China also log into all sorts of other services through WeChat, so losing that account would mean a cascade of locked doors to services that people need every day. His livelihood was literally at stake, but as many of us have experienced in this age of automation, all he could reach for help was uncaring and unhelpful machines, chatbots that led him in increasingly infuriating circles. Being in Shenzhen, he could go to Tencent's customer service center in person, but because it was Saturday, even that option was closed to him. Giving up hope, he climbed to the eleventh floor of the office tower housing Tencent's service center and jumped to his death.[3]

Tencent's decision to suspend Tang's account made sense from the company's perspective. It later emerged that someone he was contacting on WeChat had reported him for sexual harassment. But the incident raised serious concerns about tying together one's financial and business life with personal conversations in one super-app. Even more concerning, people in China regularly lose access to WeChat because their conversations or posts have fallen afoul of either automated censors or people the tech firms hired to police content, leading to warnings and temporary suspensions. People are more likely to self-censor their discussions with others when a large part of one's financial life is at stake. Super-apps, though convenient, are an excessive concentration of power, whether when used directly for the companies that run them or when they become tools for the governments that regulate them.

There are now two diametrically opposed models for the future of finance, each with its own promise and problems. The world of cryptocurrency ("web3") represents one extreme, akin to the early promise of the internet: libertarian, untethered to any nation-state, hostile to regulation, fiercely protective of users' privacy, and often decentralized. China is moving toward another: protective above all of the state's sovereign prerogatives and centralized power to monopolize money provision, supervise the financial system, and surveil its population. Neither represents a way forward for liberal democracies like the United States, which must find its own balance based on different social values than those prevalent in the cryptocurrency community or the Chinese Communist Party.

It is up to the US public to ensure that, if a digital dollar proves necessary, the technical design and governance would not create a single Orwellian repository of everyone's transactions and balances. The design of a digital currency must be one that can be shared among and traded with other like-minded countries that agree on similar standards. It is also crucial to ensure that anonymous, low-tech payment options like cash survive in the future to avoid excluding people who are not digitally savvy or have other legitimate reasons not to be tracked. When big-tech companies enter US finance or fintech firms aim to build super-apps, we have to ensure that we have lessons from China in mind. Rules must be in place to govern the interconnections between the tech side and the financial side, and also to ensure that conflicts of interest are limited and that risk cannot be hidden or offloaded onto taxpayers or depositors. The US public should demand from our government and our companies that we shake off our complacency and continue to earn our reputation for innovation in technology in finance, striving to improve our financial system—even if that means admitting that we are learning from China as it once learned from us.

Acknowledgments

I am thankful for sage advice and support from so many people who have put me in a position to write and finish this book. Its genesis is thanks to Dan Garon, who back in 2014 urged me to write a book about my front-row seat to China's advances in technology and finance. Earlier but just as crucially, Li Ling convinced me to take the Luce Scholarship to live in Beijing, reasoning that nothing could be better for a young person like me than to learn how China's rise would reshape global finance. He also connected me to Professor Yao Yang at Peking University, who gave me my first academic home in China. Dean Yao also provided a crucial introduction to Wang Haiming, secretary general of the China Finance 40 Forum, who hired me as the first-ever foreigner there, becoming my boss and mentor in Beijing. I cannot thank him enough for supporting me and teaching me so much of what I know about China, even though having a foreigner around in sensitive meetings could be controversial. While I was in China, Professor Huang Yiping and Logan Wright took me under their wings to teach me the particularities of Chinese finance. The Harvard

Kennedy School supported me with a grant to continue my research on the ground in China during graduate school.

Adam Posen, president of the Peterson Institute for International Economics, then gave me an institutional home and ample time to finish the manuscript, and his mentorship helped improve its contribution beyond a narrow niche to touch on more profound issues of finance and technology. I could not ask for a more supportive, collegial, or knowledgeable colleague than Nick Lardy, whose books I devoured while in China and whose advice has been crucial to my career. Steve Weisman helped me turn a sea of ideas into a cogent book, regularly helping get me unstuck. My agent, Rafe Sagalyn, skillfully helped me package an academic manuscript into an idea for a more popular book. Feedback from and conversations with John Mahaney, my editor, brought the book across the finish line with immense improvement to each draft thanks to his discerning eye.

Others whose advice I deeply appreciate include Adil Ababou, Peter Agree, Usman Ahmed, Kelvin Chen, Josh Freedman, Joe Gagnon, Julian Gewirtz, Robert Greene, Chad Harper, He Dong, Patrick Honohan, Huang Tianlei, Simon Johnson, Scott Kennedy, Asim Khwaja, Mary Lovely, Rory Macfarquhar, Amaad Mahmoud, Dinny McMahon, Paul Mozur, Marcus Noland, Simon Rabinovitch, Samm Sacks, Ted Truman, Eitan Urkowitz, Nicolas Veron, Michael Walton, Paul Watkins, Graham Webster, Yiping Huang, David Zou, and many Chinese friends who are best not named in the current climate. Thank you to my father for encouraging me to live and study abroad, my mother for nourishing my love of books, and my uncle Daniel for inspiring me to learn new languages and cultures. I also thank Huckleberry Cheesecake, the day care for my two children that has made it possible for me to finish this book.

Notes

Introduction

1. John Engen, "Lessons from a Mobile Payments Revolution," *American Banker*, 2018, www.americanbanker.com/news/why-chinas-mobile-payments -revolution-matters-for-us-bankers.

1. The Rise of the Super-apps

1. Zhou Xiaochuan, 金融基础设施, 科技创新与政策响应—周小川有 关讲座汇编 [A collection of Zhou Xiaochuan's lectures on financial infrastructure, technology innovation, and policy responses] (Beijing: China Financial Publishing), 10.

2. World Bank data show China's GDP per capita at $156 in current USD in 1978, compared to $496 in sub-Saharan Africa. https://data.worldbank.org /indicator/NY.GDP.PCAP.CD?locations=CN-ZG.

3. Yuen Yuen Ang, *How China Escaped the Poverty Trap* (Ithaca, NY: Cornell University Press, 2016), 17.

4. Sebastian Heilmann, "Policy Experimentation in China's Economic Rise," *Studies in Comparative International Development* 43 (2008): 9, http://citeseerx .ist.psu.edu/viewdoc/download?doi=10.1.1.1023.3162&rep=rep1&type=pdf.

5. Chaowen Li, "马化腾：模仿是最妥的创新" [Ma Huateng: Imitation is the most dependable innovation], *Daily Economic News*, August 25, 2010, https:// tech.china.com/zh_cn/news/net/domestic/11066127/20100825/16102912.html.

6. Xiaobo Wu, 腾讯传1998–2016: 中国互联网公司进化论 [Tencent biography 1998–2016: Theory of evolution of China's internet company] (Hangzhou: Zhejiang University Press, 2017), 39.

7. Wu, *Tencent Biography*, 45.

8. Wu, 50. World Bank data on GDP per capita in today's dollars.

9. Wu, 51.

10. Wu, 75.

11. Duncan Clark, *Alibaba: The House That Jack Ma Built* (New York: Ecco, 2016), loc. 2155, Kindle.

12. Wu, *Tencent Biography*, 85.

13. China's National Bureau of Statistics lists per capita annual net income of 6,280 RMB in 2000, when the exchange rate was 8.28 RMB per USD. See www.stats.gov.cn/english/statisticaldata/yearlydata/YB2001e/ml/indexE.htm. The estimate for China, based on Chinese data, is close to the World Bank's calculation for net national income per capita of $817 in 2000, which is used for comparison purposes. See https://data.worldbank.org/indicator/NY.ADJ .NNTY.PC.CD?locations=CN&most_recent_value_desc=false.

14. Wu, *Tencent Biography*, 120.

15. Quoted in Wu, 120.

16. China UnionPay, "China UnionPay Established in Shanghai," 2002, https://web.archive.org/web/20170630140149/http://en.unionpay.com/news /newsroom/file_2653330.html.

17. H. Asher Bolande, "China Unveils a Bold Plan to Boost Its Wireless Sector," *Wall Street Journal*, April 25, 2001, www.wsj.com/articles/SB988 151752939479820.

18. In 2020 Apple created a program that charges 15 percent commissions for small businesses that earn less than one million USD per year, and Google followed suit in 2021. The 30 percent fee still applies to developers making more. See Chaim Gartenberg, "Google Will Reduce Play Store Cut to 15 Percent for a Developer's First $1M in Annual Revenue," *Verge*, March 16, 2021, www.theverge.com/2021/3/16/22333777/google-play-store-fee-reduction -developers-1-million-dollars.

19. Wu, *Tencent Biography*.

20. Edward Castronova, "Virtual Worlds: A First-Hand Account of Market and Society on the Cyberian Frontier," *SSRN*, January 14, 2002, https://papers .ssrn.com/sol3/papers.cfm?abstract_id=294828.

21. Tencent Holdings, *Annual Report 2007*, March 19, 2008, 91, http://cdc -tencent-com-1258344706.image.myqcloud.com/storage/uploads/2019/11/09 /bed5cd0ddbbab97a39eea9cb1308e725.pdf.

22. China Internet Network Information Center, "The Internet Timeline of China 2004–2006," September 4, 2012, https://cnnic.com.cn/IDR/hlwfzdsj /201209/t20120904_36017.htm.

23. Rates vary, but with Square, commonly used by small merchants, an online transaction incurs a 30-cent fee plus 2.9 percent of the transaction amount. See Meredith Galante, "What Is a Card-Not-Present (CNP) Transaction and Why It Costs More," Square, December 26, 2017, https://squareup.com/us/en /townsquare/what-is-a-card-not-present-transaction.

24. Xing Wang and Shanshan Wang, "Virtual Money Poses a Real Threat," *China Daily*, December 26, 2006, accessed March 8, 2018, www.chinadaily .com.cn/china/2006-12/26/content_767335.htm.

25. Virtual Economy Research Network, "The Q Coin Secondary Market in Practice—with Screenshots," *Virtual Economy Research Network Blog*, April 27, 2007, accessed March 8, 2018, https://virtualeconomyresearchnetwork.word press.com/2007/04/27/the_q_coin_secondary_market_in.

26. Virtual Economy Research Network, "The Q Coin Secondary Market in Practice."

27. Geoffrey Fowler and Juying Qin, "QQ: China's New Coin of the Realm?," *Wall Street Journal*, March 30, 2007, www.wsj.com/articles/SB11 7519670114653518.

28. Clark, *Alibaba*, loc. 1953.

29. Clark, loc. 1388. The quotation that Ma later admitted to making up was "The Internet will change every aspect of human beings' lives," although Ma claimed that "I believed that Bill Gates would definitely say it one day."

30. Clark, loc. 1880.

31. Lucy Peng, "Injecting New Ideas into Business Models: Duncan Clark Interview with Lucy Peng," *Youku*, Stanford Business School, September 28, 2012, https://v.youku.com/v_show/id_XNjEyMDg1MzAw.html?spm=a2h0k .8191407.0.0&from=s1.8-1-1.2.

32. William Barnett and Peter Lorentzen, "EachNet.com," Stanford Business School, 2006, www.gsb.stanford.edu/faculty-research/case-studies/each netcom.

33. Wei Lian, Hui Bian, Xianghui Su, and Pengcheng Cao, 蚂蚁金服:从支付宝-到新金融生态圈 [Ant Financial: From Alipay to a new financial ecosphere] (Beijing: China Renmin University Press, 2017), 24.

34. "ICBC, Alibaba Combine Strengths to Advance Digital Business Development" [工行、阿里巴巴双强联手，共推电子商务发展], Industrial and Commercial Bank of China, May 26, 2006, www.icbc.com.cn/icbc/gxk_1/5257 .htm.

35. Zhang Ran, "More Logging On to Internet Banking," *China Daily*, December 14, 2007, www.chinadaily.com.cn/bizchina/2007-12/14/content_63212 56.htm.

36. Alibaba Group, "Alibaba Group and China Post Sign Cooperation Agreement," November 22, 2006, www.alibabagroup.com/en/news/press_pdf/ p061122.pdf.

37. Quoted in Clark, *Alibaba*, loc. 2760.

38. Xi You, 蚂蚁金服：科技金融独角兽的崛起 [Ant Financial: The emergence of a techfin unicorn] (Beijing: China Citic Press, 2017), Chapter 1.

39. Lian et al., *Ant Financial*, 28.

40. Lian et al., 29.

41. Jerome Cohen, "Written Statement to the Congressional-Executive Committee on China," September 20, 2006, https://scholarship.law.upenn.edu/cgi/viewcontent.cgi?article=1017&context=ealr.

42. World Bank and People's Bank of China, "Toward Universal Financial Inclusion in China: Models, Challenges, and Global Lessons," 2018, https://openknowledge.worldbank.org/handle/10986/29336.

43. State Council of the People's Republic of China, "国务院办公厅关于加快电子商务发展的若干意见" [State Council General Office opinions on how to accelerate e-commerce's development], January 8, 2005, www.gov.cn/gongbao/content/2005/content_63341.htm.

44. People's Bank of China, "A PBC Official Answers Questions of Reporters on the E-payment Guidance (No. 1)," October 26, 2005, https://web.archive.org/web/20051230034447/http://www.pbc.gov.cn/english/detail.asp?col=6400&id=611.

45. Mao Linsheng, "Mao Linsheng Sends a Message to Alibaba Workers," Hangzhou Municipal Government, May 8, 2003, www.hangzhou.gov.cn/art/2003/6/4/art_812381_266561.html; Shujie Leng, "'Be in Love with Them, but Don't Marry Them': How Jack Ma Partnered with Local Government to Make E-commerce Giant Alibaba, and Hangzhou, a Success," *Foreign Policy*, October 31, 2014, https://foreignpolicy.com/2014/10/31/be-in-love-with-them-but-dont-marry-them.

46. Barry Naughton, "The Rise of China's Industrial Policy 1978 to 2020," Universidad Nacional Autónoma de México, 2021, https://dusselpeters.com/CECHIMEX/Naughton2021_Industrial_Policy_in_China_CECHIMEX.pdf.

47. Julie Bick, "When PayPal Becomes the Back Office, Too," *New York Times*, December 18, 2005, www.nytimes.com/2005/12/18/business/yourmoney/when-paypal-becomes-the-back-office-too.html.

48. Quoted in "Standing Up to a Giant," *Forbes*, April 25, 2005, www.forbes.com/global/2005/0425/030.html#bc35a1916b3a.

49. Quoted in Clark, *Alibaba*, loc. 265.

50. Clark, loc. 226.

51. Clark, loc. 236–238.

52. Keith Bradsher, "For eBay, It's About Political Connections in China," *New York Times*, December 22, 2006, www.nytimes.com/2006/12/22/technology/22ebay.html.

53. "New Alipay Service Speeds E-pay," Alizila, April 9, 2011, www.alizila.com/new-alipay-service-speeds-e-pay.

54. Asli Demirgüç-Kunt, Leora Klapper, Dorothe Singer, Saniya Ansar, and Jake Hess, *The Global Findex Database 2017: Measuring Financial Inclusion and the Fintech Revolution* (Washington, DC: World Bank, 2018).

55. You, *Ant Financial*, Chapter 5.

56. You, Chapter 5.

57. World Bank and People's Bank of China, "Toward Universal Financial Inclusion in China."

58. "CCTV Exposes Behind the Scenes Promoters of Online Gambling, Many Payment Companies Implicated" [央视揭网络赌博幕后推手多家支付公司染指], China Central Television, July 13, 2010, https://tech.qq.com/a/20100713/000196_1.htm.

59. Quoted in Jialin Zhu, "Alipay, Dedicate to the Government or to the People? This Never Was a Dilemma," *Technode China*, October 16, 2014, https://cn.technode.com/post/2014-10-16/alipay-nation-people-dilemma.

60. Clark, *Alibaba*, loc. 3472.

61. Qingmin Yan and Jianhua Li, *Regulating China's Shadow Banks* (Beijing: China Renmin University Press, 2014), 153.

62. Paul Mozur, "Alibaba Unveils Wall of Shame for Deadbeat Borrowers," *Wall Street Journal*, July 12, 2013, https://blogs.wsj.com/chinarealtime/2013/07/12/alibaba-unveils-wall-of-shame-for-deadbeat-borrowers.

63. Quoted in Porter Erisman, "'We're Going to War': The Inside Story of How Jack Ma Took on eBay with Taobao," *Tech in Asia*, July 30, 2018, www.techinasia.com/were-war-story-jack-ma-ebay-taobao.

64. "The Internet Timeline of China (2012)," China Internet Network Information Center, May 8, 2013, https://cnnic.com.cn/IDR/hlwfzdsj/201305/t20130508_39415.htm.

65. "Stellar Growth Sees China Take 27% of Global Smart Phone Shipments, Powered by Domestic Vendors," Canalys, August 2, 2012, www.canalys.com/newsroom/stellar-growth-sees-china-take-27-global-smart-phone-shipments-powered-domestic-vendors.

2. Repression Ripe for a Revolution

1. For a history of China's financial system until 1990, see Nicholas Lardy, *China's Unfinished Economic Revolution* (Washington, DC: Brookings Institution Press, 1998). For most of the 2000s, see Carl Walter and Fraser Howie, *Red Capitalism: The Fragile Financial Foundation of China's Extraordinary Rise* (Singapore: Wiley, 2010).

2. Barry Naughton, "Economic Policy After the 16th Party Congress," *China Leadership Monitor* 5 (Winter 2003), www.hoover.org/sites/default/files/uploads/documents/clm5_bn.pdf.

3. Henry Paulson, *Dealing with China: An Insider Unmasks the New Economic Superpower* (London: Headline, 2015).

4. Julian Gewirtz, *Unlikely Partners: Chinese Reformers, Western Economists, and the Making of Global China* (Cambridge, MA: Harvard University Press, 2017).

5. Sebastian Heilmann, "Regulatory Innovation by Leninist Means: Communist Party Supervision in China's Financial Industry," *China Quarterly* 181 (2005): 1–21, doi:10.1017/S0305741005000019.

6. Victor Shih, *Factions and Finance in China: Elite Conflict and Inflation* (Cambridge: Cambridge University Press, 2009).

7. Lardy, *China's Unfinished Economic Revolution*; World Bank, "Bank Non-performing Loans to Gross Loans for United States," retrieved from FRED, Federal Reserve Bank of St. Louis, https://fred.stlouisfed.org/series /DDSI02USA156NWDB.

8. Quoted in "ICBC and Goldman Sachs Start Their Strategic Cooperation," Industrial and Commercial Bank of China, March 22, 2006, www.icbc.com.cn /icbc/icbc%20news/icbc%20and%20goldman%20sachs%20start%20their%20 strategic%20cooperation.htm.

9. Quoted in Richard McGregor, *The Party: The Secret World of China's Communist Rulers* (New York: Harper Perennial, 2010), loc. 1368, Kindle.

10. McGregor, *The Party*, loc. 1376.

11. Paulson, *Dealing with China*, 140–142.

12. McGregor, *The Party*, loc. 1402.

13. "China Crashes Its Stockmarket with Circuit-Breakers Meant to Save It," *Economist*, January 7, 2016, www.economist.com/free-exchange/2016/01/07 /china-crashes-its-stockmarket-with-circuit-breakers-meant-to-save-it.

14. Author's calculations based on PBOC and Tianhong data. Accessed through Wind Terminal and Federal Reserve Economic Data.

15. Emily Perry and Florian Weltewitz, "Wealth Management Products in China," *Reserve Bank of Australia Bulletin*, June 2015, www.rba.gov.au/publi cations/bulletin/2015/jun/pdf/bu-0615-7.pdf.

16. Author's calculations based on China Banking Regulatory Commission, *2012 Annual Report*, Beijing, April 23, 2013, 26, 46.

17. World Bank, "China Enterprise Survey 2012," www.enterprisesurveys .org/content/dam/enterprisesurveys/documents/country-profiles/China -2012.pdf.

18. Nicholas Lardy, *Markets over Mao: The Rise of Private Business in China* (Washington, DC: Peterson Institute for International Economics, 2014), 109, 112.

19. Author calculations based on PBOC data on sources and uses of funds of financial institutions. Accessed through Wind Terminal.

20. Demirgüç-Kunt et al., *Global Findex Database 2017*.

21. Akos Rona-Tas and Alya Guseva, *Plastic Money: Constructing Markets for Credit Cards in Eight Postcommunist Countries* (Palo Alto, CA: Stanford University Press, 2014), 220.

22. People's Bank of China, "中国支付体系发展报告2012（中英文）" [China payment system development report 2012], www.pbc.gov.cn/zhifujie suansi/128525/128545/128646/2813132/index.html.

23. Rona-Tas and Guseva, *Plastic Money*, 219.

24. Jerry Hausman, Jeffrey Yuhu, and Xinju Zhang, "Economic Analysis of Wireless Point of Sale Payment in China," Center for eBusiness at MIT paper 212, 2004, http://ebusiness.mit.edu/research/papers/212_JHausman_ChinaE Payment.pdf.

25. Joe Nocera, *A Piece of the Action: How the Middle Class Joined the Money Class* (New York: Simon and Schuster, 1994), 25, 27.

26. Qingmin Yan and Jianhua Li, *Regulating China's Shadow Banks* (New York: Routledge, 2016), Chapter 2.

27. Kellee Tsai, "Review: The State of China's Economic Miracle," *Asia Policy* 20 (July 2015): 144-148, www.jstor.org/stable/24905073.

28. Li Gan, "Findings from China Household Finance Survey," January 2013, http://people.tamu.edu/~ganli/Report-English-Dec-2013.pdf.

29. Shuxia Jiang, "The Evolution of Informal Finance in China and Its Prospects," in *Informal Finance in China: American and Chinese Perspectives*, ed. Jianjun Li and Sara Hsu (New York: Oxford University Press, 2009), 22.

30. Yan and Li, *Regulating China's Shadow Banks*, 160.

31. Hanming Fang and Rongzhu Ke, "The Insurance Role of ROSCA in the Presence of Credit Markets: Theory and Evidence," working paper, November 23, 2006, citeseerx.ist.psu.edu/viewdoc/download?doi=10.1.1.405 .1998&rep=rep1&type=pdf.

32. Keith Bradsher, "Informal Lenders in China Pose Risks to Banking System," *New York Times*, November 9, 2004, www.nytimes.com/2004/11/09 /business/worldbusiness/informal-lenders-in-china-pose-risks-to-banking.html.

33. Kellee Tsai, *Back-Alley Banking: Private Entrepreneurs in China* (Ithaca, NY: Cornell University Press, 2002), 213.

34. Nicholas Lardy and Nicholas Borst, "A Blueprint for Rebalancing China's Economy," Peterson Institute for International Economics Policy Brief 13-02, February 2013, www.piie.com/publications/pb/pb13-2.pdf.

35. Quoted in "China's Wen Urges Breakup of Bank Monopoly as Growth Slows," Reuters, April 3, 2012, www.reuters.com/article/us-china-banks /chinas-wen-urges-breakup-of-bank-monopoly-as-growth-slows-idUSBRE 83211C20120404.

36. People's Bank of China, "人民银行关于印发《关于中国支付体系发展（2011-2015年）的指导意见》的通知" [People's Bank of China publishes notice on "guiding opinions on China's payment system development (2011-2015)"], January 5, 2012, www.gov.cn/gongbao/content/2012/content _2163591.htm.

37. Quoted in Xiu Wen, Yuzhe Zhang, Tao Zhang, and Weifeng Ni, "Counting Down to the End of Unionpay's Monopoly" [终结银联垄断倒计时],

Caixin, July 23, 2012, http://magazine.caixin.com/2012-07-20/100413146.html ?p0#page2.

38. World Trade Organization, "China—Certain Measures Affecting Electronic Payment Services," Dispute Settlement Case DS413, www.wto.org/english/tratop_e/dispu_e/cases_e/ds413_e.htm.

39. Quoted in Wansheng Guo, 奔腾年代：互联网与中国: *1995-2018* [Surging period: The internet and China 1995-2018] (Beijing: Citic Press, 2018), 333.

40. Quoted in Huateng Ma, "An Appeal from Delegate Ma Huateng: Make Internet Development a Major National Development Policy," March 12, 2013, www.gov.cn/2013lh/content_2352207.htm.

41. Li Keqiang, "Report on the Work of the Government," March 5, 2014, 18, http://online.wsj.com/public/resources/documents/2014GovtWorkReport _Eng.pdf.

42. Guo, *Surging Period*, 346.

43. Zhou Xiaochuan, "Interview with Phoenix Technology," March 14, 2013, http://people.techweb.com.cn/2013-03-14/1282824.shtml.

44. People's Bank of China, "全面落实金融业信息化"十二五"发展规划 着力提升人民银行科技服务水平" [Comprehensively implement financial sector informatization "12th five-year plan" development plan, try to raise PBOC technical service level], February 23, 2012, www.pbc.gov.cn/kejisi /146812/146814/2858211/index.html.

3. Fintech Brings Financial Freedom

1. "Fintech Adoption Index 2017," EY Global Financial Services, www .ey.com/Publication/vwLUAssets/ey-fintech-adoption-index-2017/%24FILE /ey-fintech-adoption-index-2017.pdf.

2. Dan Breznitz and Michael Murphree, *Run of the Red Queen: Government, Innovation, Globalization, and Economic Growth in China* (New Haven, CT: Yale University Press, 2011), 4.

3. C. Custer, "Alipay Says Wireless Payments Up 546% in 2012," *TechInAsia*, January 15, 2013, www.techinasia.com/alipay-wireless-payments-546-2012.

4. Quoted in You, *Ant Financial*, Chapter 8.

5. You, Chapter 8.

6. Jamil Anderlini, "Explosive Growth Pushes Alibaba Online Fund Up Global Rankings," *Financial Times*, March 10, 2014, www.ft.com/content/748 a0cd8-a843-11e3-8ce1-00144feab7de#axzz38MDGQhid.

7. Quoted in Stella Yifan Xie, "Asset Growth in the World's Largest Money-Market Fund Slows Sharply," *Wall Street Journal*, February 5, 2018, www.wsj .com/articles/asset-growth-in-the-worlds-largest-money-market-fund-slows -sharply-1517826603.

8. China Securities Regulatory Commission, "证券投资基金销售管理办法" [Measures for the administration of sales practice of securities investment funds], June 9, 2011, www.csrc.gov.cn/zjhpublic/G00306201/201106/t20110621_196582.htm.

9. Nocera, *A Piece of the Action*, Chapter 4. Unlike in China, government bonds paid a market rate of interest much higher than deposits, but the United States tried to maintain repression by selling bonds only in large amounts that most households could not afford.

10. Guonan Ma and Chang Shu, "Interbank Volatility in China," *BIS Quarterly Review*, September 15, 2013, www.bis.org/publ/qtrpdf/r_qt1309u.htm.

11. Asset Management Association of China, "基金市场数据（2013年05月）" [Fund market data (May 2013)], June 13, 2013, https://web.archive.org/web/20170724190003/https://www.amac.org.cn/tjsj/xysj/jjgssj/384240.shtml.

12. Grace Zhu and Paul Mozur, "Text, Chat, Profit: Tencent Launches Investing on WeChat," *Wall Street Journal*, January 22, 2014, https://blogs.wsj.com/chinarealtime/2014/01/22/text-chat-profit-tencent-launches-investing-on-wechat; Junli Fan, "理财通上线首日吸金8亿（更新）" [Caifutong's first day online takes in 800 million in funds (updated)], *Caixin*, January 22, 2014, http://finance.caixin.com/2014-01-22/100632009.html.

13. Author calculations based on PBC: Resident Outstanding Deposit Balances at Financial Institutions. Accessed through Wind Terminal.

14. Industrial and Commercial Bank of China, *2013 Annual Report*, March 27, 2014, 11, www.icbc-ltd.com/SiteCollectionDocuments/ICBC/Resources/ICBCLTD/download/2014/2013ndbg_h_E.pdf.

15. Jack Ma, "Financial Industry Needs Disruptors," June 21, 2013, *People's Daily*, accessed November 5, 2018, http://cpc.people.com.cn/n/2013/0621/c78779-21920452.html.

16. Michael Forsythe, "Alibaba's I.P.O. Could Be a Bonanza for the Scions of Chinese Leaders," *New York Times*, July 20, 2014, https://dealbook.nytimes.com/2014/07/20/alibabas-i-p-o-could-be-a-bonanza-for-the-scions-of-chinese-leaders.

17. China Securities Regulatory Commission, "证监会：支持'余额宝'等产品市场创新" [CSRC: Support "Yu'E Bao and other products" market innovations], March 28, 2013, www.csrc.gov.cn/pub/zhejiang/xxfw/tzzsyd/201306/t20130628_229840.htm.

18. State Council of the People's Republic of China, "国务院办公厅关于金融支持经济结构调整和转型升级的指导意见" [State Council General Office guiding opinions on finance supporting economic structural adjustment, transformation, and upgrading], July 5, 2017, www.gov.cn/zwgk/2013-07/05/content_2440894.htm.

19. People's Bank of China, *年第二季度中国货币政策执行报告* [2013Q2 China monetary policy implementation report], August 2, 2013, www.pbc.gov.cn/zhengcehuobisi/125207/125227/125957/125991/2869042/index.html.

20. Kai-Fu Lee, *AI Superpowers: China, Silicon Valley, and the New World Order* (Boston: Mariner, 2018), 52.

21. "习近平：实施创新驱动不能等待观望懈怠" [Xi Jinping: Pushing and implementing innovation cannot be done with a laziness or "wait and see"], Xinhua, October 1, 2013, www.xinhuanet.com//politics/2013-10/01/c_117582 862.htm.

22. Qingmin Yan, "银监会副主席阎庆民谈民营银行试点工作" [Banking Regulatory Commission Vice Chairman Yan Qingmin discusses private banking pilot work], China Banking Regulatory Commission, March 11, 2014, www.cbrc.gov.cn/chinese/home/docView/0D1BF9561CE54D2087F2F00 AC889405F.html.

23. "中共中央关于全面深化改革若干重大问题的决定" [Decision of the Central Committee on how to deal with serious issues in comprehensively deepening reform], Xinhua, November 15, 2013, www.gov.cn/jrzg/2013-11/15/ content_2528179.htm.

24. Lingjuan Cao, "外滩金融创新试验区实施细则发布 允许获批企业冠名'外滩'" [Detailed rules implementing the Bund financial innovation experimental area published, permits authorized companies to include "Bund" in their name], *Renmin Ribao*, September 8, 2013, http://politics.people.com .cn/n/2013/0908/c1001-22847176.html.

25. Zhou Xiaochuan, "Interview with *Caijing*," *Caijing*, December 16, 2013, http://misc.caijing.com.cn/chargeFullNews.jsp?id=113695309&time=2013 -12-16&cl=106.

26. Yun Ma, Speech at China Business Leaders Annual Conference, December 7, 2008, http://finance.sina.com.cn/hy/20081207/18215601586.shtml.

27. Patrick Boehler, "Fangs Are Out After Chinese Broadcaster's 'Vampire' Slur on Online Funds," *South China Morning Post*, February 24, 2014, www.scmp.com/news/china-insider/article/1434035/fangs-are-out-after -chinese-broadcasters-vampire-slur-online.

28. David Keohane, "Alibaba and the 40 Cannibals," *FT Alphaville*, March 12, 2014, https://ftalphaville.ft.com/2014/03/12/1798122/alibaba-and -the-40-cannibals.

29. Xueqing Jiang, "Banks Strike Back at Online Financial Startups," *China Daily*, February 11, 2014, www.chinadaily.com.cn/business/2014-02/11 /content_17277806_2.htm.

30. He Wei, "Alipay to Discontinue Offline-Payment Service," *China Daily*, August 28, 2013, http://usa.chinadaily.com.cn/epaper/2013-08/28/content_16 926518.htm.

31. Terri Bradford and Fumiko Hayashi, "Complex Landscapes: Mobile Payments in Japan, South Korea, and the United States," Federal Reserve Bank of Kansas City, 2007, https://pdfs.semanticscholar.org/c07a/5db553474 bf87afdf5ec3dac60bbd43a93b1.pdf.

32. Quoted in Claire Cain Miller, "At Checkout, More Ways to Avoid Cash or Plastic," *New York Times*, November 16, 2009, www.nytimes.com/2009/11/16/technology/start-ups/16wallet.html.

33. Austin Carr, "Google Wallet Creators Reflect on Its Failures, Lessons," *Fast Company*, November 20, 2013, www.fastcompany.com/3021913/google-wallet-creators-reflect-on-its-failures-lessons.

34. Mancy Sun, Piyush Mubayi, Tian Lu, and Stanley Tian, "The Rise of China FinTech," Goldman Sachs Equity Research, August 7, 2017, https://hybg.cebnet.com.cn/upload/gaoshengfintech.pdf.

35. Aaron Klein, "Testimony to the US House Committee on Financial Services Task Force on Financial Technology," January 30, 2020, www.congress.gov/116/meeting/house/110420/witnesses/HHRG-116-BA00-Wstate-KleinA-20200130-U1.pdf.

36. Denso Wave, "History of QR Code," www.qrcode.com/en/history/#:~:text=In%201994%2C%20DENSO%20WAVE%20(then,placed%20on%20high%2Dspeed%20reading; Nicole Jao, "A Short History of the QR Code in China and Why Southeast Asia Is Next," *Technode*, September 20, 2018, https://technode.com/2018/09/10/qr-code-payment-overseas-china.

37. Roy Furchgott, "From Starbucks, Coffee from the Future," *New York Times*, September 23, 2009, https://gadgetwise.blogs.nytimes.com/2009/09/23/from-starbucks-coffee-from-the-future.

38. "Alipay Introduces a Mobile Wallet App," Alizila, January 18, 2013, www.alizila.com/alipay-introduces-a-mobile-wallet-app; Tracey Xiang, "[Updated] Alipay Beta-Testing New Mobile Financial Service, More Than a Passbook Clone," *Technode*, December 10, 2012, https://technode.com/2012/12/10/alipay-beta-testing-new-mobile-financial-service; Xiang, "Alipay App Has a Major Update Again, Wants More Control over Your Mobile Life," *Technode*, June 8, 2013, https://technode.com/2013/06/08/alipay-app-has-a-major-update-again-wants-more-control-over-your-mobile-life.

39. Li Tao, "Former Tokyo-Based Engineer Emerges as Big Winner from China's Love Affair with the QR Code," *South China Morning Post*, August 14, 2018, www.scmp.com/tech/article/2159452/former-tokyo-based-engineer-emerges-big-winner-chinas-love-affair-qr-code.

40. You, *Ant Financial*, Chapter 9.

41. Francis Tan, "Tencent Launches Kik-Like Messaging App in China," *Next Web*, January 21, 2011, accessed November 7, 2018, https://thenextweb.com/asia/2011/01/21/tencent-launches-kik-like-messaging-app-in-china.

42. Lee, *AI Superpowers*.

43. Steven Millward, "7 Years of WeChat," *TechInAsia*, January 20, 2018, www.techinasia.com/history-of-wechat.

44. You, *Ant Financial*, Chapter 9.

45. Quoted in Chen Tian, "WeChat Challenges Alipay," *Global Times*, February 11, 2014, accessed November 12, 2018, www.globaltimes.cn/content /841861.shtml.

46. You, *Ant Financial*, Chapter 9.

47. Tracey Xiang, "WeChat Creates a Social Game for Giving Away New Year Lucky Money: WeChat Payment Will Be the Biggest Winner," *Technode*, January 27, 2014, https://technode.com/2014/01/27/wechat-creates-a-social -game-for-giving-away-new-year-lucky-money-wechat-payment-will-be-the -biggest-winner.

48. Jing Meng, "Technology Giants in a Flap over Gift Envelopes," *China Daily*, February 6, 2015, www.chinadaily.com.cn/a/201502/06/WS5a2b5065a 310eefe3e99fa3b.html.

49. "Alipay Spends Big to Promote Online Payment Service," Xinhua, January 23, 2014, www.china.org.cn/china/Off_the_Wire/2014-01-23/content _31288548.htm.

50. "China Third-Party Mobile Payment GMV Rises to 1.43 Tn Yuan," iResearch, December 15, 2014, www.iresearchchina.com/content/details7 _18384.html; "GMV of China's Third-Party Mobile Payment Market Topped 27 Tn Yuan in Q2," iResearch, October 23, 2017, www.iresearchchina.com /content/details7_37999.html.

51. Quoted in Gillian Wong, "New Version of Alipay App Sparks Privacy Concerns," *Wall Street Journal*, July 14, 2015, https://blogs.wsj.com /chinarealtime/2015/07/15/new-version-of-alipay-app-sparks-privacy-concerns.

52. China Internet Network Information Center, "June 2014 Statistical Report," https://webcache.googleusercontent.com/search?q=cache:SKpLYibIBh4J :https://cnnic.com.cn/IDR/ReportDownloads/201411/P02014110257431 4897888.pdf+&cd=2&hl=en&ct=clnk&gl=hk#17.

53. Demirgüç-Kunt et al., *Global Findex Database 2017*.

54. As Reuters reported in 2015, "Analysts said that much of that money has historically fallen to the bottom line." David Henry, "JPMorgan Uses Its Might to Cut Costs in Credit Card Market," Reuters, September 8, 2015, www.reuters .com/article/us-jpmorganchase-creditcards-insight/jpmorgan-uses-its-might -to-cut-costs-in-credit-card-market-idUSKCN0R80B620150908.

55. JP Morgan Chase, *2019 Annual Report*, 197, www.jpmorganchase.com /corporate/investor-relations/document/annualreport-2019.pdf; ICBC, *2013 Annual Report*, www.icbc-ltd.com/SiteCollectionDocuments/ICBC/Resources /ICBCLTD/download/2014/2013ndbg_h_E.pdf.

56. Demirgüç-Kunt et al., *Global Findex Database 2017*.

57. Wei He, "Alipay to Discontinue Offline-Payment Service," *China Daily*, August 28, 2013, http://usa.chinadaily.com.cn/epaper/2013-08/28/content_169 26518.htm.

58. Lieyunwang, "马云谈四大行封杀支付宝：最艰难最光荣时刻" [Jack Ma says four large banks shut out Alipay, most difficult and glorious time], March 24, 2014, www.lieyunwang.com/archives/37021.

59. Xie Wen and Yuzhe Zhang, "Alipay and UnionPay Battle over How Payments Are Processed," *Caixin Global*, September 6, 2013, www.caixinglobal.com/2013-09-06/alipay-and-unionpay-battle-over-how-payments-are-processed-101014108.html.

60. Jinran Zheng, "Smartphone Users Victims of Scams," *China Daily*, March 16, 2013, www.chinadaily.com.cn/business/2013-04/16/content_16409686_3.htm.

61. "China's Central Bank Mulls Alibaba, Tencent Payment Curbs—State Media," Reuters, March 17, 2014, www.reuters.com/article/us-china-payments/chinas-central-bank-mulls-alibaba-tencent-payment-curbs-state-media-idUSBREA2G12P20140317.

62. Min Qin and Yunxu Qu, "二维码支付安全之争" [The debate on QR code security], *Caixin*, March 24, 2014, http://magazine.caixin.com/2014-03-21/100654599.html.

63. "China Issues Banking Rules to Strengthen Online Payment Security," Reuters, April 18, 2014, www.reuters.com/article/china-banking-internet/china-issues-banking-rules-to-strengthen-online-payment-security-idUSL3N0NA06W20140418.

64. Industrial and Commercial Bank of China, "Industrial and Commercial Bank of China Announces 2013 Results," March 28, 2014, www.icbc.com.cn/icbc/en/newsupdates/icbc%20news/industrialandcommercialbankofchinaannounces2013results.htm.

65. Juro Osawa and Ken Brown, "New Alibaba CEO Jonathan Lu Pushes Chinese E-commerce Firm to Adapt," *Wall Street Journal*, July 10, 2013, www.wsj.com/articles/SB10001424127887323823004578595083736296600.

66. Jack Ma, "让信用等于财富" [Make credit equal wealth], September 12, 2012, *Sina Tech*, accessed February 19, 2019, http://tech.sina.com.cn/i/2012-09-12/13477609753.shtml.

67. Jonathan Shaw, "Why 'Big Data' Is a Big Deal," *Harvard Magazine*, March–April 2014, accessed February 12, 2019, https://harvardmagazine.com/2014/03/why-big-data-is-a-big-deal.

68. Tracey Xiang, "Alibaba's Finance Arm to Launch User Data-Based Credit Scoring System Sesame," *Technode*, October 28, 2014, https://technode.com/2014/10/28/alibabas-sesame-credit-scoring-system.

69. Alibaba Group, "Ant Financial Unveils China's First Credit-Scoring System Using Online Data," January 28, 2015, accessed February 6, 2019, www.alibabagroup.com/en/news/article?news=p150128.

70. Xiaoxiao Li, "Ant Financial Subsidiary Starts Offering Individual Credit Scores," *Caixin Global*, March 2, 2015, accessed February 13, 2019, www.caixinglobal.com/2015-03-02/101012655.html.

71. Alibaba Group, "Ant Financial Unveils China's First Credit-Scoring System Using Online Data."

72. Ta Licai, "支付宝芝麻信用750可走安检专用通道" [Alipay Sesame Credit 750 can go through dedicated security check], *Douban*, September 21, 2015, accessed February 15, 2019, www.douban.com/note/517804916; Fast Science and Technology, "芝麻信用首推"大学生信用节"" [Sesame Credit first promotion of "University Students' Credit Day"], September 9, 2015, accessed February 15, 2019, https://news.mydrivers.com/1/446/446185.htm.

73. Charles Clover, "China P2P Lender Banks on Social Media Usage," *Financial Times*, August 30, 2015, accessed February 19, 2019, www.ft.com /content/673d9608-4d83-11e5-b558-8a9722977189.

74. Quoted in Eva Xiao, "Tencent's New Credit System to Use Payments, Social Data," *TechInAsia*, January 31, 2018, accessed February 19, 2019, www .techinasia.com/tencent-credit-launch.

75. Qun Hu, "8机构等待19个月 个人征信牌照为何一证难求" [How can eight institutions wait 19 months for individual credit evaluation licenses —proof of difficulty to request], *Economic Observer*, July 31, 2016, accessed February 20, 2019, http://m.eeo.com.cn/2016/0731/290369.shtml.

76. Jing Meng, "Tencent to Use Social Networks for Credit-Rating Services," *China Daily*, August 8, 2015, accessed February 19, 2019, www .chinadaily.com.cn/business/tech/2015-08/08/content_21535587.htm; Ling Wu, "腾讯也有了信用分，除了免押金骑摩拜还能干什么？" [Tencent now has credit points too, other than shared bikes without a deposit, what else can you do with it?], *Sohu Tech*, August 7, 2017, accessed February 19, 2019, www .sohu.com/a/162878300_114778.

77. Quoted in Gabriel Wildau, "Tencent Launches China's First Online-Only Bank," *Financial Times*, January 4, 2015, accessed February 20, 2019, www.ft.com/content/ccc5a6dc-9488-11e4-82c7-00144feabdc0.

78. China Banking Regulatory Commission, "11家民营银行已获批建 银监会:首批整体运行审慎稳健" [11 privately operated banks already been approved for establishment: First complete prudential operating report], December 9, 2016, www.cbrc.gov.cn/chinese/home/docView/49A00896C4C24 C0D8EC5AE8212BBBD9A.html.

79. Tracey Xiang, "Online Offerings Are Shaping the Future of China's Consumer Credit Market," *Technode*, November 19, 2015, https://technode .com/2015/11/19/online-offerings-are-shaping-the-future-of-chinas-consumer -credit-market.

80. Wei He, "Ant Financial Extends Online Credit Service to Retailers," *China Daily*, June 9, 2017, www.chinadaily.com.cn/business/2017-06/09/con tent_29678804.htm.

81. WeBank, "微众银行年报披露：累计发放贷款逾200亿" [WeBank publishes annual report: Cumulative loans issued exceeds 20 billion], March 30, 2016, www.webank.com/announcement/mediareport-detail09.html.

82. WeChat, "The 2016 WeChat Data Report," December 29, 2016, https://blog.wechat.com/2016/12/29/the-2016-wechat-data-report.

83. CB Insights, "Disrupting Banking: The Fintech Startups That Are Unbundling Wells Fargo, Citi and Bank of America," November 19, 2015, www.cbinsights.com/research/disrupting-banking-fintech-startups.

84. Quoted in Xin Fu, Yifan He, and Jing Yang, "马明哲豪言做金融界天猫要求舍弃传统金融路径" [Ma Mingzhe's grand word: To become finance's Tmall requires giving up the traditional methods of finance], *Entrepreneur*, December 25, 2013, http://finance.sina.com.cn/360desktop/money/insurance/bxyx/20131225/141917747378.shtml.

4. A Fintech Wild West

1. Bai Yang and Chen Ji, "e租宝"非法集资案真相调查" [Investigating the truth of the Ezubao illegal financing case], Xinhua, January 31, 2016, accessed February 4, 2019, www.chinacourt.org/article/detail/2016/01/id/1801878.shtml.

2. Benoît Cœuré, "Financial Regulation and Innovation: A Two-Way Street," speech at a Finleap roundtable, March 14, 2018, www.ecb.europa.eu/press/key/date/2018/html/ecb.sp180314.en.html.

3. I recommend *Digital Gold*, by Nathaniel Popper, for those who want to go deeper into an overview of Bitcoin and its early history. See Popper, *Digital Gold: Bitcoin and the Inside Story of the Misfits and Millionaires Trying to Reinvent Money* (New York: Harper Paperbacks, 2016), 256.

4. Sourceforge, "Download Statistics," https://sourceforge.net/projects/bitcoin/files/stats/map?dates=2013-04-01+to+2013-04-30.

5. Michael Bedford Taylor, "The Evolution of Bitcoin Hardware," *Computer*, 2017, https://cseweb.ucsd.edu/~mbtaylor/papers/Taylor_Bitcoin_IEEE_Computer_2017.pdf.

6. Adrianne Jeffries, "FTC Shuts Down Butterfly Labs, the Second-Most Hated Company in Bitcoinland," *Verge*, September 23, 2014, www.theverge.com/2014/9/23/6833047/bitcoin-conspiracy-theorists-vindicated-as-ftc-shuts-down-butterfly-labs.

7. The first part of the documentary can be viewed at www.youtube.com/watch?v=aw3OSTkdE-s.

8. Popper, *Digital Gold*, 263; Zennon Kapron, *Chomping at the Bitcoin: The Past, Present, and Future of Bitcoin in China* (Melbourne, Australia: Penguin Specials, 2014).

9. Kapron, *Chomping at the Bitcoin*.

10. Kapron.

11. Ju Lan, Timothy Lu, and Zhiyong Tu, "Capital Flight and Bitcoin Regulation," *International Review of Finance* 16, no. 3 (2015): 445–455, doi:10.1111/irfi.12072.

12. LendingClub called itself a "marketplace lender" rather than a P2P. By the time of its IPO, many of its investors were institutions.

13. Bryan Zhang, Luke Deer, Robert Wardrop, Andrew Grant, Kieran Garvey, Susan Thorp, Tania Ziegler, Kong Ying, Zheng Xinwei, Eva Huang, John Burton, Hung-Yi Chen, Alexis Lui, and Yvonne Gray, "Harnessing Potential: The Asia-Pacific Alternative Finance Benchmarking Report," Cambridge Center for Alternative Finance, March 2016, 19, www.jbs.cam.ac.uk/fileadmin /user_upload/research/centres/alternative-finance/downloads/harnessing -potential.pdf; Robert Wardrop, Robert Rosenberg, Bryan Zhang, Tania Ziegler, Rob Squire, John Burton, Eduardo Arenas Hernandez Jr., and Kieran Garvey, "Breaking New Ground: The Americas Alternative Finance Benchmarking Report," Cambridge Center for Alternative Finance, April 2016, 19, www.jbs. cam.ac.uk/fileadmin/user_upload/research/centres/alternative-finance/down loads/2016-americas-alternative-finance-benchmarking-report.pdf.

14. KPMG, "The Pulse of Fintech Q4 2016," February 21, 2017, https:// assets.kpmg/content/dam/kpmg/xx/pdf/2017/02/pulse-of-fintech-q4-2016 .pdf.

15. Ping An, *2012 Annual Report*, http://doc.irasia.com//listco/hk/pingan /annual/ar106101-e_101.pdf.

16. Ping An, "A Profile of Lufax," June 24, 2014, http://resources.pingan .com/app_upload/file/ir/c261968d105847e98718f3be809ed880.pdf; Kane Wu, "Ping An–Backed Lufax Raises $1.3 Billion at Lower Valuation: Sources," Reuters, December 3, 2018, www.reuters.com/article/us-lufax-fundraising/ping-an -backed-lufax-raises-1-3-billion-at-lower-valuation-sources-idUSKBN1O20HG.

17. Kwong Man-ki, "Lufax Rides Internet Finance Boom," *South China Morning Post*, April 12, 2015, www.scmp.com/business/companies/article/1764866/ lufax-rides-internet-finance-boom.

18. Xiaoxiao Li and Lu Yang, "Central Bank Raises the Red Flag over P2P Lending Risks," *Caixin Global*, July 4, 2013, www.caixinglobal.com/2013-07-04 /101014280.html.

19. Quoted in Frank Tang, "Why Ponzi Schemes Are Thriving in China Despite Crackdowns," *South China Morning Post*, July 25, 2017, www.scmp .com/news/china/money-wealth/article/2104062/chinese-ponzi-schemes -feed-publics-lack-financial-knowledge.

20. Logan Wright and Daniel Rosen, "Credit and Credibility: Risks to China's Economic Resilience," Center for Strategic and International Studies, https:// csis-website-prod.s3.amazonaws.com/s3fs-public/publication/181003_Credit andCredibility_final.PDF?_WNS0vtP_qsWMtScnNdT.wxxnyEd1pUf.

21. Quoted in "Some Chinese Are Taking 22% Margin Loans to Finance Stock Purchases," *Bloomberg News*, June 30, 2015, accessed January 28, 2019, www.bloomberg.com/news/articles/2015-06-30/hidden-china-stock-debt -revealed-in-online-loans-at-22-interest.

22. Chuin-Wei Yap, "China Crackdown on Margin Lending Hits Peer-to-Peer Lenders," *Wall Street Journal*, July 13, 2015, accessed January 30, 2019, www.wsj.com/articles/china-crackdown-on-margin-lending-hits-peer-to-peer-lenders-1436789145?mod=article_inline.

23. For more background, see Jiangze Bian, Zhiguo He, Kelly Shue, and Hao Zhou, "Leverage-Induced Fire Sales and Stock Market Crashes," National Bureau of Economic Research Working Paper 25040, September 2018, accessed January 30, 2019, www.nber.org/papers/w25040.pdf.

24. Wright and Rosen, "Credit and Credibility," 85.

25. An investigation by LendingClub's board found that Laplanche had not properly disclosed loans that the company issued to himself and family members. In addition, it found that LendingClub staff had altered loan documents on $3 million in loans to make them appear that they fit the investor's criteria. See Peter Rudegeair, "LendingClub CEO Fired over Faulty Loans," *Wall Street Journal*, May 9, 2016, www.wsj.com/articles/lendingclub-ceo-resigns-over-sales-review-1462795070; and Nathaniel Popper, "LendingClub Founder, Ousted in 2016, Settles Fraud Charges," *New York Times*, September 28, 2018, www.nytimes.com/2018/09/28/technology/lendingclub-renaud-laplanche-fraud.html.

26. Quoted in Lulu Yilun Chen, "Alibaba Arm to Create $163 Billion Loans Marketplace," *Bloomberg News*, September 23, 2014, https://web.archive.org/web/20150708191414/http://www.bloomberg.com/news/articles/2014-09-23/alibaba-arm-aims-to-create-163-billion-loans-marketplace.

27. "中国证监会约束私募债以大拆小套利 阿里'招财宝'模式受限—报载" [Report: CSRC restricts arbitrage of trimming large private debt into small pieces: Alibaba's "Zhaocaibao" model will be constrained], Reuters, September 27, 2015, https://cn.reuters.com/article/csrc-ali-idCNKCS0RS02N20150928.

28. Quoted in James T. Areddy, "A Default in China Spreads Anxiety Among Investors," *Wall Street Journal*, January 27, 2017, www.wsj.com/articles/a-default-in-china-spreads-anxiety-among-investors-1485513181.

29. Xin Zhou, "China's HK$59 Billion Online Ponzi Scheme: Who Started It, How Did It Happen and Now What?," *South China Morning Post*, February 1, 2016, accessed February 5, 2019, www.scmp.com/news/china/money-wealth/article/1908096/chinas-hk59-billion-online-ponzi-scheme-who-started-it-how.

30. "e租宝：100亿融资租赁公司进军P2P" [Ezubao: 10 billion financing leasing company enters the P2P battle], China Economic Net, October 17, 2014, accessed February 5, 2019, http://iof.hexun.com/2014-10-17/169439029.html.

31. Video of the event is available at www.youtube.com/watch?v=WChCzVGQqYE.

32. "e租宝."

33. Quoted in Neil Gough, "Ponzi Scheme in China Gained Credibility from State Media," *New York Times*, February 5, 2016, www.nytimes.com/2016/02/06 /business/dealbook/alleged-china-ponzi-scheme-ezubao.html.

34. Yang and Ji, "e租宝."

35. Rong 360, "2015年网贷评级报告" [2015 Online Lending Ranking Report], accessed February 5, 2019, https://ss0.rong360.com/dl/pdf/wdpj_201502 .pdf; Rong 360, "e租宝被评为C-级 融360发3大风险提示" [Ezubao ranked C– level, Rong 360 issues three major risk warnings], June 6, 2015, www.rong 360.com/gl/2015/06/06/72855.html.

36. Beijing Business Paper Financial Investigation Small Group, "揭e租宝 背后黑洞：涉嫌自融 虚假标的内控不严" [Exposing the black hole behind Ezubao: Self-financing, fake project list, and weak internal controls], June 29, 2015, http://tech.sina.com.cn/i/2015-06-29/doc-ifxemzau8812893.shtml.

37. "Five on Trial Linked to US$7.6b China 'Ponzi Scheme,'" Agence France Presse, November 25, 2016, www.businesstimes.com.sg/banking-finance/five -on-trial-linked-to-us76b-china-ponzi-scheme.

38. "Petitioning Clients of Ezubao P2P Investing Platform Arrested," *EJ Insight*, January 11, 2016, accessed August 1, 2016, www.ejinsight.com /20160111-petitioning-clients-ezubo-p2p-investing-platform-arrested.

39. Quoted in Jennifer Li, "P2P Has a Bright Future, Insists Dianrong Founder, as He Plans IPO Within Two Years," *South China Morning Post*, June 30, 2016, accessed August 8, 2016, www.scmp.com/business/companies/article/1983671 /p2p-has-bright-future-insists-dianrong-founder-he-plans-ipo.

40. Li Keqiang, "Annual Work Report of the Government to the 12th National People's Congress," March 5, 2016, accessed February 25, 2019, www .gov.cn/guowuyuan/2016-03/05/content_5049372.htm.

5. Social Credit and Crackdown on Risk

1. As of late June 2021, according to the *Forbes* real-time billionaires list: www.forbes.com/real-time-billionaires/#8a75f973d788.

2. State Council of the People's Republic of China, "Planning Outline for the Construction of a Social Credit System," trans. Rogier Creemers, June 14, 2014, accessed June 6, 2018, https://chinacopyrightandmedia.word press.com/2014/06/14/planning-outline-for-the-construction-of-a-social -credit-system-2014-2020.

3. Susan Finder, "Supreme People's Court, CSRC, SAIC, and PBOC Tighten the Regulatory Net," *Supreme People's Court Monitor*, December 20, 2014, https://supremepeoplescourtmonitor.com/2014/12/20/supreme-peoples-court -csrc-saic-and-pboc-tighten-the-regulatory-net.

4. Yang Yuan, "China Penalises 6.7m Debtors with Travel Ban," *Financial Times*, February 15, 2017, www.ft.com/content/ceb2a7f0-f350-11e6-8758-6876 151821a6.

5. Yuen-Quan Leung, "Blacklisting Default Debtors," *Tsinghua China Law Review* 2–14 (2014): 135–137, www.tsinghuachinalawreview.org/articles/PDF /TCLR_0601_ChinaLawUpdate.pdf.

6. Shazeda Ahmed, "The Messy Truth About Social Credit," *ChinaFile*, April 22, 2019, www.chinafile.com/reporting-opinion/viewpoint/messy-truth -about-social-credit.

7. Jay Stanley, "China's Nightmarish Citizen Scores Are a Warning for Americans," *ACLU Blog*, October 5, 2015, www.aclu.org/blog/privacy -technology/consumer-privacy/chinas-nightmarish-citizen-scores-are-warning -americans.

8. Karen Chiu, "Even Prisons Accept Mobile Payment in China's Cashless Society," *South China Morning Post*, January 14, 2019, www.abacusnews.com /digital-life/even-prisons-accept-mobile-payment-chinas-cashless-society /article/3000461.

9. Shazeda Ahmed and Bertram Lang, "Central Planning, Local Experiments: The Complex Implementation of China's Social Credit System," Mercator Institute for China Studies, December 12, 2017, accessed on June 14, 2018, www .merics.org/en/report/central-planning-local-experiments.

10. Brianna McGurran, "Can Having More Credit Cards Help Your Credit Score?," *Experian Blog*, May 19, 2021, www.experian.com/blogs/ask-experian /getting-more-credit-cards-to-help-credit-scores.

11. "Humiliating the Big Vs," *Economist*, September 16, 2013, www.econo mist.com/analects/2013/09/16/humiliating-the-big-vs.

12. Bank for International Settlements, "Total Credit to the Non-financial Sector (Core Debt)," Table F1.1, 2021, https://stats.bis.org/statx/srs/table/f1.1.

13. Barry Naughton, "Two Trains Running: Supply-Side Reform, SOE Reform and the Authoritative Personage," *China Leadership Monitor* 50 (2016), www.hoover.org/sites/default/files/research/docs/clm50bn.pdf#overlay -context=publications/china-leadership-monitor.

14. Jingxia Li, "独家丨银监会开展'四不当'专项整治 银行全面自查同 业、理财不当交易" [Exclusive: CBRC unfolds special enforcement action against "four inappropriates," banks must comprehensively self-examine inappropriate transactions in their interbank and wealth management activities], *Yicai*, April 12, 2017, www.yicai.com/news/5265115.html.

15. Quoted in Zen Soo, "TechFin: Jack Ma Coins Term to Set Alipay's Goal to Give Emerging Markets Access to Capital," *South China Morning Post*, December 2, 2016, www.scmp.com/tech/article/2051249/techfin-jack-ma-coins -term-set-alipays-goal-give-emerging-markets-access.

16. Author calculations based on data from Online Lending House and PBOC. Accessed through Wind Terminal.

17. Gabriele Galati and Richhild Moessner, "Macroprudential Policy—a Literature Review," BIS Working Paper 337, February 2011, www.bis.org/publ /work337.pdf.

18. Zhou Xiaochuan, "周小川行长与拉加德总裁问答环节实录" [Transcript of Zhou Xiaochuan and Managing Director Lagarde's question and answer segment], PBOC Communication and Exchange, June 25, 2016, www.pbc.gov.cn/goutongjiaoliu/113456/113469/3090405/index.html.

19. Xiaoqing He, "支清会拟发起成立网联平台 争夺线上支付入口" [Payments and Clearing Association approves establishment of Wanglian platform: Fight over online payment entry], *21st Century Business Herald*, April 14, 2016, https://m.21jingji.com/article/20160414/d9a0e94332f843698b603a168291f8a7.html.

20. Yuzhe Zhang and Timmy Shen, "How China's New Online Payments Clearinghouse Survived 'Double 11,'" *Caixin Global*, November 22, 2018, www.caixinglobal.com/2018-11-22/how-chinas-new-online-payments-clearinghouse-survived-double-11-101350944.html.

21. Ben Norman, Rachel Shaw, and George Speight, "The History of Interbank Settlement Arrangements: Exploring Central Banks' Role in the Payment System," Bank of England Working Paper 412, June 2011, www.ecb.europa.eu/home/pdf/research/Working_Paper_412.pdf.

22. Yi Gang, "Remarks at the BIS Annual General Meeting in Basel," June 30, 2019, YouTube, www.youtube.com/watch?v=KMJDuRWKB5M.

23. Xie Yu, "Tycoon Zhang Zhenxin, Owner of Troubled Chinese Financial Conglomerate UCF Group, Dies Aged 48 as Company Struggles with Mountain of Debt," *South China Morning Post*, October 7, 2019, www.scmp.com/business/companies/article/3031881/tycoon-zhang-zhenxin-owner-troubled-chinese-financial.

24. Gabriel Wildau, "Tencent and Alipay Set to Lose $1bn in Revenue from Payment Rules," *Financial Times*, July 15, 2018, www.ft.com/content/b472f73c-859e-11e8-96dd-fa565ec55929.

25. "Expansion of Yu'e Bao Slows in Q1 After Fund Limits Daily Deposits," *Global Times*, March 23, 2018, www.globaltimes.cn/content/1099298.shtml.

26. People's Bank of China, "2018 Financial Stability Report," November 2, 2018, 78, www.pbc.gov.cn/jinrongwendingju/146766/146772/3656006/index.html.

27. Ping Xie and Chuanwei Zou, "Opinion: Why China Needs Independent Credit Reporting Agencies," *Caixin Global*, February 17, 2017, www.caixinglobal.com/2017-02-17/opinion-why-china-needs-independent-credit-reporting-agencies-101056262.html.

28. Xiao Liu, "Microlenders' Debt Sales Slump as Crackdown Bites," *Caixin Global*, January 10, 2018, www.caixinglobal.com/2018-01-10/microlenders-debt-sales-slump-as-crackdown-bites-101196154.html.

29. "Bitcoin Trading Volume," Bitcoinity, https://data.bitcoinity.org/markets/volume/5y?c=e&t=b. Data are for BTC China, Huobi, and OKCoin. However, much of this volume was likely exaggerated by the free trading offered at the

time, which made it easy to execute fraudulent "wash trades" in which a trader sells assets to itself on the exchange to manipulate prices.

30. People's Bank of China Shanghai Branch, "人民银行上海总部、上海市金融办联合相关监管部门约见上海市比特币交易平台主要负责人" [PBOC Shanghai Headquarters, Shanghai Municipal Finance Office with other regulatory departments arranged an interview with the primary responsible individuals for Shanghai's Bitcoin exchanges], January 6, 2017, https://www.financialnews.com.cn/if/jgzc/201701/t20170107_110760.html.

31. William Suberg, "China: PBOC Says Exchanges 'Violated Rules,' Repeats Investor Warnings," January 18, 2017, *Bitcoinist*, https://bitcoinist.com/china-pboc-exchanges-investor-warning.

32. Matt Levine [@matt_levine], "my explanation is that they're like if the Wright Brothers sold air miles to finance inventing the airplane," Twitter, August 29, 2017, https://twitter.com/matt_levine/status/902617398620168196.

33. Arjun Kharpal, "Initial Coin Offerings Have Raised $1.2 Billion and Now Surpass Early Stage VC Funding," CNBC, August 9, 2017, www.cnbc.com/2017/08/09/initial-coin-offerings-surpass-early-stage-venture-capital-funding.html.

34. Guohui Li, "ICO甚嚣尘上 监管应尽快落地" [ICOs raise a clamor, regulation should land as soon as possible], Xinhua, September 1, 2017, www.xinhuanet.com//fortune/2017-09/01/c_129694158.htm.

35. Jin Yu, Quanhao Wang, and Xing Zhu, "ICO from Start to Bottom: Projects and Teams Are All Fake, Investors Are Betting Later Money Will Hold the Bag," Xinhua, August 27, 2017, www.xinhuanet.com//fortune/2017-08/28/c_1121552253.htm.

36. Shangyue Feng, "Five Billion USD Atmosphere: The History of ICO Craziness," *36Kr*, August 17, 2017, https://36kr.com/p/1721772638209.

37. Yu, Wang, and Zhu, "ICO from Start to Bottom."

38. Li, "ICOs Raise a Clamor."

39. Martin Chorzempa, "Why China Is Cracking Down on Cryptocurrencies and ICOs," *Peterson Institute for International Economics China Economic Watch*, September 15, 2017, https://piie.com/blogs/china-economic-watch/why-china-cracking-down-cryptocurrencies-and-icos#_ftnref5.

40. Qinqin Peng, Yujian Wu, and Wei Han, "China Steps Up Curbs on Virtual Currency Trading," *Caixin Global*, September 9, 2017, accessed March 6, 2019, www.caixinglobal.com/2017-09-09/china-steps-up-curbs-on-virtual-currency-trading-101142821.html.

41. Yi Han and Denise Jia, "China's Central Bank Warns of New Crypto Risks," *Caixin Global*, September 19, 2018, www.caixinglobal.com/2018-09-19/chinas-central-bank-warns-of-new-crypto-risks-101327753.html.

42. Aaron Klein, "Is China's New Payment System the Future?," Brookings Institution, June 2019, 10, www.brookings.edu/wp-content/uploads/2019/06/ES_20190617_Klein_ChinaPayments.pdf.

43. Thomas Graziani, "What Are WeChat Mini-programs? A Simple Introduction," *Walkthechat*, November 6, 2019, https://walkthechat.com/wechat-mini-programs-simple-introduction; Graziani, "Taobao Launches Mini-program to Compete Against WeChat," *Walkthechat*, February 18, 2019, https://walkthechat.com/taobao-launches-mini-program-to-compete-against-wechat.

44. Jialu Shan and Michael Wade, "How China Is Revolutionising E-commerce with an Injection of Entertainment," *Conversation*, April 2, 2020, https://theconversation.com/how-china-is-revolutionising-e-commerce-with-an-injection-of-entertainment-131728.

45. Bank for International Settlements, "Big Tech in Finance: Opportunities and Risks," *BIS Annual Economic Report*, June 2019, www.bis.org/publ/arpdf/ar2019e3.pdf.

46. "China Moves to Regulate 'Blind' Business Expansion of Financial Holding Firms," Reuters, July 26, 2019, www.reuters.com/article/us-china-finance-holding-firms/china-moves-to-regulate-blind-business-expansion-of-financial-holding-firms-idUSKCN1UL12C.

47. Sherisse Pham, "Once China's Richest Man, Wang Jianlin Is Selling Off His Global Empire," CNN, January 24, 2018, https://money.cnn.com/2018/01/24/investing/wanda-china-wang-jianlin-selling-assets/index.html.

48. Tingbing Guo, "In Depth: A Maze of Capital Leads to Anbang's Aggressive Expansion," *Caixin Global*, April 30, 2017, www.caixinglobal.com/2017-04-30/a-maze-of-capital-leads-to-anbangs-aggressive-expansion-101084940.html.

49. Nicholas Lardy, *The State Strikes Back: The End of Economic Reform in China?* (Washington, DC: Peterson Institute for International Economics, 2019), 16–21.

50. Jinping Xi, "Full Text of Xi Jinping's Report at 19th CPC National Congress," Xinhua, October 18, 2017, www.chinadaily.com.cn/china/19thcpcnationalcongress/2017-11/04/content_34115212.htm.

51. Manya Koetse, "'Daddy Ma, Are You OK?'—Jack Ma's Situation Discussed on Chinese Social Media," *What's on Weibo*, January 9, 2021, www.whatsonweibo.com/daddy-ma-are-you-ok-jack-mas-situation-discussed-on-chinese-social-media.

6. Chinese Fintech Goes Abroad

1. Quoted in Cyril Altmeyer, "China's Alipay Deepens Push into Europe with Ingenico Partnership," Reuters, August 18, 2016, www.reuters.com/article/us-ingenico-group-alipay-idUSKCN10T0G9.

2. Eric Jing, "Interview with CNBC," CNBC, January 19, 2017, www.cnbc.com/video/2017/01/19/ant-financial-aims-for-2-billion-users-in-a-decade.html.

3. United Nations World Tourism Organization, "UNWTO Tourism Highlights," 2018, https://doi.org/10.18111/9789284419876.

4. Ingenico, "Ingenico Group and Alipay Partner to Provide Both Online and In-Store Payment Solutions to Europe-Wide Acquirers and Merchants," August 18, 2016, www.ingenico.com/press-and-publications/press-releases /all/2016/08/alipay-partnership.html.

5. Leena Rao, "Apple Pay Volume Is Up 450% over Past Year," *Fortune*, May 2, 2017, https://fortune.com/2017/05/02/apple-pay-volume-up.

6. Elisabeth Rosen, "US Merchants Adopt Chinese App Payments to Draw Big Spenders," *Nikkei Asia*, December 17, 2017, https://asia.nikkei.com /Business/Banking-Finance/US-merchants-adopt-Chinese-app-payments -to-draw-big-spenders.

7. "Kenya Bank to Boost WeChat Pay, Alipay Presence in Africa," Xinhua, March 25, 2019, http://en.people.cn/n3/2019/0326/c90000-9560607.html.

8. Stella Yifan Xie and Krishna Pokharel, "China's Mobile-Payment Giants Come Under Fire in Nepal," *Wall Street Journal*, May 22, 2019, www .wsj.com/articles/chinas-mobile-payment-giants-come-under-fire-in-nepal -11558530770.

9. Cyril Han, "Alibaba Investor Day Presentation," Alibaba Group, June 2016, www.alibabagroup.com/en/ir/pdf/160614/12.pdf.

10. "Alibaba's Ant Financial to Buy 25 Pct of India's One97," Reuters, February 5, 2015, www.reuters.com/article/alibaba-group-one97/update-1-alibabas -ant-financial-to-buy-25-pct-of-indias-one97-idUSL4N0VF43L20150205.

11. You, *Ant Financial*.

12. Stephanie Findlay, "Paytm Founder Hails Hitting 8m Users in Japan," *Financial Times*, July 13, 2019, www.ft.com/content/7338948c-a20a-11e9-974c -ad1c6ab5efd1.

13. You, *Ant Financial*, Chapter 15.

14. "Alipay: Global Users Exceed 1 Billion," *Techweb*, January 10, 2019, www.techweb.com.cn/internet/2019-01-10/2720002.shtml.

15. Shadma Shaikh, "How WeChat Faded into the Silence in India," *Factor Daily*, October 8, 2018, https://factordaily.com/how-wechat-faded-into -the-silence-in-india.

16. Thomas K. Thomas, "Messaging Platform WeChat Under Security Scanner," *Hindu Business Line*, June 13, 2013, www.thehindubusinessline.com /info-tech/messaging-platform-wechat-under-security-scanner/article2062 3988.ece1.

17. Tiisetso Motsoeneng, "China's WeChat Takes on WhatsApp in Africa," Reuters, July 21, 2016, https://ca.reuters.com/article/idUSKCN10205A.

18. Kavin Bharti Mittal, "2017—We Explored. 2018—We Focus," *Hike Blog*, May 28, 2018, https://blog.hike.in/2017-we-explored-2018-we-focus-3bf3766 ee85b?gi=b5edaa09c40b.

19. Ant Financial, "Ant Financial Raises Approximately US$14 billion in Series C Equity Financing to Accelerate Globalization and Technology

Innovation," June 8, 2018, https://web.archive.org/web/20200414104316/https://www.antfin.com/newsDetail.html?id=5b19ed5ef86ebdaa6985060f.

20. Liza Lin and Josh Chin, "China's Tech Giants Have a Second Job: Helping Beijing Spy on Its People," *Wall Street Journal*, November 30, 2017, www.wsj.com/articles/chinas-tech-giants-have-a-second-job-helping-the-government-see-everything-1512056284.

21. Quoted in "Payment with WeChat Pay, Alipay Only for Foreign Tourists: BI," *Jakarta Post*, December 14, 2018, www.thejakartapost.com/news/2018/12/14/payment-with-wechat-pay-alipay-only-for-foreign-tourists-bi.html.

22. Sanchita Dash, "Amazon and Flipkart Have More Than Twice the Site Visits of Next 5 Other E-commerce Companies Combined," *Business Insider*, October 21, 2019, www.businessinsider.in/business/ecommerce/news/amazon-flipkart-site-visits-compared-to-snapdeal-clubfactory-paytm-mall-and-other-peers/articleshow/71689839.cms.

23. Brenda Ngari, "Bitcoin Surges After Fed Chair Powell Declares That the US Is Working on a Digital Dollar," *ZyCrypto*, February 11, 2020, https://hill.house.gov/news/documentsingle.aspx?DocumentID=6628.

24. Chris Welch, "Read Mark Zuckerberg's Letter on Facebook's Privacy-Focused Future," *Verge*, March 6, 2019, www.theverge.com/2019/3/6/18253472/mark-zuckerberg-facebook-letter-privacy-encrypted-messaging.

25. Iris Deng, "Mark Zuckerberg Says He Should Have Listened to Earlier Advice About Learning from WeChat," *South China Morning Post*, March 11, 2019, www.scmp.com/tech/apps-social/article/2189449/mark-zuckerberg-says-he-should-have-listened-earlier-advice-about.

26. Sam Schechner, "France Hardens Position Against Facebook's Libra Currency," *Wall Street Journal*, September 12, 2019, www.wsj.com/articles/france-hardens-position-against-facebooks-libra-currency-11568295458.

7. Techlash

1. Quoted in Yiting Sun, "China's Citizens Do Care About Their Data Privacy, Actually," *MIT Technology Review*, March 28, 2018, www.technologyreview.com/the-download/610708/chinas-citizens-do-care-about-their-data-privacy-actually.

2. Sachin Mittal and James Lloyd, "The Rise of Fintech in China," EY and DBS joint report, November 2016, https://www.finyear.com/attachment/785371/.

3. "Baidu Chief Under Fire for Privacy Comments," *People's Daily*, March 28, 2018, http://en.people.cn/n3/2018/0328/c90000-9442509.html.

4. Boston Consulting Group, "Data Privacy by the Numbers," February 19, 2014, www.bcg.com/publications/2014/data-privacy-numbers.

5. Cited in Li Yuan, "Personal-Privacy Concerns Grip China," *Wall Street Journal*, August 31, 2016, www.wsj.com/articles/personal-privacy-concerns -grip-china-1472665341.

6. Timothy Morey, Theodore Forbath, and Allison Schoop, "Customer Data: Designing for Transparency and Trust," *Harvard Business Review*, May 2015, https://hbr.org/2015/05/customer-data-designing-for-transparency-and-trust.

7. Bing Jia, "China: Consumer Protection Law Revamped for First Time in 20 Years," *Law Library of Congress Global Legal Monitor*, January 29, 2014, www .loc.gov/item/global-legal-monitor/2014-01-29/china-consumer-protection -law-revamped-for-first-time-in-20-years.

8. Yuan, "Personal-Privacy Concerns Grip China."

9. Xiangwei Wang, "How Rampant Phone Scams Highlight China's Need for Tighter Privacy Laws," *South China Morning Post*, May 2, 2016, www .scmp.com/comment/insight-opinion/article/1940394/how-rampant-phone -scams-highlight-chinas-need-tighter.

10. Samm Sacks, Paul Triolo, and Graham Webster, "Beyond the Worst-Case Assumptions on China's Cybersecurity Law," New America Foundation Cybersecurity Initiative, October 13, 2017, www.newamerica.org/cybersecurity -initiative/blog/beyond-worst-case-assumptions-chinas-cybersecurity-law.

11. Samm Sacks, "China's Emerging Data Privacy System and GDPR," Center for Strategic and International Studies, March 9, 2018, www.csis.org /analysis/chinas-emerging-data-privacy-system-and-gdpr.

12. Quoted in Yuan Yang, "China's Data Privacy Outcry Fuels Case for Tighter Rules," *Financial Times*, October 1, 2018, www.ft.com/content/fdea f22a-c09a-11e8-95b1-d36dfef1b89a.

13. Li Tao and Andrew Barclay, "Tencent Denies Storing WeChat Records After Chinese Billionaire Reportedly Questions Monitoring," *South China Morning Post*, January 2, 2018, www.scmp.com/tech/social-gadgets/article /2126516/tencent-denies-storing-wechat-records-after-chinese-billionaire.

14. Rogier Creemers, Paul Triolo, and Graham Webster, "Translation: Cybersecurity Law of the People's Republic of China (Effective June 1, 2017)," New America Foundation Cybersecurity Initiative, June 29, 2018, www.newamerica.org/cybersecurity-initiative/digichina/blog/translation -cybersecurity-law-peoples-republic-china.

15. "Consumer Rights Group Withdraws Complaint Against Baidu," Xinhua, March 15, 2018, https://www.chinadailyhk.com/articles/248/127 /148/1521095625083.html.

16. Quoted in Meng Jing, "China Warns Internet Companies over Weak Data Protection Policies," *South China Morning Post*, January 12, 2018, www.scmp.com/tech/china-tech/article/2128043/china-warns-internet -companies-over-weak-data-protection-policies.

17. Yuzhe Zhang, Timmy Shen, and Isabelle Li, "In Depth: China's Big Data Clampdown Leaves Online Lenders in a Bind," *Caixin Global*, October 30, 2019,

www.caixinglobal.com/2019-10-30/in-depth-chinas-big-data-clampdown
-leaves-online-lenders-in-a-bind-101476995.html?cxg=web&Sfrom=twitter.

18. Jeffrey Ding, "ChinAI Newsletter #19: Is the Wild East of Big Data Coming to an End? A Turning Point Case in Personal Information Protection," *ChinAI Newsletter*, July 16, 2018, https://chinai.substack.com/p/chinai-new sletter-19-is-the-wild-east-of-big-data-coming-to-an-end-a-turning-point -case-in-personal-information-protection.

19. Quoted in Yin Cao, "Lawmakers, Political Advisers Focus on Personal Data Protection," *China Daily*, March 20, 2019, http://global.chinadaily.com .cn/a/201903/20/WS5c9187e4a3104842260b1788.html.

20. Shoshana Zuboff, *The Age of Surveillance Capitalism: The Fight for a Human Future at the New Frontier of Power* (New York: PublicAffairs, 2019).

21. Zhong Xu, "大技术公司如何影响金融发展?" [How do large technology companies influence financial development?], *Yicai*, November 18, 2018, www.yicai.com/news/100061767.html.

22. Zhou Xiaochuan, "Speech at the 9th Caixin Summit in Beijing," trans. Han Wei, *Caixin Global*, November 18, 2018, www.caixinglobal.com/2018-11-23 /ex-central-bank-head-warns-about-techs-influence-on-finance-101351415 .html.

23. Shu Zhang and John Ruwitch, "Exclusive: Ant Financial Shifts Focus from Finance to Tech Services: Sources," Reuters, June 5, 2018, www.reuters .com/article/us-china-ant-financial-regulation-exclus/exclusive-ant-financial -shifts-focus-from-finance-to-tech-services-sources-idUSKCN1J10WV.

24. Zhang and Ruwitch, "Ant Financial Shifts Focus from Finance to Tech Services."

25. Zhou Xiaochuan, *Collection of Zhou Xiaochuan's Lectures*.

26. Zining Gong, "P2P行业敏感期 不仅投资人 平台也是如履薄冰" [P2P industry sensitive period, not just investors, also platforms are on thin ice], Online Lending House, May 10, 2018, www.wdzj.com/zhuanlan/guancha /17-7830-1.html.

27. "Chinese Banking Regulator Warns Yields in Excess of 10% Mean Automatic Loss for Investors," *China Banking News*, June 14, 2018, www.china bankingnews.com/2018/06/14/chinese-banking-regulator-warns-yields-excess -10-mean-automatic-loss-investors.

28. Xiaoping Li, "杭州P2P暴风眼:连踩数弹者多 2体育馆成受害人集中营" [Eye of the Hangzhou P2P storm: Many invested in defaulted P2P products, two stadiums become camps for victims], 证券时报 [*Securities Times*], July 10, 2018, http://finance.jrj.com.cn/2018/07/10101524793926.shtml.

29. Cited in Hu Yue and Denise Jia, "China's 4-Year Crackdown Leaves Just Three P2P Lenders Standing," *Caixin Global*, November 7, 2020, www.caixin global.com/2020-11-07/chinas-3-year-crackdown-leaves-just-3-p2p-lenders -standing-101624086.html.

30. Becky Davis, "China Deploys Huge Police Force to Prevent Fraud Protest," *Hong Kong Free Press*, August 8, 2018, www.hongkongfp.com /2018/08/08/china-deploys-huge-police-force-prevent-fraud-protest; "How China's Peer-to-Peer Lending Crash Is Destroying Lives," *Bloomberg News*, October 2, 2018, www.bloomberg.com/news/articles/2018-10-02/peer-to-peer -lending-crash-in-china-leads-to-suicide-and-protest.

31. Quoted in Nicole Jao, "Don't Blame Internet Finance for All of the Problems in P2P Lending: Jack Ma," *Technode*, August 27, 2019, https://technode .com/2019/08/27/dont-blame-internet-finance-for-all-of-the-problems-in -p2p-lending-jack-ma.

32. Karen Gilchrist, "Alibaba Founder Jack Ma Says Working Overtime Is a 'Huge Blessing,'" CNBC, April 15, 2019, www.cnbc.com/2019/04/15/alibaba s-jack-ma-working-overtime-is-a-huge-blessing.html.

33. Koetse, "'Daddy Ma, Are You OK?'"; Zhiser, "Why Has Jack Ma's Reputation Collapsed?," January 1, 2021, *Zhihu*, https://zhuanlan.zhihu.com/p /340919282.

34. "外卖骑手，困在系统里" [Delivery drivers' hardship is in the system], *People (人物) Magazine*, September 9, 2020, https://mp.weixin.qq.com/s /Mes1RqIOdp48CMw4pXTwXw.

35. Siyuan Meng, "'A Painful Read': New Report on the Dangers Facing China's Delivery Drivers Goes Viral," *Radii China*, September 8, 2020, https://radi ichina.com/delivery-china-driver-safety.

36. Koetse, "'Daddy Ma, Are You OK?'"

37. Angela Zhang, *Chinese Antitrust Exceptionalism: How the Rise of China Challenges Global Regulation* (Oxford: Oxford University Press, 2021).

38. Zhang, *Chinese Antitrust Exceptionalism*.

39. Sheng Wei, "China's Antitrust Law Doesn't Seem to Apply to Internet Giants," *Technode*, April 26, 2020, https://technode.com/2020/04/26 /chinas-antitrust-law-doesnt-seem-to-apply-to-internet-giants.

40. Martin Chorzempa, "Who Likes Facebook's Digital Currency? Not the Chinese," *Peterson Institute for International Economics China Economic Watch*, July 16, 2019, www.piie.com/blogs/realtime-economic-issues-watch /who-likes-facebooks-libra-currency-not-chinese.

41. Richard Von Glahn, *The Economic History of China: From Antiquity to the Nineteenth Century* (Cambridge: Cambridge University Press, 2016), 233; "Digital Currency Research Institute of the People's Bank of China," *China Banking News*, October 2, 2018, www.chinabankingnews.com/wiki /digital-currency-research-institute-peoples-bank-china.

42. State Council of the People's Republic of China, "国务院关于印发'十三五'国家信息化规划的通知" [State Council notice on the issuance of the "13th five-year" national informatization plan], December 15, 2016, www.gov.cn /zhengce/content/2016-12/27/content_5153411.htm.

43. Quoted in Frank Tang, "Facebook's Libra Forcing China to Step Up Plans for Its Own Cryptocurrency, Says Central Bank Official," *South China Morning Post*, July 8, 2019, www.scmp.com/economy/china-economy/article/3017716/facebooks-libra-forcing-china-step-plans-its-own.

44. "习近平在中央政治局第十八次集体学习时强调 把区块链作为核心技术自主创新重要突破口 加快推动区块链技术和产业创新发展" [At Politburo 18th group study session, Xi Jinping emphasizes making blockchain into a core technology and important breakthrough opportunity for self-reliant innovation, accelerate and push blockchain technology and industry innovation and development], Xinhua, October 25, 2019, www.xinhuanet.com/politics/2019-10/25/c_1125153665.htm.

45. Changchun Mu, "Opinion: Facebook's Libra Needs Central Bank Supervision," *Caixin Global*, July 9, 2019, www.caixinglobal.com/2019-07-09/opinion-facebooks-libra-needs-central-bank-supervision-101437334.html.

46. "Tencent Says Libra Could Deal Crushing Blow to Chinese Payments Giants," *China Banking News*, October 24, 2019, www.chinabankingnews.com/2019/10/24/tencent-concerned-about-threat-posed-by-libra-to-chinese-payments.

47. Quoted in Ryohei Yasoshima and Alex Fang, "Doubts over Facebook's Libra Swirl at G-7 and US Congress," *Nikkei Asia*, July 18, 2019, https://asia.nikkei.com/Spotlight/Bitcoin-evolution/Doubts-over-Facebook-s-Libra-swirl-at-G-7-and-US-Congress.

48. Tommaso Mancini-Griffoli, Maria Soledad Martinez Peria, Itai Agur, Anil Ari, John Kiff, Adina Popescu, and Celine Rochon, "Casting Light on Central Bank Digital Currencies," International Monetary Fund, November 12, 2018, www.imf.org/en/Publications/Staff-Discussion-Notes/Issues/2018/11/13/Casting-Light-on-Central-Bank-Digital-Currencies-46233.

49. Martin Chorzempa, "China's Central Bank–Backed Digital Currency Is the Anti-Bitcoin," *Peterson Institute for International Economics China Economic Watch*, January 31, 2018, https://piie.com/blogs/china-economic-watch/chinas-central-bank-backed-digital-currency-anti-bitcoin.

50. Martin Chorzempa, "Promise and Peril of Digital Money in China," *Cato Journal*, Spring/Summer 2021, www.cato.org/cato-journal/spring/summer-2021/promise-peril-digital-money-china.

51. Chorzempa, "Promise and Peril of Digital Money in China."

52. Maggie Zhang, "Revealed: Chinese State TV Airs Footage of US$31 Million Worth of Cash Hidden in Corrupt Official's Flat," *South China Morning Post*, October 21, 2016, www.scmp.com/news/china/society/article/2038939/revealed-chinese-state-tv-airs-footage-huge-stash-cash-hidden.

53. Martin Chorzempa, "China's Pursuit of Leadership in Digital Currency," testimony before the US-China Economic and Security Review Commission, April 15, 2021, www.piie.com/commentary/testimonies/chinas-pursuit-leadership-digital-currency.

54. International Monetary Fund, "Official Foreign Exchange Reserves (COFER) Database," updated September 2021, https://data.imf.org/?sk=E6A5 F467-C14B-4AA8-9F6D-5A09EC4E62A4; SWIFT, "RMB Tracker," July 2020, www .swift.com/our-solutions/compliance-and-shared-services/business-intelligence /renminbi/rmb-tracker/rmb-tracker-document-centre.

55. Chorzempa, "China's Pursuit of Leadership in Digital Currency."

56. "腾讯牵头起草首个'防疫出行码'团体标准，为疫情防控和复工复产助力" [Tencent leads drafting team of first "epidemic protection code for going out" standard, helping epidemic control, returning to work and returning to production], *China Economic News*, March 6, 2020, www.xinhuanet .com/tech/2020-03/06/c_1125674248.htm; Dan Grover, "How Chinese Apps Handled Covid-19," *Dan Grover Blog*, April 5, 2020, http://dangrover.com /blog/2020/04/05/covid-in-ui.html.

57. Xu Han, "Trending in China: Elderly Left Behind in Tech Fight Against Covid-19," *Caixin Global*, January 8, 2021, www.caixinglobal.com/2021-01 -08/trending-in-china-elderly-left-behind-in-tech-fight-against-covid-19 -101648179.html.

58. I highly recommend this post by Dan Grover for an overview: Dan Grover, "How Chinese Apps Handled Covid-19," *Dan Grover Blog*, April 5, 2020, http://dangrover.com/blog/2020/04/05/covid-in-ui.html.

59. Paul Mozur, Raymond Zhong, and Aaron Krolik, "In Coronavirus Fight, China Gives Citizens a Color Code, with Red Flags," *New York Times*, March 1, 2020, www.nytimes.com/2020/03/01/business/china-coronavirus-survei llance.html.

60. Shaun Ee, "Beijing Taps Telecoms Data in Search of Covid-19," *Technode*, June 19, 2020, https://technode.com/2020/06/19/beijing-taps-telecoms -data-in-search-of-covid-19.

61. Wan Yu and Lihua Qiu, "健康码功能'迭代升级'须审慎" [Health code function "iterative upgrade" must be cautious], Xinhua, June 4, 2020, https:// web.archive.org/web/20200612082450/http://www.zj.xinhuanet.com/2020 -06/04/c_1126073732.htm.

8. The Costliest Speech in History

1. "中共中央政治局召开会议 习近平主持" [Politburo opens meeting, Xi Jinping chairs], Xinhua, December 11, 2020, www.xinhuanet.com/politics /leaders/2020-12/11/c_1126850644.htm.

2. Julie Zhu, "Exclusive: Alibaba's Ant Plans Hong Kong IPO, Targets Valuation over $200 Billion, Sources Say," Reuters, July 8, 2020, www.reuters .com/article/us-ant-financial-ipo-exclusive/exclusive-alibabas-ant-plans -hong-kong-ipo-targets-valuation-over-200-billion-sources-say-idUSKBN 2491JU.

3. Ant Group Initial Public Offering Prospectus, August 25, 2020, 1, 41–42, https://web.archive.org/web/20200917154430/https://www1.hkexnews.hk /app/sehk/2020/102484/documents/sehk20082500535.pdf.

4. Eric Jing, "Ant Financial—A Global Leading Techfin Company," Alibaba Group, September 23–24, 2019, www.alibabagroup.com/en/ir/presentations/ Investor_Day_2019_AntFinancial.pdf.

5. Tencent, "Tencent Announces 2019 Fourth Quarter and Annual Results," March 18, 2020, https://cdc-tencent-com-1258344706.image.myqcloud.com /uploads/2020/03/18/7fceaf3d1b264debc61342fc1a27dd18.pdf.

6. Pengbo Wang, "移动支付行业数字化进程分析—易观：2020年第1季度中国第三方支付移动支付市场交易规模534878.3亿元人民币" [Analyzing the progress of mobile payment industry digitization—Analysys: 2020Q1 China third-party mobile payment market scale reached 53.48783 trillion RMB], *Analysys*, June 30, 2020, www.analysys.cn/article/detail/20019826; People's Bank of China, "2019年支付体系运行总体情况" [Overall conditions in the payment system's operation 2019], March 17, 2020, www.pbc.gov.cn /zhifujiesuansi/128525/128545/128643/3990497/2020031714061362010.pdf.

7. Stella Yifan Xie, "More Than a Third of China Is Now Invested in One Giant Mutual Fund," *Wall Street Journal*, March 27, 2019, www.wsj.com /articles/more-than-a-third-of-china-is-now-invested-in-one-giant-mutual -fund-11553682785.

8. "China Plans Caps on Ant's Lending Rates to Control Risk," *Bloomberg News*, September 6, 2020, www.caixinglobal.com/2020-09-07/china-plans-caps -on-ants-lending-rates-to-control-risk-101602081.html.

9. Xiaomeng Wu, Qinqin Ping, and Denise Jia, "Banks Told to Report Data on Consumer Lending Via Ant's Platforms," *Caixin Global*, July 29, 2020, www .caixinglobal.com/2020-07-29/banks-told-to-report-data-on-consumer-lending -via-ants-platforms-101585742.html; China Banking and Insurance Regulatory Commission, "中国银保监会办公厅关于加强小额贷款公司监督管理的通知" [CBIRC notice on strengthening microlending company supervision and management], September 16, 2020, www.cbirc.gov.cn/cn/view/pages/ItemDetail .html?docId=929448&itemId=928&generaltype=0.

10. State Council of the People's Republic of China, "国务院关于实施金融控股公司准入管理的决定" [State Council decision on implementing supervision of entry for financial holding companies], September 13, 2020, www.gov .cn/zhengce/content/2020-09/13/content_5543127.htm.

11. Hui Li, "范一飞提示支付新风险：互联网企业应切实整顿超范围信贷业务" [Fan Yifei warns of payment risk: Internet companies must thoroughly clean up credit activity happening outside their scope of business], *Sina Finance*, September 24, 2020, https://finance.sina.com.cn/china/gncj/2020 -09-24/doc-iivhuipp6258420.shtml.

12. Keith Zhai and Julie Zhu, "Exclusive: China's Central Bank Urges Antitrust Probe into Alipay, WeChat Pay—Sources," Reuters, July 31, 2020, www

.reuters.com/article/us-alipay-wechat-pay-china-exclusive/exclusive-chinas
-central-bank-urges-antitrust-probe-into-alipay-wechat-pay-sources-id
USKCN24W0XD.

13. Author interviews with multiple PBOC officials.

14. Yejie Wang, "90后成短期消费贷款主力军 被花呗'困住'的年轻人怎样了" [Post-90s become mainstays of short-term consumption loans, how is it going for the young people "trapped" by Huabei?], Xinhua, September 11, 2020, www.xinhuanet.com/fortune/2020-09/11/c_1126479776.htm.

15. "如何看待用花呗给女儿过生日的广告？" [What to think about the advertisement in which Huabei is used to give a girl a birthday celebration?], Zhihu, October 9, 2020, https://www.zhihu.com/question/423848622.

16. Yang Zeyi, "Chinese Microlending Is Getting Weird and Dangerous," *Protocol*, February 9, 2021, www.protocol.com/china/chinese-micro lending-out-of-control.

17. Logan Wright and Allen Feng, "COVID-19 and China's Household Debt Dilemma," Rhodium Group, May 12, 2020, https://rhg.com/research /china-household-debt.

18. Julie Zhu and Zhang Yan, "Exclusive: Chinese Regulatory Probe Delays Approval for Ant's IPO, Sources Say," Reuters, October 13, 2020, www.reuters .com/article/us-ant-group-ipo-regulation-exclusive-idUKKBN26Y18S.

19. Yun Ma, "Speech at the Second Bund Summit," October 24, 2020, trans. Kevin Xu, https://interconnected.blog/jack-ma-bund-finance-summit-speech.

20. Ma, "Speech at the Second Bund Summit."

21. China Government Net, "习近平主持中共中央政治局第十三次集体学习并讲话" [Xi Jinping chairs Politburo Standing Committee 13th group study session and makes a speech], February 22, 2019, www.gov.cn/xinwen /2019-02/23/content_5367953.htm.

22. Quoted in Keith Zhai, Julia Zhu, and Cheng Leng, "How Billionaire Jack Ma Fell to Earth and Took Ant's Mega IPO with Him," Reuters, November 5, 2020, www.reuters.com/article/us-ant-group-ipo-suspension-regulators-i /how-billionaire-jack-ma-fell-to-earth-and-took-ants-mega-ipo-with-him-id USKBN27L1BB.

23. China Government Net, "刘鹤主持召开国务院金融稳定发展委员会专题会议" [Liu He chairs and opens State Council Financial Stability and Development Committee special meeting], October 31, 2020, www.gov.cn /guowuyuan/2020-10/31/content_5556394.htm.

24. Jing Yang and Lingling Wei, "China's President Xi Jinping Personally Scuttled Jack Ma's Ant IPO," *Wall Street Journal*, November 12, 2020, www.wsj .com/articles/china-president-xi-jinping-halted-jack-ma-ant-ipo-11605 203556.

25. Zhou Jueshou, "大型互联网企业进入金融领域的潜在风险与监管" [The hidden risk of large internet platforms entering the finance area, and

regulation], *Caixin*, November 1, 2020, https://opinion.caixin.com/2020-11
-01/101621303.html.

26. Wuping Guo, "银保监会消费者权益保护局局长郭武平：'花呗'、
'借呗'侵害消费者权益值得高度关注" [CBIRC Financial Consumer Protec-
tion Bureau Head Guo Wuping: "Just Spend" and "Ant Check Later" hurt consumer interests and deserve a high degree of attention], *21st Century Business
Herald*, November 2, 2020, https://m.21jingji.com/article/20201102/herald
/62dfca7696f0148a9353a88dbd9eedf5.html.

27. China Securities Regulatory Commission, "四部门联合约谈蚂蚁集
团有关人员" [Four departments jointly interview related personnel of Ant
Group], November 2, 2020, www.csrc.gov.cn/pub/newsite/zjhxwfb/xwdd
/202011/t20201102_385514.html.

28. Eliza Gkritsi, "CHINA VOICES | The Unsigned Op-eds That Fore-
shadowed Ant Group IPO Suspension," *Technode*, November 9, 2020, https://
technode.com/2020/11/09/china-voices-the-unsigned-op-eds-that-foreshad
owed-ant-group-ipo-suspension.

29. Haibo Sun, "重磅！蚂蚁小贷监管银行化！联合贷款出资不低于
30%，单户余额不超30万或年均收入1/3！" [Serious! Ant small loan regula-
tion becomes more like a bank's! Co-loan capital contribution minimum 30%,
each customer amount cannot exceed 300,000 or 1/3 of their annual income!],
November 2, 2020, https://mp.weixin.qq.com/s/_1J3De6MeyfhPRX_Xg6S4g.

30. Shanghai Stock Exchange, "关于暂缓蚂蚁科技集团股份有限公司
科创板上市的决定" [Decision to postpone Ant Technology Group Holding Limited's IPO on the STAR market], November 3, 2020, www.sse.com.cn
/disclosure/announcement/general/c/c_20201103_5253315.shtml.

31. Shuli Ren, "The Day Jack Ma Became Ray Dalio's Nightmare," *Bloomberg
News*, November 4, 2020, www.bloomberg.com/opinion/articles/2020-11-04
/ant-group-s-suspended-ipo-turns-jack-ma-into-ray-dalio-s-nightmare
?sref=ATN0rNv3; Yang and Wei, "China's President Xi Jinping Personally
Scuttled Jack Ma's Ant IPO."

32. Rui Ma, "Ant Group: The Biggest IPO That Wasn't," *Technode*, November 14,
2020, https://technode.com/2020/11/14/ant-group-the-biggest-ipo-that-wasnt.

33. Chad Bray and Enoch Yiu, "Fintech Giant Ant Group Wins Approval from
China's Securities Regulator for Jumbo IPO in Hong Kong," *South China Morning
Post*, October 19, 2020, www.scmp.com/business/companies/article/3106046
/fintech-giant-ant-group-wins-approval-chinas-securities; Shen Lu and Clara
Wang, "Data: IPO Path Narrows on China's STAR Market," *Protocol*, April 13,
2021, www.protocol.com/china/shanghai-star-ipo-termination-data.

34. Lingling Wei, "Ant IPO Approval Process Under Investigation by
Beijing," *Wall Street Journal*, April 27, 2021, www.wsj.com/articles/ant
-ipo-approval-process-under-investigation-by-beijing-11619532022.

35. Xinxin Lin, "腾讯刘炽平：对风险管理的强烈尊重是金融市场中金
融服务的基础" [Tencent's Liu Chiping: Strong respect for risk management is

the foundation of financial market services], *21st Century Business Herald*, November 4, 2020, https://m.21jingji.com/article/20201104/herald/b3b952ef0e733ad64720649f35d53a66.html.

36. State Administration for Market Regulation (SAMR), "市场监管总局关于《关于平台经济领域的反垄断指南（征求意见稿）》公开征求意见的公告" [SAMR announces the publication of "Antimonopoly Guidelines in the Platform Economy (draft version)" for public comment], November 10, 2020, www.samr.gov.cn/hd/zjdc/202011/t20201109_323234.html.

37. Eustance Huang, "China's Tech Giants Have Lost More Than \$280 Billion in Market Value as Regulatory Concerns Mount," CNBC, November 11, 2020, www.cnbc.com/2020/11/11/china-tech-giants-lost-250-billion-in-market-value-amid-potential-regulations.html.

38. State Administration for Market Regulation (SAMR), "市场监管总局依法对京东、天猫、唯品会　三家平台不正当价格行为案作出行政处罚决定" [SAMR decision to issue administrative penalty to JD, Tmall, and Vipshop for the three platforms' improper pricing practices], December 30, 2020, www.samr.gov.cn/xw/zj/202012/t20201230_324826.html.

39. State Administration for Market Regulation (SAMR), "市场监管总局依法对阿里巴巴集团 涉嫌垄断行为立案调查" [SAMR registers investigation into Alibaba on suspicion of monopolistic practices], December 24, 2020, www.samr.gov.cn/xw/zj/202012/t20201224_324638.html.

40. Alessandro Acquisti, Curtis Taylor, and Liad Wagman, "The Economics of Privacy," *Journal of Economic Literature* 54, no. 2 (June 2016), www.aeaweb.org/articles?id=10.1257/jel.54.2.442.

41. Quan Du, "银保监会：蚂蚁集团的问题具有普遍性，建议所有互联网平台对照自查" [CBIRC: Ant Group issues are universal, recommend all internet platforms make self-examination], *Yicai*, January 4, 2021, www.yicai.com/news/100898134.html.

42. China Securities Regulatory Commission (CSRC), "关于修改《科创属性评价指引（试行）》的决定" [Decision on amending provisional guidelines for evaluating science and technology companies], April 16, 2021, www.gov.cn/zhengce/zhengceku/2021-04/17/content_5600280.htm.

43. People's Bank of China, "中国人民银行关于《非银行支付机构条例（征求意见稿）》公开征求意见的通知" [People's Bank of China notice on making public and seeking comments on the "Nonbank Payment Institutions Rules" (draft measures)], January 20, 2021, www.pbc.gov.cn/rmyh/105208/4166553/index.html.

44. State Administration for Market Regulation (SAMR), "市场监管总局依法对阿里巴巴集团控股有限公司在中国境内网络零售平台服务市场实施'二选一'垄断行为作出行政处罚" [SAMR issues administrative penalty according to the law to Alibaba Group Holding for implementing the "two choose one" monopolistic practice in China's domestic e-commerce

platform service market], April 10, 2021, www.samr.gov.cn/xw/zj/202104/t20210410_327702.html.

45. Heather Mowbray, "Trending in China: Baidu Blocking Caixin's Criticism of Search Engines Goes Viral," *Caixin Global*, November 23, 2020, www.caixinglobal.com/2020-11-23/trending-in-china-baidu-blocking-caixins-criticism-of-search-engines-goes-viral-101631522.html.

46. Jing Yang, "Beijing Asks Alibaba to Shed Its Media Assets," *Wall Street Journal*, March 16, 2021, www.wsj.com/articles/beijing-asks-alibaba-to-shed-its-media-assets-11615809999.

47. People's Bank of China, "中国人民银行副行长潘功胜就金融管理部门约谈蚂蚁集团有关情况答记者问" [PBOC Vice Governor Pan Gongsheng answers journalist questions on the circumstances of financial regulatory agencies interview with Ant Group], December 27, 2020, www.pbc.gov.cn/goutongjiaoliu/113456/113469/4153479/index.html.

48. Barry Naughton and Jude Blanchette, "The Party Politics Driving Xi Jinping," *The Wire China*, October 3, 2021, www.thewirechina.com/2021/10/03/the-party-politics-driving-xi-jinping.

49. Nuala O'Connor, "Reforming the U.S. Approach to Data Protection and Privacy," Council on Foreign Relations, January 30, 2018, www.cfr.org/report/reforming-us-approach-data-protection.

50. National People's Congress, "Personal Information Protection Law of the People's Republic of China," August 20, 2021, https://digichina.stanford.edu/work/translation-personal-information-protection-law-of-the-peoples-republic-of-china-effective-nov-1-2021.

51. Samm Sacks, "New China Data Privacy Standard Looks More Far-Reaching Than GDPR," Center for Strategic and International Studies, January 29, 2018, www.csis.org/analysis/new-china-data-privacy-standard-looks-more-far-reaching-gdpr.

52. Alexa Lee, Mingli Shi, Qiheng Chen, Jamie Horsley, Kendra Schaefer, Rogier Creemers, and Graham Webster, "Seven Major Changes in China's Finalized Personal Information Protection Law," Stanford University Digichina, September 15, 2021, https://digichina.stanford.edu/work/seven-major-changes-in-chinas-finalized-personal-information-protection-law.

53. People's Bank of China, "中国货币政策执行报告2020 年第四季度" [China monetary policy implementation report, 2020 Q4], February 8, 2021, www.pbc.gov.cn/goutongjiaoliu/113456/113469/4190887/2021020821282167078.pdf.

54. National Development and Reform Commission, "国家发展改革委等部门关于推动平台经济规范健康持续发展的若干意见" [National Development and Reform Commission and other departments release some opinions concerning promoting the standardized, healthy, and sustained development of the platform economy], December 24, 2021, www.ndrc.gov.cn/xxgk/zcfb/tz/202201/t20220119_1312326.html?code=&state=123.

55. "Ant's Consumer Finance Unit to Boost Its Capital to $4.7 Bln," Reuters, December 24, 2021, www.reuters.com/business/finance/ants-consumer-finance-unit-boost-its-capital-47-bln-2021-12-24.

56. Rui Ma, "Does Beijing's Tech Crackdown Threaten China's Entrepreneurial Sphere?," *Protocol*, November 30, 2021, www.protocol.com/china/china-tech-crackdown-entrepreneurial-future?rebelltitem=2#rebelltitem2.

57. Tianlei Huang and Nicholas Lardy, "Is the Sky Really Falling for Private Firms in China?," *Peterson Institute for International Economics China Economic Watch*, October 14, 2021, www.piie.com/blogs/china-economic-watch/sky-really-falling-private-firms-china.

58. Sun Yu, "Jack Ma's Ant Group Implicated in Corruption Scandal by Chinese State Media," *Financial Times*, January 20, 2022, www.ft.com/content/aac4b040-e349-4feb-9030-bc49ab568c22.

59. Central Commission for Discipline Inspection, "中国共产党第十九届中央纪律检查委员会第六次全体会议公报" [Chinese Communist Party ninth CCDI plenum, sixth meeting report], January 20, 2022, www.gov.cn/xinwen/2022-01/20/content_5669518.htm.

9. From Liberator to Oppressor?

1. Kenrick Davis, "In Cashless China, Criminals Are Punished with Payment App Bans," *Sixth Tone*, November 12, 2020, www.sixthtone.com/news/1006443/in-cashless-china%2C-criminals-are-punished-with-payment-app-bans.

2. Mark Bergen, "Google Hires PayPal Vet to Reset Strategy After Its Banking Retreat," *Bloomberg News*, January 19, 2022, www.bloomberg.com/news/articles/2022-01-19/google-hires-paypal-vet-to-reset-strategy-after-banking-retreat?sref=ATN0rNv3.

3. Yumeng Bao, "21岁男子在腾讯客户中心坠楼身亡 起因各方持不同看法" [21-year-old man dies after jumping off Tencent's customer service center, all sides have different view of the reason], *21st Century Business Herald*, August 27, 2020, https://m.21jingji.com/article/20200827/herald/eb1c906d26ec48e694bc97e5969edb9c_zaker.html.

Index

early system backwardness,
27–28
expansion after successes, 48–49
fees, 86
need for in China, 21–22, 27
opportunity for fintech to
"leapfrog," 57–58, 60, 67, 73,
104–105
regulation, 150–151
scandals and abuses, 44–46
size in China, 159–160, 210–211
support of governments, 39–40
See also mobile-payment
systems; super-apps;
individual tools and apps

paper money, 196, 200
parking, payment for, 159
party-state. *See* government of
China
payment method
as battleground, 82–83
change in China, 58–59
criticism of UnionPay, 64
legality, 2, 31, 38
subsidies in, 91
payment tools for online
transactions. *See* online
payment system
PayPal, 40, 41–42, 85
PayTM, 171–172, 178
PBOC. *See* People's Bank of China
peer-to-peer (P2P) lending
as bubble, 116–123
collapse and losses, 192–194
description as system, 116–117
Ezubao scandal and collapse,
129–133
hype globally, 127
move abroad, 173

as promise in China, 118–120
regulation, 120–123, 126–128,
131, 133, 145
risk in, 117, 120, 133–134
for stock market investment,
125, 126
in USA, 117, 127
Zhaocaibao model and Cosun
dispute, 127–129
Peng, Lucy, 36
People's Bank of China (PBOC)
and Bitcoin, 115, 116
change of governor, 162–163
control over finance, 14
credit evaluation and scoring, 97
and cryptocurrencies, 154–155,
157
digital currency plan, 196–204
and "float" interest earnings, 151
invite of big tech into finance, 9,
23, 140–141, 152, 190
loans through Ant Group,
211–212
mobile-payment systems
restrictions, 95, 96
and online payment system, 39
and P2P, 120–121
and privacy, 201, 221
"rectification" demands on Ant
Group, 221–224
regulation for online payments,
39, 44, 150–151, 160
reversal on big-tech policy,
190–191, 192
role in financial system, 51
See also Zhou Xiaochuan
People's Daily, 54, 78–79, 82, 95,
185
People's Republic of China. *See*
China

support for private innovation, 65, 80

support of state companies, 161

Xiao Jianhua, 161

Yahoo!, 40–41, 45

Yan Qingmin, 46, 60

Yang, Jerry, 45

Yi Gang, 150–151, 162–163

Yuan Leiming, 128

Yucheng group, 129–130, 132

Yu'E Bao

description and size, 76, 78, 151–152, 211

expansion and impact, 82, 151–152, 211

as money-market fund, 5–6, 76, 77–78, 82

in "rectification" demands of PBOC, 222

support by authorities, 79

Zhang Min, 131

Zhang Minmin, 124

Zhang Yiming, 229

Zhao Xijun, 122

Zhaocaibao, 127–128

Zhongguancun, 80

Zhou Jiangyong, 230

Zhou Xiaochuan

background and early career, 53

development of fintech in China, 19, 20–21, 22, 39, 66–67, 81–83

on finance as tech, 192

and internet in finance, 19

invite of big tech into finance, 9, 23, 140–141, 190–191

protection of fintech, 79

reforms in finance, 53, 54–55

retirement, 162, 163, 190

reversal of opinion on fintech, 149, 190–191

work in finance and as banker, 53–55, 66–67

Zhu Rongji, 55

Zhuang Chengzhan, 76

Zuckerberg, Mark, 4, 13–14, 139, 179, 180

MARTIN CHORZEMPA is a Senior Fellow at the Peterson Institute for International Economics. He lived in China from 2013 to 2015, where he conducted research on China's economy and financial system, first as a Luce Scholar at Peking University's China Center for Economic Research and then at the China Finance 40 Forum, China's leading independent think tank. Martin graduated from the Harvard Kennedy School of Government with a master's degree in public administration in international development. He has appeared on NPR multiple times, including recently to discuss issues including digital currency and the fate of Chinese firms in US equity markets. He is regularly cited in major media on issues of Chinese technology regulation, digital currency, fintech, and US-China economic relations, including in the *Wall Street Journal*, *New York Times*, *Financial Times*, *Economist*, *Washington Post*, *MIT Technology Review*, and *Foreign Affairs*.

PublicAffairs is a publishing house founded in 1997. It is a tribute to the standards, values, and flair of three persons who have served as mentors to countless reporters, writers, editors, and book people of all kinds, including me.

I. F. STONE, proprietor of *I. F. Stone's Weekly*, combined a commitment to the First Amendment with entrepreneurial zeal and reporting skill and became one of the great independent journalists in American history. At the age of eighty, Izzy published *The Trial of Socrates*, which was a national bestseller. He wrote the book after he taught himself ancient Greek.

BENJAMIN C. BRADLEE was for nearly thirty years the charismatic editorial leader of *The Washington Post*. It was Ben who gave the *Post* the range and courage to pursue such historic issues as Watergate. He supported his reporters with a tenacity that made them fearless and it is no accident that so many became authors of influential, best-selling books.

ROBERT L. BERNSTEIN, the chief executive of Random House for more than a quarter century, guided one of the nation's premier publishing houses. Bob was personally responsible for many books of political dissent and argument that challenged tyranny around the globe. He is also the founder and longtime chair of Human Rights Watch, one of the most respected human rights organizations in the world.

. . .

For fifty years, the banner of Public Affairs Press was carried by its owner Morris B. Schnapper, who published Gandhi, Nasser, Toynbee, Truman, and about 1,500 other authors. In 1983, Schnapper was described by *The Washington Post* as "a redoubtable gadfly." His legacy will endure in the books to come.

Peter Osnos, *Founder*